Beginning Entity Framework Core 2.0

Database Access from .NET

Derek J. Rouleau

Apress®

Beginning Entity Framework Core 2.0

Derek J. Rouleau
East Baldwin, Maine, USA

ISBN-13 (pbk): 978-1-4842-3374-0
https://doi.org/10.1007/978-1-4842-3375-7

ISBN-13 (electronic): 978-1-4842-3375-7

Library of Congress Control Number: 2018935922

Managing Director, Apress Media LLC: Welmoed Spahr
Acquisitions Editor: Jonathan Gennick
Development Editor: Laura Berendson
Coordinating Editor: Jill Balzano

Cover designed by eStudioCalamar

Cover image designed by Freepik (www.freepik.com)

Distributed to the book trade worldwide by Springer Science+Business Media New York, 233 Spring Street, 6th Floor, New York, NY 10013. Phone 1-800-SPRINGER, fax (201) 348-4505, e-mail orders-ny@springer-sbm.com, or visit www.springeronline.com. Apress Media, LLC is a California LLC and the sole member (owner) is Springer Science + Business Media Finance Inc (SSBM Finance Inc). SSBM Finance Inc is a **Delaware** corporation.

For information on translations, please e-mail rights@apress.com, or visit http://www.apress.com/rights-permissions.

Apress titles may be purchased in bulk for academic, corporate, or promotional use. eBook versions and licenses are also available for most titles. For more information, reference our Print and eBook Bulk Sales web page at http://www.apress.com/bulk-sales.

Any source code or other supplementary material referenced by the author in this book is available to readers on GitHub via the book's product page, located at www.apress.com/9781484233740. For more detailed information, please visit http://www.apress.com/source-code.

Printed on acid-free paper

To my best friend Chris and his father Paul Champagne. If it wasn't for you two, I may have never gotten interested in computer science.

Table of Contents

About the Author

Derek J. Rouleau is a Computer and Information Systems Manager for a small company in the greater Portland, Maine area. He has been working with computers since the mid 1990s thanks to a friend's father, who got him interested in hardware and the workings of the operating system. Derek started professionally programming while working for an educational publishing and software company in the Quality Assurance department. He has been using Visual Basic since VB 6 and C# since 2010. Although he now manages the department where he works, Derek still makes time each week to write code and research new and exciting technologies. When he's not working, he is involved with Off Track Standardbreds, and he competes in Dressage.

About the Technical Reviewer

Doug Holland is a Technical Evangelist at Microsoft. Before joining Microsoft in 2010, he was awarded the Microsoft MVP (C#) and Intel Black Belt Developer awards. He has presented sessions at the Microsoft BUILD conference and frequently speaks at other events about Microsoft technologies, from cloud computing to mixed reality. He holds a Master's Degree in Software Engineering from Oxford University, as well as certifications from Microsoft and Unity Technologies. You can follow him on Twitter @dougholland or connect with him on LinkedIn at `https://www.linkedin.com/in/dougholland/`.

Acknowledgments

I would like to thank Jonathan Gennick and Jill Balzano for having the faith in me and for helping me bring this book to you. If it weren't for them and all the great people at Apress, this would not have been possible.

I also need to thank my Uncle "Doc" and Don Rahmlow of TC2 Consulting Services for reminding me that we always need to keep trying to learn new things and for pushing me to keep improving myself. As we get along in our careers, we tend to stick with what we know, but in this industry you need to keep up with the ever-changing environment, which isn't always easy.

Introduction

We decided to try a different approach at writing a technical book, and that is to convey the information through examples, rather than long paragraphs of text you are only going to forget later. The hope is that this will give you a good foundation to start your Entity Framework Core 2.0 journey and that, when you complete the book and start working on your own projects, you'll have a good understanding of the material.

Even though this is a book on Entity Framework Core 2.0, we are going to cover some C# topics that you might not be familiar with, so I hope you find those parts helpful.

In the second part of this book, we cover some aspects of ASP.NET MVC Core. If you are interested in that topic, Apress has some very good books on the subject. I highly recommend that you look into them. Although you will have a working web application by the end, it will behoove you to do some more reading on the subject.

Who This Book Is For

This book is for someone who has never used Entity Framework Core and is looking for a new way to access databases. Although we focus on SQL Server in this book, according to Microsoft, it is possible to connect to MySQL, PostgreSQL, and MyCAT as well. (However, there is no Oracle support for EF Core yet, but hopefully there will be in the future.) If you have not programmed in any language before, you may have a little bit of trouble, as we don't explain the basics of C# or ASP.NET. You may not understand or might miss some key concepts. If you are coming over from Visual Basic, you will probably do fine, although you need to remember to add those pesky semicolons at the end of your code lines.

Although we do use quite a bit of LINQ in this book, it is not required that you have any background in LINQ prior to running any of the examples. It would be wise to do some follow-up reading on LINQ after you complete this book, but you should be able to piece together most of what you need to do after completing these examples. If you get stuck, an Internet search will give you a better idea of what you are looking at so you can make a better decision as to what to use.

Requirements

When writing this book, I did everything in Visual Studio 2017 Preview and SQL Server 2014. The free version of SQL Server and Visual Studio works with all the examples in this book. Since this is a beginner book, I thought it best to use the tools that someone just starting might be using. You can use any version of SQL Server 2008 or newer with Entity Framework Core 2.0; however, you will run into issues when you try to do the paging examples if you have an older version of SQL Server, so try to use at least version 2014 if at all possible.

Although you do create a web application in the second section of this book, it is not required that you have a web server. You need one only if you want to deploy the project or one like it. Otherwise, you can run and test everything through Visual Studio.

Notes About NuGet Packages

At the time of the writing of this book, some of the packages that we use were still only available in preview1-final or preview2-final. If you find that you are getting errors with your application, it may be due to a mixture of the preview and the release versions. It's better to either use all preview or all release versions with your application, as that seems to be the safest. When you use the preview packages, sometimes you will get warnings in which it's trying to find the best match. Normally those warnings won't cause you any problems when you run your code and are more of an annoyance than anything.

Before We Begin

One final note before we begin. I generally try to live my programming life by two of my favorite quotes. The first is "never remember anything you can look up" which I'm pretty sure is paraphrased from Albert Einstein. Now I'm not saying that you shouldn't remember how to use an `int` without having to look it up online or in a book. But for those things that you hardly ever do, don't take the time to commit them to memory. The second is "frustration begins where knowledge ends". This quote I know for sure is from Clinton Anderson. This is by far the hardest to implement. If you are getting frustrated with something, take a step back and try to figure out why. If you are honest with yourself, it's probably because you have run out of knowledge on the subject. Try to figure out where the problem is and which part you are missing. Then learn about it and try again. By doing this, you will likely have more success than just plugging away and blindly trying different things.

CHAPTER 1

Getting Started

We are going to jump right into an example, as I think that is the best way to learn something. As we cover new topics, we explain them as we work on them. This is better than a general overview at the start of the chapter or section, because that won't mean much to you while you are reading it. I personally dislike it when books show you the wrong way of doing something and then show you how to do it "correctly" after you just spent five minutes typing in the wrong way, so I'm not going to do that to you. However, I do explain why we are doing something and explain what would be wrong. Since this is a "getting started" type of book, all the examples work as written, although they may not be the best way of getting it done. As you get more comfortable with this technology and as your skills grow, you'll come up with your own way of doing things. I'm just here to help you started down the path to greatness.

For those of you who are like me and skipped the Introduction, you should be using the latest build of Visual Studio 2017 and at least .NET Framework 4.6.1. At the time of this writing, the latest build of Visual Studio was 15.3.3 with the .NET Framework build 4.7.02046. These build numbers can be found in the Visual Studio About window.

What Is .NET Core

Let's take a quick moment to cover something that some of you may be wondering—what is the difference between .NET and .NET Core? First off, .NET Core is cross platform, so if you want to run an application on Windows, Linux, or Mac, .NET Core is your tool. Due to its compact nature, .NET Core also gives better performance. The other nice thing is that you can always start with .NET Core and, if you find you need more features, you can switch to the full version of the .NET Framework. This is especially true if you are writing a service.

© Derek J. Rouleau 2018
D. J. Rouleau, *Beginning Entity Framework Core 2.0*, https://doi.org/10.1007/978-1-4842-3375-7_1

The application created here is used throughout the first section of this book and each section builds off the last, so you really can't skip around. With that being said, let's get started!

Setting Up Your Application

Follow these steps to set up the application:

Step 1: Create a new Visual C# Console App (.NET Core) Application in Visual studio called ComputerInventory. Again, make sure you are using at least .NET Framework 4.6.1 for your application.

Step 2: Open the NuGet package browser by clicking on Project ➤ Manage NuGet Packages (see Figure 1-1).

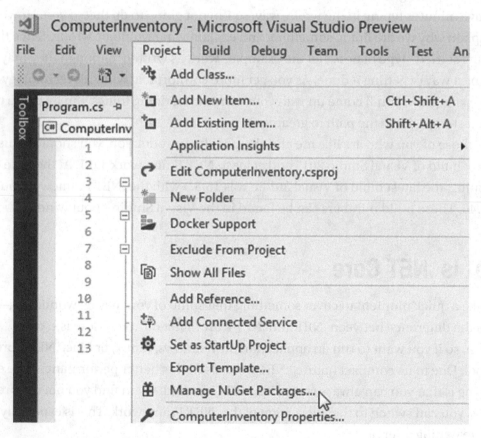

Figure 1-1. *Location of NuGet package manager*

Step 3: Add the following packages:

- Microsoft.EntityFrameworkcore.SqlServer v2.0.0

- Microsoft.EntityFrameworkcore.Tools v2.0.0

- Microsoft.EntityFrameworkcore.SqlServer.Design v2.0.0

Note   As of the writing of this book, only the preview packages were available. If you can't find version 2.0.0, check the preview packages.

Figure 1-2 shows what it looks like when you search for a package. Once you have selected the package you want to install, just click on the Install button to the right and click I Accept for any prompts that come up.

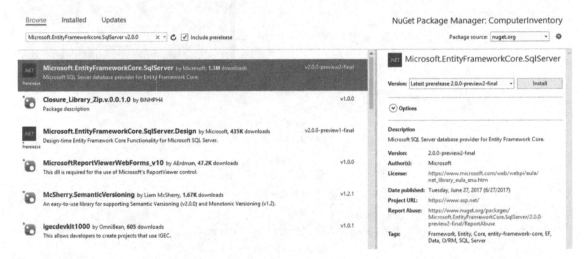

Figure 1-2. *NuGet package manager*

That completes the basic setup of your application. Feel free to save your work before you continue.

Creating the Database and Tables (Entities)

If you have used Entity Framework 6.x or one of the other versions in the past, this next part will be a little new to you (or perhaps not). We are going to start with a code-first Entity Framework type of application, as that is somewhat easier when using EF

Core. Later in the book, we use an application that is database-first, so you can see the difference. If you were to create an application based on an existing database, database-first is the choice you'd probably use.

We are going to follow the model that is generally used by most people who design websites, so we need to create two folders in our application—Models and Data. If you have never done this before, it's simple. Just right-click on the ComputerInventory project in the Solution Explorer and select Add and then New Folder. Then change the name to Models. See Figure 1-3. Each of our eventual tables will have a corresponding class file in the Models folder. I'll take you step by step through the first one and then you should be able to create the remaining ones on your own (you just change the name of the class).

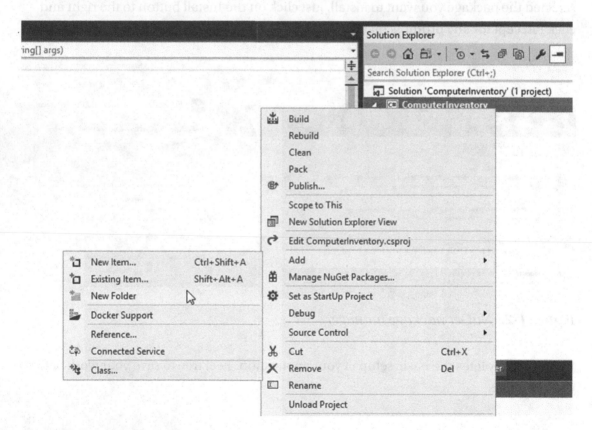

Figure 1-3. *Adding a new folder*

Let's create our first class file. Right-click on the `Models` folder, select Add, and then select Class (should be at the bottom of the list). Make sure that Class is selected and change the name to `OperatingSys.cs`. Figure 1-4 shows you what it should look like when you are creating the new class file. We are using `OperatingSys` rather than `OperatingSystem`, as `OperatingSystem` is a reserved type in C# and we'd have to put `Models.OperatingSystem` in our code each time we wanted to use it.

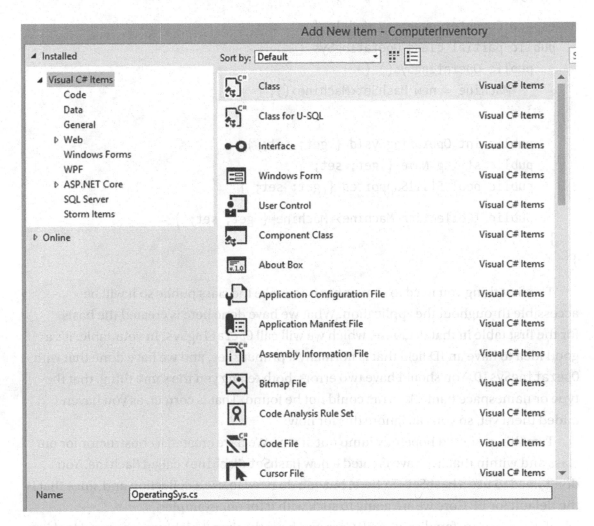

Figure 1-4. Creating a new class

Once you click on Add, `OperatingSys.cs` will be created and load for you to start working on it. Listing 1-1 shows the code for this new class.

Listing 1-1. OperatingSys.cs After You Changed It

```
using System;
using System.Collections.Generic;

namespace ComputerInventory.Models {
    public partial class OperatingSys {
        public OperatingSys() {
            Machine = new HashSet<Machine>();
        }

        public int OperatingSysId { get; set; }
        public string Name { get; set; }
        public bool StillSupported { get; set; }

        public ICollection<Machine> Machine { get; set; }
    }
}
```

The first thing you need to remember is to make the class public so it will be accessible throughout the application. What we have done here is created the basis for the first table in that database, which we will call `OperatingSys`. In your table, it's a good idea to have an ID field that is normally a primary key, and we have done that with `OperatingSysID`. You should have two errors, both telling you the same thing, that the type or namespace name `Machine` could not be found. That is correct, as you haven't added them yet, so you can ignore this for now.

Two things should hopefully jump out at you. We have created a constructor for our class and within that, we have created a new `HashSet<Machine>` called `Machine`. You don't need to use a `HashSet<T>` here, but you do need to use a collection and since that is the default for EF Core we are going to stick with it for our examples.

If you are more familiar with EF Core and have the time, I highly recommend looking at the other set types as there are cases in which using a `HashSet` isn't needed and there is a better fit. We then have our `ICollection<Machine>`, which provides an interface to the `Machine` table. After all, one OS could have multiple machines, but one machine generally only has one OS (we aren't going to handle multi-boot systems in this simple example).

For a simple class like this, that is all there is to it. We will set up all of our tables that don't have any linking via foreign keys first.

Now create the next class and call it MachineType. Listing 1-2 shows all the code you need to create the class.

Listing 1-2. MachineType.cs

```
using System;
using System.Collections.Generic;

namespace ComputerInventory.Models {
    public partial class MachineType {
        public MachineType() {
            Machine = new HashSet<Machine>();
        }

        public int MachineTypeId { get; set; }
        public string Description { get; set; }
        public ICollection<Machine> Machine { get; set; }
    }
}
```

As you can see, this is very similar to the OperatingSys class. We have one basic class left, the WarrantyProvider class. Its code is shown in Listing 1-3.

Listing 1-3. WarrantyProvider.cs

```
using System;
using System.Collections.Generic;

namespace ComputerInventory.Models {
    public partial class WarrantyProvider {
        public WarrantyProvider() {
            MachineWarranty = new HashSet<MachineWarranty>();
        }
```

```
    public int WarrantyProviderId { get; set; }
    public string ProviderName { get; set; }
    public int? SupportExtension { get; set; }
    public string SupportNumber { get; set; }

    public ICollection<MachineWarranty> MachineWarranty { get; set; }
  }
}
```

There are a couple of things with this class that you need to be aware of. First of all, the SupportNumber property is a string. This was done so that we can limit the number of characters to 10 (this is the number of digits that United States telephone numbers have; if you need to add a number from another country, this may need to be increased). We will take care of the field length in a little bit. SupportExtension is not required, as you could have a direct number to support and thus no value here, so we add the question mark after int to make it nullable (int?). You should have two new errors about MachineWarranty, but they will go away soon, so you can ignore those as well. If you were going to put this into production, you could increase the length of the ProviderName, as you may have a support contract with a company such as "Bob's Computer Repair Service of Northern California," which would not fit into a 30-character field.

Now for the first class that has a foreign key in it. Listing 1-4 shows the code for Machine.cs, which will be the "base class" for most of what you'll be working on in this project.

Listing 1-4. Machine.cs

```
using System;
using System.Collections.Generic;

namespace ComputerInventory.Models {
  public partial class Machine {
    public Machine() {
      SupportTicket = new HashSet<SupportTicket>();
    }
```

```
    public int MachineId { get; set; }
    public string Name { get; set; }
    public string GeneralRole { get; set; }
    public string InstalledRoles { get; set; }
    public int OperatingSysId { get; set; }
    public int MachineTypeId { get; set; }

    public MachineType MachineType { get; set; }
    public OperatingSys OperatingSys { get; set; }
    public ICollection<SupportTicket> SupportTicket { get; set; }
  }
}
```

The first three quarters of this code contains all things that you have already seen, except for the new error for SupportTicket. Then we get to public int OperatingSysId { get; set; }. In and of itself, there isn't anything special about it, until you realize that we created a property called OperatingSysId in the OperatingSys class. You then see the line public OperatingSys OperatingSys { get; set; } at the bottom, and this is what makes all the difference. Hopefully up until now, you have been wondering why we haven't specified which field is the primary key. That is because Entity Framework Core is nice enough to do it if it's obvious enough, plus we'll be doing a bit more with our database fields when we set up our DBContext class, but we are getting ahead of ourselves. As you'll see later, specifying the primary key is good practice for making your code easier to read and for maintainability purposes. The first property we created in each class so far has the name ID in it. Well, the great folks at Microsoft added logic that gives EF the ability to pick the most logical choice for the key.

Now that makes sense for the first part, but what about for OperatingSysId? How is it to know that we want that to be a foreign key? Well, that second line tells EF that we are going to be adding a reference to the OperatingSys class/table and it assumes that you want to link it with the OperatingSysId field to create the foreign key. I strongly encourage you to look into this further if you aren't going to create your tables in SQL Server Management Studio or another DBMS, because a good table structure is like a foundation; the stronger it is, the better it will perform/hold up.

The code for the three remaining tables you need to create are shown in Listings 1-5, 1-6, and 1-7.

Listing 1-5. MachineWarranty.cs

```csharp
using System;
using System.Collections.Generic;

namespace ComputerInventory.Models {
    public partial class MachineWarranty {
        public int MachineWarrantyId { get; set; }
        public string ServiceTag { get; set; }
        public DateTime WarrantyExpiration { get; set; }
        public int MachineId { get; set; }
        public int WarrantyProviderId { get; set; }

        public WarrantyProvider WarrantyProvider { get; set; }
    }
}
```

Listing 1-6. SupportTicket.cs

```csharp
using System;
using System.Collections.Generic;

namespace ComputerInventory.Models {
    public partial class SupportTicket {
        public SupportTicket() {
            SupportLog = new HashSet<SupportLog>();
        }

        public int SupportTicketId { get; set; }
        public DateTime DateReported { get; set; }
        public DateTime? DateResolved { get; set; }
        public string IssueDescription { get; set; }
        public string IssueDetail { get; set; }
        public string TicketOpenedBy { get; set; }
        public int MachineId { get; set; }
```

```
        public Machine Machine { get; set; }
        public ICollection<SupportLog> SupportLog { get; set; }
    }
}
```

Listing 1-7. SupportLog.cs

```
using System;
using System.Collections.Generic;

namespace ComputerInventory.Models {
    public partial class SupportLog {
        public int SupportLogId { get; set; }
        public DateTime SupportLogEntryDate { get; set; }
        public string SupportLogEntry { get; set; }
        public string SupportLogUpdatedBy { get; set; }
        public int SupportTicketId { get; set; }

        public SupportTicket SupportTicket { get; set; }
    }
}
```

Now you have what you need to start creating the seven tables used in this first section of the book. As I mentioned, each class created in the Models folder represents a table in the database. The next thing we need to do is set up our DBContext, which is the Grand Poobah of Entity Framework and Entity Framework Core. It's the connection between your entity classes and the database. Without this primary class, we wouldn't have Entity Framework and we'd be back to setting up database connections using the SQL client and creating instances of the DataSet and DataTables classes while putting things in memory and using lots of big SQL queries. You'll see better how great it is once you use it.

Since we are talking about DBContext, let's create a Context class so we can get to writing some code to interact with our database that much quicker. Remember that folder we created called Data? That is where we are going to put our class, so create a new class in the Data folder and call it MachineContext.cs. Listing 1-8 shows the code we'll use for MachineContext.cs. You could have called this class anything you wanted and you'll want to give it a name that makes sense to you when you create your own projects. Okay, this is going to be a big one, so get ready.

Listing 1-8. MachineContext.cs

```csharp
using System;
using Microsoft.EntityFrameworkCore;
using ComputerInventory.Models;

namespace ComputerInventory.Data {
    class MachineContext : DbContext {
        public virtual DbSet<Machine> Machine { get; set; }
        public virtual DbSet<MachineType> MachineType { get; set; }
        public virtual DbSet<MachineWarranty> MachineWarranty { get; set; }
        public virtual DbSet<OperatingSys> OperatingSys { get; set; }
        public virtual DbSet<SupportLog> SupportLog { get; set; }
        public virtual DbSet<SupportTicket> SupportTicket { get; set; }
        public virtual DbSet<WarrantyProvider> WarrantyProvider { get; set; }

        protected override void OnConfiguring(DbContextOptionsBuilder
        optionsBuilder) {
        if (!optionsBuilder.IsConfigured) {

            optionsBuilder.UseSqlServer(@"Server=ServerName;Database=BegEFCore2;
            Trusted_Connection=false;User ID=sa;Password= ");
        }
    }

    protected override void OnModelCreating(ModelBuilder modelBuilder) {
        modelBuilder.Entity<Machine>(entity => {
        entity.Property(e => e.MachineId).HasColumnName("MachineID");

        entity.Property(e => e.GeneralRole)
            .IsRequired()
            .HasMaxLength(25)
            .IsUnicode(false);

        entity.Property(e => e.InstalledRoles)
            .IsRequired()
            .HasMaxLength(50)
            .IsUnicode(false);
```

```
entity.Property(e => e.MachineTypeId).HasColumnName("MachineTypeID");

entity.Property(e => e.Name)
    .IsRequired()
    .HasMaxLength(25)
    .IsUnicode(false);

entity.Property(e => e.OperatingSysId).HasColumnName("OperatingSysID");

entity.HasOne(d => d.MachineType)
    .WithMany(p => p.Machine)
    .HasForeignKey(d => d.MachineTypeId)
    .OnDelete(DeleteBehavior.ClientSetNull)
    .HasConstraintName("FK_MachineType");

entity.HasOne(d => d.OperatingSys)
    .WithMany(p => p.Machine)
    .HasForeignKey(d => d.OperatingSysId)
    .OnDelete(DeleteBehavior.ClientSetNull)
    .HasConstraintName("FK_OperatingSys");
});

modelBuilder.Entity<MachineType>(entity => {
    entity.Property(e => e.MachineTypeId).HasColumnName("MachineTypeID");

    entity.Property(e => e.Description)
        .HasMaxLength(15)
        .IsUnicode(false);
});

modelBuilder.Entity<MachineWarranty>(entity => {
    entity.Property(e => e.MachineWarrantyId).HasColumnName
    ("MachineWarrantyID");

    entity.Property(e => e.MachineId).HasColumnName("MachineID");

    entity.Property(e => e.ServiceTag)
        .IsRequired()
```

```
            .HasMaxLength(20)
            .IsUnicode(false);

        entity.Property(e => e.WarrantyExpiration).HasColumnType("date");

        entity.Property(e => e.WarrantyProviderId).HasColumnName
        ("WarrantyProviderID");

        entity.HasOne(d => d.WarrantyProvider)
            .WithMany(p => p.MachineWarranty)
            .HasForeignKey(d => d.WarrantyProviderId)
            .OnDelete(DeleteBehavior.ClientSetNull)
            .HasConstraintName("FK_WarrantyProvider");
    });

    modelBuilder.Entity<OperatingSys>(entity => {
        entity.Property(e => e.OperatingSysId).HasColumnName
        ("OperatingSysID");

        entity.Property(e => e.Name)
            .IsRequired()
            .HasMaxLength(35)
            .IsUnicode(false);
    });

    modelBuilder.Entity<SupportLog>(entity => {
        entity.Property(e => e.SupportLogId).HasColumnName("SupportLogID");

        entity.Property(e => e.SupportLogEntry)
            .IsRequired()
            .IsUnicode(false);

        entity.Property(e => e.SupportLogEntryDate).HasColumnType("date");

            entity.Property(e => e.SupportLogUpdatedBy)
                .IsRequired()
                .HasMaxLength(50)
                .IsUnicode(false);
```

```
        entity.Property(e => e.SupportTicketId).HasColumnName
        ("SupportTicketID");

        entity.HasOne(d => d.SupportTicket)
            .WithMany(p => p.SupportLog)
            .HasForeignKey(d => d.SupportTicketId)
            .OnDelete(DeleteBehavior.ClientSetNull)
            .HasConstraintName("FK_SupportTicket");
    });

    modelBuilder.Entity<SupportTicket>(entity => {
        entity.Property(e => e.SupportTicketId).HasColumnName
        ("SupportTicketID");

        entity.Property(e => e.DateReported).HasColumnType("date");

        entity.Property(e => e.DateResolved).HasColumnType("date");

        entity.Property(e => e.IssueDescription)
            .IsRequired()
            .HasMaxLength(150)
            .IsUnicode(false);
        entity.Property(e => e.IssueDetail).IsUnicode(false);

            entity.Property(e => e.MachineId).HasColumnName("MachineID");

        entity.Property(e => e.TicketOpenedBy)
            .IsRequired()
            .HasMaxLength(50)
            .IsUnicode(false);

        entity.HasOne(d => d.Machine)
            .WithMany(p => p.SupportTicket)
            .HasForeignKey(d => d.MachineId)
            .OnDelete(DeleteBehavior.ClientSetNull)
            .HasConstraintName("FK_Machine");
    });
```

```
modelBuilder.Entity<WarrantyProvider>(entity => {
    entity.Property(e => e.WarrantyProviderId).HasColumnName
    ("WarrantyProviderID");

    entity.Property(e => e.ProviderName)
        .IsRequired()
        .HasMaxLength(50)
        .IsUnicode(false);

    entity.Property(e => e.SupportNumber)
        .IsRequired()
        .HasMaxLength(10)
        .IsUnicode(false);
    });
  }
 }
}
```

Let's take a look at the first DBSet line and figure out what is going on. We are creating a new public property for the MachineContext class of type DBSet<TEntity> in our case it's a <Machine>. We are going to use this to query and save instances of our entity type using our DBContext variable MachineContext. When we create LINQ queries against our DBSet<Machine> (or any other entity for that matter), it will be translated by EF into a query against the underlying database. One point to keep in mind is that the results you see will be from the database and not from other contexts that haven't been saved back to the database. In short, we will interact with the entity class we created and thus with the database table associated with said class.

We then create OnConfiguring(), which is our database connection. It's not good form to leave this in the application, but since we are at the beginning stage of our Entity Framework Core career, we'll leave it here. There is good documentation from Microsoft about how to handle this better if you need to remove it from the application. That being said, take a look at the string so you know what is going on:

```
optionsBuilder.UseSqlServer(@"Data Source=ServerName;Initial
Catalog=BegEFCore;Integrated Security=false;User ID=sa;Password= ;");
```

My good friend Doug brought something to my attention here and as a result I'm going to bring it up. I did mention that I wasn't going to show you the wrong way to do something and then fix it later. Well, we technically aren't going to fix this part later, as I'm going to leave that up to you, but leaving your connection in your code isn't a good habit to get into.

We need to tell it the data source, which is the name of the database server. The initial catalog is the name of the database. The next part depends on your connection. I'm not using integrated security, so I set that to `false`. I'm using the sa user account for my database and for obvious reasons I have deleted the password I'm using. However, you would put it after `Password=` with no space or quotes.

If you have one of those jobs where you can work on this during your lunch or breaks at work and they'll let you create a database, get the login information from your DBA. If you are in charge of your own database or it's at home, you just need to be sure you have the ability to create and modify databases and tables. Many of you will be able to use Windows Integrated Security for your application and it uses your user account (the one you logged into the Windows Environment with) to gain access to the database. For this to work, the user or users need to be given permission to access the SQL Server database.

Note   If you are working for a company or doing a project for someone else, be sure to find out if you should be using SQL Server or integrated security.

The last part of this class is the `OnModelCreating()` method. Let's take a look at the `Machine` entity first, as this covers about 90% of what we'll be doing for the rest of them. This might look complicated and scary, but once you do it a few times, it's less so. We are using our `ModelBuilder` parameter that was passed into the method to do all this work. We need to work with each of the entities, so that's pretty straight forward: `modelBuilder.Entity<Machine>`. This is where it gets a little confusing if you aren't used to inline and lambda functions, which we'll be using a lot in this book. We create our *entity* property then use our lambda operator (`=>`), followed by listing the properties in braces `{}`. These braces are a terrific way to get this done. If you aren't familiar with them, check out MSDN for more information, as they will save you a lot of time.

Let's look at each of these property types one at a time to make it a little bit easier to follow. The first one is the ID field, which I mentioned earlier. Because the ID is the same name as our entity, EF Core knows to make it the primary key:

```
entity.Property(e => e.MachineId).HasColumnName("MachineID");
```

So what are we saying here? We have our entity and we are working with a property. We create an operator called e (this could be anything, but when you are working with multiples, it's very important to keep them straight) and we are going to work with MachineId, so we tell it that is the property from our Machine class that we are using. We then tell it that it has a name and its name is MachineID. You might wonder why they are different. That's because when I created the class Machine I forgot to hold down the Shift key and the D ended up being lowercase. I could fix this, but it illustrates how the name of the field in the database could be different than in the code. This can be helpful when working with a database that already exists and contains inconsistencies like these. This is also common when you want a different naming convention from the database and the EF Source code.

On to the next property, which is the GeneralRole property. In Machine.cs this is:

```
public MachineType MachineType { get; set; }
entity.Property(e => e.GeneralRole).IsRequired().HasMaxLength(25).
IsUnicode(false);
```

You can put this all on one line or split it into multiple lines like we did in Listing 1-8. Because the name hasn't changed, we don't need to tell it that it has a different name but we do need to tell it that it "is required" and that it has a maximum length of 25 characters. The last property, called .IsUnicode(false), makes the field a varchar rather than a nvarchar. Since we aren't storing any Unicode characters and they take up two bytes each rather than one, this saves space.

Next in the code, note the MachineType property. We are going to create a relationship in which this entity points to a single instance of another entity. In this case, it's a MachineType. This is where it's important to keep track of your variables. We are going to use d when referring to MachineType. We will then use p for our current property. By using .WithMany we are creating a many-to-one relationship when going from MachineType to Machine, as each MachineType could have many different Machines associated with it.

We then have a property about what happens when we try to delete a field in a table that is a primary key and has associated foreign keys. For now, just go with this. When you have time, look at the different options, as this could prove useful to you in the future. Lastly, we have to give our foreign key a name and we do so with .HasConstraintName with the name in parentheses.

Let's skip down to the OperatingSys entity, since it doesn't have a foreign key association.

```
modelBuilder.Entity<OperatingSys>(entity => {
entity.Property(e => e.OperatingSysId).HasColumnName("OperatingSysID");

entity.Property(e => e.Name).IsRequired().HasMaxLength(35).IsUnicode(false);});
```

This looks pretty boring in comparison to what we have for our Machine entity. All we have is our OperatingSysId and the Name properties. There is another field in the OperatingSys class, but the only thing we are concerned about with the Model Builder is the properties that aren't easily defined data types or that require a little tweaking to get working. If you look at the entry for SupportTicket, you'll notice that we had to specify the data type for the Date fields and the string properties are not accepting Unicode characters.

Take a look at everything we have done in MachineContext.cs and read through it once or twice using the compiler. Hover over the parts that you don't quite understand. Sometimes IntelliSense can be helpful in trying to understand what is going on.

Creating the Database

Okay, it's time for the moment of truth. Let's see if everything we did is going to work and create the database. Open the NuGet Package Manager console by choosing Tools ➤ NuGet Package Manager ➤ Package Manager Console. Then type the following into the console (your PMC host version may be different):

```
Package Manager Console Host Version 4.3.0.4315
Type 'get-help NuGet' to see all available NuGet commands.
PM> Add-Migration ComputerInventory.Data.MachineContext
```

You should then see this after it has completed:

```
To undo this action, use Remove-Migration.
PM>
```

You don't want to do that, so instead enter Update-Database. Once it's done, you'll have a new database on your server. Figure 1-5 shows my database in SQL Server Management Studio.

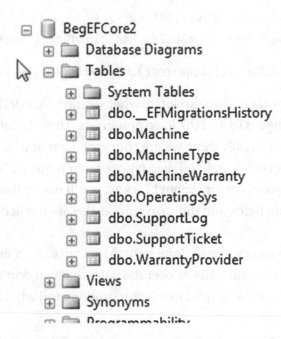

Figure 1-5. *View of the database from SSMS*

If you look in Solution Explorer for this project, you'll see that a Migrations folder was created and there are a couple of class files in there. They were created for the database and tables. Take some time to look through them. It's pretty interesting what EF Core does for you.

Now that you have some tables set up in the database, you might as well start adding something to it. The next section covers adding data to the table and then you'll see how to retrieve data from it. You could use SSMS to add data, but why not do it in code since you'll have to do it eventually anyway.

Adding Data to a Table

Open `Program.cs` and delete `Console.WriteLine("Hello World!");` as you don't need that. Listing 1-9 shows `Program.cs` after we delete this line and add a few using statements.

Listing 1-9. Program.cs Before Coding

```
using Microsoft.EntityFrameworkCore;
using System;
using System.Collections.Generic;
using System.Linq;

using ComputerInventory.Data;
using ComputerInventory.Models;

namespace ComputerInventory {
    class Program {
        static void Main(string[] args) {

        }
    }
}
```

Now that we have our project ready, let's get started. Listings 1-10 through 1-13 show the code added to `Program.cs` in digestible chunks. I explain each section after you add it. There is a lot here that we need to get set up. Once it's there, though, it'll make your life easier in the long run. Without further ado, here we go.

Listing 1-10. Program.cs: Setting Up the Menus

```
static void Main(string[] args) {
    // Set a color you like other than green or red as this will be used later
    Console.ForegroundColor = ConsoleColor.Black;
    int result = -1;
    while (result !- 9) {
        result = MainMenu();
    }
}
```

21

```
static int MainMenu() {
    int result = -1;
    ConsoleKeyInfo cki;
    bool cont = false;
    do {
        Console.Clear();
        WriteHeader("Welcome to Newbie Data Systems");
        WriteHeader("Main Menu");
        Console.WriteLine("\r\nPlease select from the list below for what you
        would like to do today");
        Console.WriteLine("1. List All Machines in Inventory");
        Console.WriteLine("2. List All Operating Systems");
        Console.WriteLine("3. Data Entry Menu");
        Console.WriteLine("9. Exit");
        cki = Console.ReadKey();
        try {
            result = Convert.ToInt16(cki.KeyChar.ToString());
            if (result == 1) {
                //DisplayAllMachines();
            }
            else if (result == 2) {
                //DisplayOperatingSystems();
            }
            else if (result == 3) {
                DataEntryMenu();
            }
            else if (result == 9) {
                // We are exiting so nothing to do
                cont = true;
            }
        }
        catch (System.FormatException) {
            // a key that wasn't a number
        }
```

```
    } while (!cont);

    return result;
}

static void DataEntryMenu() {
    ConsoleKeyInfo cki;
    int result = -1;
    bool cont = false;
    do {
        Console.Clear();
        WriteHeader("Data Entry Menu");
        Console.WriteLine("\r\nPlease select from the list below for what you
        would like to do today");
        Console.WriteLine("1. Add a New Machine");
        Console.WriteLine("2. Add a New Operating System");
        Console.WriteLine("3. Add a New Warranty Provider");
        Console.WriteLine("9. Exit Menu");
        cki = Console.ReadKey();
        try {
            result = Convert.ToInt16(cki.KeyChar.ToString());
            if (result == 1) {
                //AddMachine();
            }
            else if (result == 2) {
                AddOperatingSystem();
            }
            else if (result == 3) {
                //AddNewWarrantyProvider();
            }
            else if (result == 9) {
                // We are exiting so nothing to do
                cont = true;
            }
```

```
        }
        catch (System.FormatException) {
            // a key that wasn't a number
        }
    } while (!cont);
}
```

Note   I set my `Console.ForegroundColor` = `ConsoleColor.Black`, as I have to use a white background for the book. If you are using a black background, you'll need to use another color for the console.

That was quite a bit, I know and unfortunately we haven't gotten to any Entity Framework Core yet, but don't worry we are almost there. Let's go over a couple of things first. As I hope you have guessed, we are creating a menu-based console application so every time we get to a new menu we are calling `Console.Clear()` to clear the old screen. We are doing some basic error handling to check for proper user input, although if you want, you can make it more robust.

I have a couple of things commented out that we will be using shortly, so if you didn't add them you can now or when we add the new methods. I set the font color to white as we'll be making some changes to it shortly and this way I can change it back and forth. You should have gotten a few errors in your error list and we'll take care of a few of them right now. Listing 1-11 shows the helper methods.

Listing 1-11. Helper Methods in Program.cs

```
static void WriteHeader(string headerText) {
    Console.WriteLine(string.Format("{0," + ((Console.WindowWidth / 2) +
headerText.Length / 2) + "}", headerText));
}

static bool ValidateYorN(string entry) {
    bool result = false;
    if (entry.ToLower() == "y" || entry.ToLower() == "n") {
```

```
        result = true;
    }
    return result;
}
```

These two little helper methods will save you a lot of typing later, as you add to the application. The first will center the text in the console window when it displays the header line. This makes the text more readable and somewhat more professional looking. The second you'll see in action in Listing 1-12, but basically it's validating user input when they are asking to enter a y or n. This one is where the real savings is, as you'll be using that one quite a lot. You finally get some Entity Framework Core to look at in Listing 1-12.

Listing 1-12. Finally Some EF Core

```
static bool CheckForExistingOS(string osName) {
    bool exists = false;
    using (var context = new MachineContext()) {
        var os = context.OperatingSys.Where(o => o.Name == osName);
        if (os.Count() > 0) {
            exists = true;
        }
    }
    return exists;
}
```

Well, that was worth the wait, right? Okay, it doesn't look like a lot, but you did quite a bit of work in just a couple of lines. As mentioned earlier, DBContext (MachineContext here) is our connection to the database, so we create a new local variable in this case for ease of reading we called context. The next thing we do is throw in some LINQ magic to create a IQueriable<OperatingSys> (var is so much easier to type) object and write a basic LINQ query to see if there is an entry in the OperatingSys table that matches the OS. If there is a result, os.Count() will return a value greater than 0. Think of how many lines that would have been if you did it without EF Core. Finally, let's get the last piece in so we can at least enter some data into the table. Listing 1-13 shows you just that.

Listing 1-13. Method for Entering Data Into the Table

```
static void AddOperatingSystem() {
    Console.Clear();
    ConsoleKeyInfo cki;
    string result;
    bool cont = false;
    OperatingSys os = new OperatingSys();
    string osName = "";
    do {
        WriteHeader("Add New Operating System");
        Console.WriteLine("Enter the Name of the Operating System and hit Enter");
        osName = Console.ReadLine();
        if (osName.Length >= 4) {
            cont = true;
        }
        else {
            Console.WriteLine("Please enter a valid OS name of at least 4
            characters.\r\nPress and key to continue...");
            Console.ReadKey();
        }
    } while (!cont);
    cont = false;
    os.Name = osName;
    Console.WriteLine("Is the Operating System still supported? [y or n]");

    do {
        cki = Console.ReadKey();
        result = cki.KeyChar.ToString();
        cont = ValidateYorN(result);
    } while (!cont);

    if (result.ToLower() == "y") {
        os.StillSupported = true;
    }
```

```
else {
   os.StillSupported = false;
}
cont = false;
do {
   Console.Clear();
   Console.WriteLine($"You entered {os.Name} as the Operating
   System Name\r\nIs the OS still supported, you entered {os.
   StillSupported}.\r\nDo you wish to continue? [y or n]");
   cki = Console.ReadKey();
   result = cki.KeyChar.ToString();
   cont = ValidateYorN(result);
} while (!cont);
if (result.ToLower() == "y") {
   bool exists = CheckForExistingOS(os.Name);
   if (exists) {
      Console.WriteLine("\r\nOperating System already exists in the
      database\r\nPress any key to continue...");
      Console.ReadKey();
   }
   else {
      using (var context = new MachineContext()) {
         Console.WriteLine("\r\nAttempting to save changes...");
         context.OperatingSys.Add(os);
         int i = context.SaveChanges();
         if (i == 1) {
            Console.WriteLine("Contents Saved\r\nPress any key to
            continue...");
            Console.ReadKey();
         }
      }
   }
}
}
```

The first part of this method is basic question and answer type code with some very basic validation and error handling. If you are new to C# 6.0, one of the lines may look a bit new to you:

```
Console.WriteLine($"You entered {os.Name} as the Operating System Name\r\nIs the OS still supported, you entered {os.StillSupported}.\r\nDo you wish to continue? [y or n]");
```

This uses a feature new to C# 6.0 called *string interpolation*. My goal is to stick with new features as much as possible, but you'll probably still find a couple of `string.format`s in the book, as old habits are hard to break. Note at the top that we created a new `OperatingSystem` object outside the `DBContext` loop. We did this for two reasons:

- To show you that they are accessible outside of the loop.

- To keep the connection open only as long as we need it.

Let's take a look at the EF Core code and see what is going on. Just like before, we get our local `DBContext` variable and put it into a `using` block. We then have the `context.OperatingSys.Add(os)` line, which makes a lot of sense. Let's break it down into parts.

`context` is our connection to the database. `OperatingSys` in this case is the table. If you hover over it, you'll see that it's `DBSet<OperatingSys>`. Lastly, what we are trying to do is add an object, so we call the `Add` method. However, there is one thing that we need to remember. We have added it only to our local copy, which is `context`. The next line saves the data to the table: `context.SaveChanges()`. Then `SaveChanges()` returns the number of rows affected as the return value.

Now that you have all that done, it's time to take this baby for a test drive. Run the application by pressing F5. After it complies and loads, you should see a window similar to Figure 1-6.

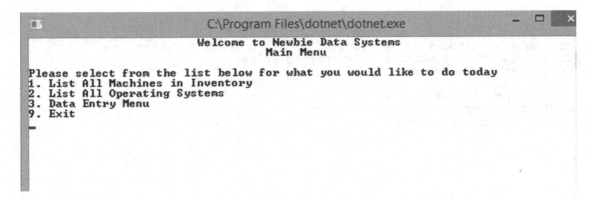

Figure 1-6. *Running the application*

Right now the only options that work are 3 and 9, but since we want to add data to the database, let's do some data entry. Choose option 3. Then choose option 2 to add a new operating system. For the name of the operating system, enter Windows Server 2003 R2 and press Enter. When asked if the OS is still supported, choose n for no. If you have entered your information correctly, you should see output like in Figure 1-7.

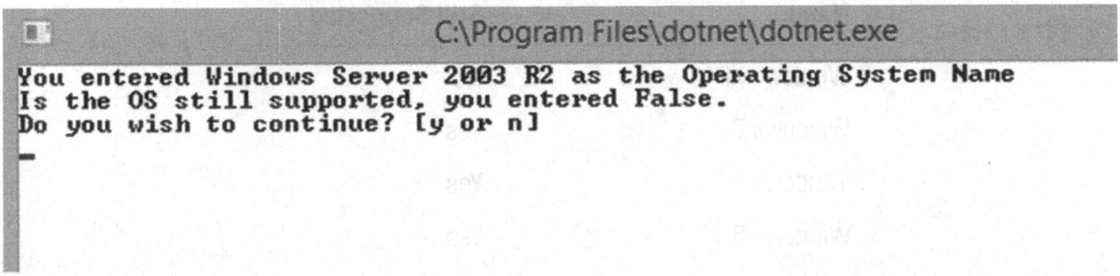

Figure 1-7. *Data entry, new operating system*

If it's correct, press y. After a second or so (depending on the speed of your database server and local machine), you should see output in your console window similar to Figure 1-8.

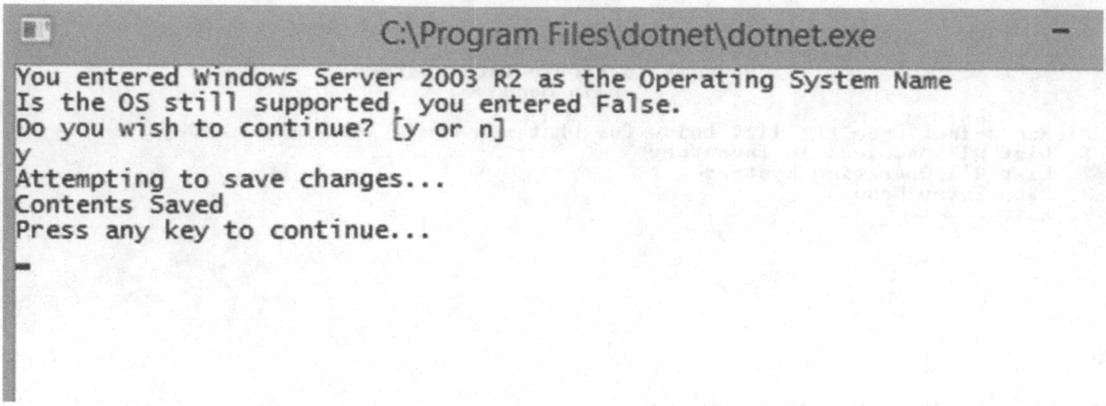

```
C:\Program Files\dotnet\dotnet.exe                    –
You entered Windows Server 2003 R2 as the Operating System Name
Is the OS still supported, you entered False.
Do you wish to continue? [y or n]
y
Attempting to save changes...
Contents Saved
Press any key to continue...
```

Figure 1-8. *You have successfully added a record with EF Core*

When you press Enter, you'll be brought back to the Data Entry menu. From there, go back to option 2 and enter the contents of Table 1-1 into the table.

Table 1-1. *Operating System Table Entries*

Name	Still Supported
Windows XP	No
Windows 7	Yes
Windows 8	Yes
Windows 8.1	Yes
Windows 10	Yes
Windows Server 2000	No
Windows Server 2008	Yes
Windows Server 2008 R2	Yes
Windows Server 2012	Yes
Windows Server 2012 R2	Yes
Windows Server 2016	Yes
Ubuntu Server 16.14.2 LTS	Yes
Ubuntu Server 17.04	Yes

You now have a few that are no longer supported and a good number that are supported. For now, we'll stick with this list, but we'll be adding some more to the table later when we start doing some more interesting things with EF Core. In the "Summary" section of this chapter, you'll find code you can use if you want to seed the table without having to use the console.

Now that we have some data, we need a way of looking at it. Option 2 in the Main menu will list all operating systems, so that seems like a good place to start. Feel free to add a couple of others, but just be sure that your listing in SSMS matches Table 1-1 (including Windows Server 2003 R2, false that we entered earlier). See what happens when you don't capitalize the entries; does it still load or throw an error?

If you want to save some time, use the method for seeding the OperatingSys table at the end of the chapter (Listing 1-20). You can also use it later to repopulate the table after you make some changes to it.

Retrieving Data from a Database and Displaying It

We technically have already retrieved results in the last example, but we need a way to check if a record is already in the table before we add it (as long as we spell it the same). Since this is the first chapter, we are going to make this as simple as possible. Listing 1-14 shows the method for displaying the contents of the OperatingSys table.

Listing 1-14. DisplayOperatingSystems() Added to Program.cs

```
static void DisplayOperatingSystems() {
    Console.Clear();
    Console.WriteLine("Operating Systems");
    using (var context = new MachineContext()) {
        foreach (var os in context.OperatingSys.ToList()) {
            Console.Write($"Name: {os.Name,-39}\tStill Supported = ");
            if (os.StillSupported == true) {
                Console.ForegroundColor = ConsoleColor.Green;
            }
            else {
                Console.ForegroundColor = ConsoleColor.Red;
            }
```

```
        Console.WriteLine(os.StillSupported);
        Console.ForegroundColor = ConsoleColor.Black;
      }
    }
    Console.WriteLine("\r\nAny key to continue...");
    Console.ReadKey();
}
```

Before you can run your code, go to the Main menu and uncomment
DisplayOperatingSystems(). Now, when you run your application and chose Option 2
from the Main menu, you should see output similar to Figure 1-9 (although the order of
the values may be different).

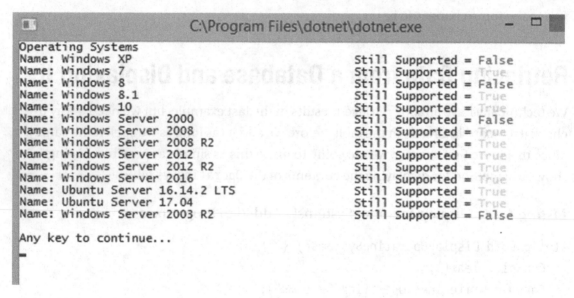

Figure 1-9. *A list of operating systems*

Take a look at the code. You can see that not a whole lot is new; we create our
MachineContext object and this time we put our query into a foreach loop. So what are
we saying here? It's quite simple: to each operating system object in our list of objects
from the OperatingSys table, we are going to do something. We are doing some line
formatting in the first Console.Writeline() so that everything lines up a little better (if
this is new to you, I highly recommend looking up formatting in console applications as
it will help things look a lot better and more readable). Now if you'll recall, I said the font
color of our console was going to be used; well, here it is. If the operating system is still

supported, we output True in green. If the OS is not supported, we output False in red. We then have to change the color back to the original selection; otherwise, it will look off. You can choose any colors you like, but green and red seem to make the most sense to me.

Deleting Data from a Database

Anytime you are going to delete data from a database, you need to be careful as it's quite easy to delete the wrong data. It's always a good idea to verify with the user that data should in fact be deleted. We will do some basic checking, but in your applications the amount of validation you do is entirely up to you. There are a couple of different methods that you can use to delete/remove records with EF. We will cover a couple of different ways in this book so you can determine which way you like best.

Deleting a Single Record

In this example, we are going to work a little backwards. We create the method in which we delete the record and then we create all the menu objects. Listing 1-15 shows the code for this deletion method.

Listing 1-15. DeleteOperatingSystem()

```
static void DeleteOperatingSystem(int id) {
    OperatingSys os = GetOperatingSystemById(id);
    if (os != null) {
        Console.WriteLine($"\r\nAre you sure you want to delete {os.Name}?
        [y or n]");
        ConsoleKeyInfo cki;
        string result;
        bool cont;
        do {
            cki = Console.ReadKey(true);
            result = cki.KeyChar.ToString();
            cont = ValidateYorN(result);
        } while (!cont);
        if ("y" == result.ToLower()) {
            Console.WriteLine("\r\nDeleting record");
```

33

```
            using (var context = new MachineContext()) {
                context.Remove(os);
                context.SaveChanges();
            }
            Console.WriteLine("Record Deleted");
            Console.ReadKey();
        }
        else {
            Console.WriteLine("Delete Aborted\r\nHit any key to continue...");
            Console.ReadKey();
        }
    }
    else {
        Console.WriteLine("\r\nOperating System Not Found!");
        Console.ReadKey();
        SelectOperatingSystem("Delete");
    }
}
```

This method starts off with a call to a helper method to retrieve an `OperatingSys()` object, which we'll get to in a minute, and then it checks to see if the result is null. We then do some basic checking to be sure that the user does want to delete the record. Once we have determined that the user does want to delete this record, we create the `using` statement to get our `DBContext` object and then we call `context.Remove(os)` to remove our `os` object from the context. Then we call `context.SaveChanges()` to save our changes to the database. Just like when we added records to the database, nothing is written back to the database until `SaveChanges()` is called. Now, some may argue that this is not the best way to do it. That you should instead add the object to the context first and then remove it, which would look like this:

```
Context.Add(os);
Context.Remove(os);
Context.SaveChanges();
```

You are free to use this method, but it is not required. Once we add the rest of the code, we'll step through it and you'll get a better understanding of what is going on with this function of Entity Framework Core.

Listing 1-16 shows how to add the other methods and Listing 1-17 shows how to add the menu updates.

Listing 1-16. More Helper Methods

```
static OperatingSys GetOperatingSystemById(int id) {
   var context = new MachineContext();
   OperatingSys os = context.OperatingSys.FirstOrDefault(i =>
   i.OperatingSysId == id);
   return os;
}

static void SelectOperatingSystem(string operation) {
   ConsoleKeyInfo cki;
   Console.Clear();
   WriteHeader($"{operation} an Existing Operating System Entry");
   Console.WriteLine($"{"ID",-7}|{"Name",-50}|Still Supported");
   Console.WriteLine("-------------------------------------- -----------");
   using (var context = new MachineContext()) {
      List<OperatingSys> lOperatingSystems = context.OperatingSys.ToList();
      foreach (OperatingSys os in lOperatingSystems) {
         Console.WriteLine($"{os.OperatingSysId,-7}|{os.Name,-50}|
         {os.StillSupported}");
      }
   }
   Console.WriteLine($"\r\nEnter the ID of the record you wish to
   {operation} and hit Enter\r\nYou can hit Esc to exit this menu");
   bool cont = false;
   string id = "";
   do {
      cki = Console.ReadKey(true);
      if (cki.Key == ConsoleKey.Escape) {
         cont = true;
         id = "";
      }
```

```
      else if (cki.Key == ConsoleKey.Enter) {
          if (id.Length > 0) {
              cont = true;
          }
          else {
              Console.WriteLine("Please enter an ID that is at least 1 digit.");
          }
      }
      else if (cki.Key == ConsoleKey.Backspace) {
          Console.Write("\b \b");
          try {
              id = id.Substring(0, id.Length - 1);
          }
          catch (System.ArgumentOutOfRangeException) {
              // at the 0 position, can't go any further back
          }
      }
      else {
          if (char.IsNumber(cki.KeyChar)) {
              id += cki.KeyChar.ToString();
              Console.Write(cki.KeyChar.ToString());
          }
      }
  } while (!cont);

  int osId = Convert.ToInt32(id);
  if ("Delete" == operation) {
     DeleteOperatingSystem(osId);
  }
  else if ("Modify" == operation) {
     //ModifyOperatingSystem(osId);
  }
}
```

The GetOperatingSystemById method returns an operating system object. There shouldn't be anything new here. We created this method to call this code more than once from different locations. However, note that we aren't using our usual using statement here. You don't need to always use the using statement in your operations. As with many of the aspects of EF Core, it comes down to how you like to do things and what makes the most sense to you. Sometimes I like to have the using statement with brackets to keep things together and tidy. However, one more thing that I should mention is that the using statement will call the Dispose method once the object is no longer needed.

Listing 1-15 includes a call back to SelectOperatingSystem when the user enters an invalid operating system from the menu. This method takes a string variable as an argument, which we use to determine if we are trying to delete a record or update a record. Since the initial code of both pieces was the same, it made sense to create a single method that we could use for both operations. Our first bit of EF Core code gets our list of operating systems and, as you more than likely noticed, we decided to not use a var this time. We specifically used a List<OperatingSys> instead, just to show you that you can. Whichever method you use is up to you, although I do use both depending on what I'm doing for notation purposes. In this case, I know I'm creating a list instead of just getting a single object.

We then loop through our results, putting them into a nice formatted "table" to read on the screen. Because we didn't specify anything in our query, we will be retrieving all records from the OperatingSys table, which in this case is fine. We'll get into filtering results in the upcoming chapters. We then have some more basic C# code. Toward the bottom is the call to DeleteOperatingSystem(osId) to do the actual deletion and right under that is the call to modify a record, which we'll get to later, so for now just leave it commented out. Listing 1-17 shows the DataModificationMenu code, which looks just like our other menus. Feel free to cut and paste and then change it as needed to save yourself some typing.

Listing 1-17. The Data Modification Menu

```
static void DataModificationMenu() {
    ConsoleKeyInfo cki;
    int result = -1;
    bool cont = false;
    do {
        Console.Clear();
```

```
    WriteHeader("Data Modification Menu");
    Console.WriteLine("\r\nPlease select from the list below for what you
    would like to do today");
    Console.WriteLine("1. Delete Operating System");
    Console.WriteLine("2. Modify Operating System");
    Console.WriteLine("3. Delete All Unsupported Operating Systems");
    Console.WriteLine("9. Exit Menu");
    cki = Console.ReadKey();
    try {
        result = Convert.ToInt16(cki.KeyChar.ToString());
        if (result == 1) {
            SelectOperatingSystem("Delete");
        }
        else if (result == 2) {
            //SelectOperatingSystem("Modify");
        }
        else if (result == 3) {
            //DeleteAllUnsupportedOperatingSystems();
        }
        else if (result == 9) {
            // We are exiting so nothing to do
            cont = true;
        }
    }
    catch (System.FormatException) {
        // a key that wasn't a number
    }
} while (!cont);
}
```

The only thing left to do is update the Main menu so we can get to the new menu and code. The following are a couple of lines from the MainMenu method to show the changes that you need to make:

```
Console.WriteLine("3. Data Entry Menu");
Console.WriteLine("4. Data Modification Menu");
Console.WriteLine("9. Exit");
```

```
else if (result == 3) {
   DataEntryMenu();
}
else if (result == 4) {
   DataModificationMenu();
}
else if (result == 9) {
   // We are exiting so nothing to do
   cont = true;
}
```

Before we run this, let's add a breakpoint to context.Remove(os); so we can take a look at our variables. Run your code and choose the Data Modification menu and then Delete Operating System. We will delete Windows Server 2000 so enter its ID and press Enter. When you press Enter, you should hit your breakpoint. If you expand the context variable, you should see something similar to Figure 1-10.

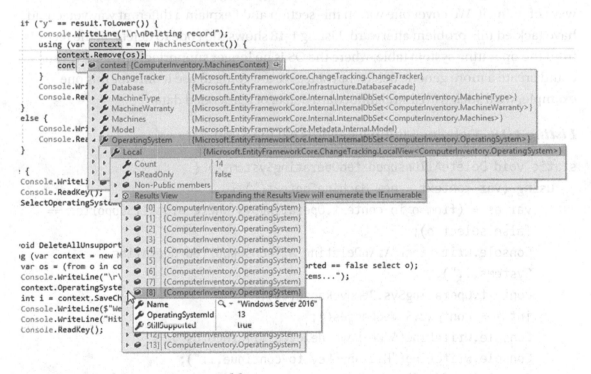

Figure 1-10. *The context variable*

As you can see, the context already knows a lot about our database just by connecting to it. This also shows you that you didn't need to add the operating system variable to the context, as the system already knew about it. If you step through the code, you will see that after the Remove is called, the local count drops by one, but the results view still has all the original values in it. Once you step past SaveChanges(), you'll see that the Results view now matches your local copy in context. If you go back to the Main menu and choose List All Operating Systems, you should now see that Windows Server 2000 is no longer on the list.

Although we cover this in detail later, I wanted to show you what is happening with DBContext so you have a better understanding of what is available to you. You can see how using smart SELECT statements is important once you start working on larger and more complex tables and table structures.

Deleting Multiple Records

Deleting multiple records is just as easy as deleting a single record and there are multiple ways of doing it. We cover one way in this section and I explain a different way you could have tackled this problem afterward. Listing 1-18 shows the code to delete all the records from the operating system table, where the OS is no longer supported. Obviously, you could create a more generic delete, but since we are going to use it only for this one example, we'll stick with a straightforward delete of hardcoded data.

Listing 1-18. Deleting Multiple Records at One Time

```
static void DeleteAllUnsupportedOperatingSystems() {
    using (var context = new MachineContext()) {
        var os = (from o in context.OperatingSys where o.StillSupported ==
        false select o);
        Console.WriteLine("\r\nDeleting all Unsupported Operating
        Systems...");
        context.OperatingSys.RemoveRange(os);
        int i = context.SaveChanges();
        Console.WriteLine($"We have deleted {i} records");
        Console.WriteLine("Hit any key to continue...");
        Console.ReadKey();
    }
}
```

I hope this is starting to sense and you can see what is going on before I explain it to you. We have our usual `using` statement to create our instance of `DBContext` followed by our `SELECT`. If you hover over `os`, you should see that we are creating an `IQueriable<OperatingSys>` variable type. We then let the users know that they are about to delete some data with no way of stopping it.

Unlike in the last example, this delete is handled a little differently because we are deleting a group of one or more records. To do this, we use `RemoveRange()` in order to delete the entity or entities that we have chosen from our `DBContext` object. We then call `SaveChanges()` to write those changes back to the database. We get back the number of rows that were affected and we are done. Uncomment your code as follows in the Data Modification menu and you can delete all those pesky unsupported operating systems from the table.

```
else if (result == 3) {
    DeleteAllUnsupportedOperatingSystems();
}
```

If you run your code multiple times, you will find that instead of throwing an error, it just tells you that you have deleted zero records. You could have determined if your initial query returned any results before calling `RemoveRange()` and you may want to do that in future projects, but in the interest of brevity, I left that out.

Now let's say you wanted to validate each record for some reason or you didn't want to use `RemoveRange()` to delete the entire group at one time. You could get the list of operating systems and then just do a loop, going through each one and deleting them in the same manner that we did when we deleted the single record. You wouldn't need to get a new `DBContext` each time, but you would have to be sure to call the `Remove()` for each record. You could either make one call to `SaveChanges()` or do it with each iteration; it's up to you, but you do need to do it before you close your connection.

This should make you dangerous enough for now; you have a database and can delete records from it. Remember you need to be careful before you delete something from a database. If you aren't careful, pray that you have a good and recent backup.

Updating Data in a Table

This last section covers the process of updating data in your database/tables. Listing 1-19 shows the code for modifying an operating system entity and the table. As you can see, we are using our GetOperatingSystemById() helper method to get an OperatingSystem object that we'll use to do our update.

Listing 1-19. Updating an Operating System Entry

```
static void ModifyOperatingSystem(int id) {
   OperatingSys os = GetOperatingSystemById(id);
   Console.Clear();
   char operation = 'O';
   bool cont = false;
   ConsoleKeyInfo cki;
   WriteHeader("Update Operating System");
   if (os != null) {
      Console.WriteLine($"\r\nOS Name: {os.Name}  Still Supported:
      {os.StillSupported}");
      Console.WriteLine("To modify the name press 1\r\nTo modify if the OS
      is Still Supported press 2");
      Console.WriteLine("Hit Esc to exit this menu");

      do {
         cki = Console.ReadKey(true);
         if (cki.Key == ConsoleKey.Escape)
            cont = true;
         else {
            if (char.IsNumber(cki.KeyChar)) {
               if (cki.KeyChar == '1') {
                  Console.WriteLine("Updated Operating System Name: ");
                  operation = '1';
                  cont = true;
               }
               else if (cki.KeyChar == '2') {
```

```
                        Console.WriteLine("Update if the OS is Still Supported
                        [y or n]: ");
                        operation = '2';
                        cont = true;
                    }
                }
            }
        } while (!cont);
    }
    if (operation == '1') {
        string osName;
        cont = false;
        do {
            osName = Console.ReadLine();
            if (osName.Length >= 4) {
                cont = true;
            }
            else {
                Console.WriteLine("Please enter a valid OS name of at least 4
                characters.\r\nPress and key to continue...");
                Console.ReadKey();
            }
        } while (!cont);
        os.Name = osName;
    }
    else if (operation == '2') {
        string k;
        do {
            cki = Console.ReadKey(true);
            k = cki.KeyChar.ToString();
            cont = ValidateYorN(k);
        } while (!cont);
        if (k == "y") {
            os.StillSupported = true;
        }
```

43

```
    else {
        os.StillSupported = false;
    }
}
using (var context = new MachineContext()) {
    var o = context.OperatingSys.FirstOrDefault(i => i.OperatingSysId ==
    os.OperatingSysId);
    if (o != null) {
        // just making sure
        o.Name = os.Name;
        o.StillSupported = os.StillSupported;
        Console.WriteLine("\r\nUpdating the database...");
        context.SaveChanges();
        Console.WriteLine("Done!\r\nHit any key to continue...");
    }
}
Console.ReadKey();
}
```

After we make our selection and retrieve our data from the database, we give the user some options to change what they see. At the end of our code sample, we do a restrictive SELECT just like we did in GetOperatingSystemById() to get the one entry we want to update and we double-check that we didn't get a null result, as that would cause some problems. We then simply change the Name and StillSupported values to those that we originally modified and save our changes. We also could have checked here to see if any of the values changed. We'll do that in a future example, but I just wanted to give you a simple way to update your records. Could we have done this all while leaving the connection open versus getting two OperatingSys objects? Yes, we could have retrieved our OperatingSys object and done all of this work while we left the connection open and then saved the original object back to the database. However, when you start working with websites, everything is done separately, so you should get in the habit of doing that now.

Another thing that we'll cover later, but that you need to keep in mind, is that you should validate your update in the same manner that you do your initial insert. You wouldn't want a user attempting to insert a date into a name field or something along those lines. It's good practice to have the validation in both places or to use the same validation in both places.

Before you can try this, don't forget that you need to uncomment `ModifyOperating` `System(osId);` within `SelectOperatingSystem()` and then uncomment `SelectOpera` `tingSystem("Modify");` from within `DataModificationMenu()`. Once you have done that, you can run the application and make a change. It's getting pretty close, which I'm sure is upsetting to many of you out there, so let's change Windows 7 so it's no longer supported.

Follow the prompts as if you were an end user. If you do everything correctly, you should see that Windows 7 is no longer supported. Choose Main Menu ➤ List All Operating Systems to see the list, as shown in Figure 1-11 (although your order may be a little bit different).

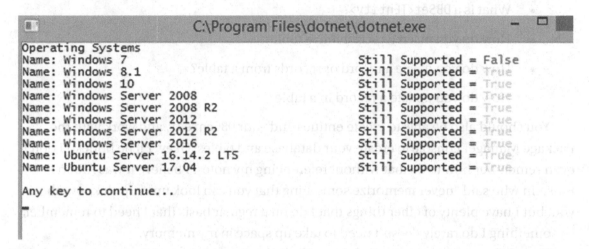

Figure 1-11. *Results after updating Windows 7 to not be supported*

Feel free to play around with everything that you have done until now. Once you are done, be sure to put everything back as it was (don't forget Windows Server 2003 R2) for Chapter 2. Don't worry about the order or the `OperatingSysId` numbers. We haven't done anything with the operating systems yet, so the ID doesn't matter.

Summary

By now you should be fairly comfortable with getting and using your `DBContext` object for some basic database manipulation. We covered how to create entities through code and how to then have those entities turn into a database and tables in the database. You created the `DBContext` class and the `DBSet<TEntity>` objects to query and save instances of the TEntities (this allows you to save your local copy of the entity back to the database). You then typed in some regular old C# code to create a working console application, and in the process you learned something new that you can use in the future. In the process of selecting, deleting, and updating the data, you learned how to use LINQ, which is something we'll discuss in greater detail in upcoming chapters.

Before going on, you should be able to explain the following:

- What is DBContext?

- Why do you have to call SaveChanges() even though you already added or updated DBContext?

- What is a DBSet<TEntity>?

- How do you insert a record into a table?

- How do you delete a record or records from a table?

- How do you update a record in a table?

You should also be able to create entities and your DBContext, and work with the Package Manager console to create your database and tables. Okay, I'll be honest; I don't even remember how to do that without referencing my notes. I believe it was Albert Einstein who said "never memorize something that you can look up". I don't know about you, but I have plenty of other things that I do on a regular basis that I need to remember, so something I do rarely doesn't need to take up space in my memory.

Hopefully, you are now comfortable with the basic operations of Entity Framework Core 2.0, as with these basic skills you can do quite a bit of work on a small project of your own if you are so inclined. Plus, what better way to learn something than to put it to use? You could create a simple application to track the daily temperatures and weather where you live. You could then figure out trends and averages once you have enough data (and get better with LINQ) and come up with an algorithm to do it. Have some fun with it.

One last thing before we go on. As I mentioned earlier, I created a method for seeding the OperatingSys table with data initially instead of using the interface to enter it manually. For those who read the chapter first, feel free to use this code to seed the database. Before you run the following code, you'll need to delete all the records or comment out the existing records as well as the Add line. I leave it up to you which method you use, but Listing 1-20 shows you one way that you can do this. Either add another item to the menu or modify one of them to run the seed operation and then comment it out once you are done.

Listing 1-20. Seeding the Table with Some Data

```
static void SeedOperatingSystemTable() {
    using (var context = new MachineContext()) {
        var os = new OperatingSys { Name = "Windows XP", StillSupported =
        false };
        context.OperatingSys.Add(os);
        os = new OperatingSys { Name = "Windows 7", StillSupported = true };
        context.OperatingSys.Add(os);
        os = new OperatingSys { Name = "Windows 8", StillSupported = false };
        context.OperatingSys.Add(os);
        os = new OperatingSys { Name = "Windows 8.1", StillSupported = true };
        context.OperatingSys.Add(os);
        os = new OperatingSys { Name = "Windows 10", StillSupported = true };
        context.OperatingSys.Add(os);
        os = new OperatingSys { Name = "Windows Server 2000", StillSupported
        = false };
        context.OperatingSys.Add(os);
        //os = new OperatingSys { Name = "Windows Server 2003 R2",
        StillSupported = false };
        //context.OperatingSys.Add(os);
        os = new OperatingSys { Name = "Windows Server 2008", StillSupported
        = true };
        context.OperatingSys.Add(os);
        os = new OperatingSys { Name = "Windows Server 2008 R2",
        StillSupported = true };
        context.OperatingSys.Add(os);
        os = new OperatingSys { Name = "Windows Server 2012", StillSupported
        = true };
        context.OperatingSys.Add(os);
        os = new OperatingSys { Name = "Windows Server 2012 R2",
        StillSupported = true };
        context.OperatingSys.Add(os);
        os = new OperatingSys { Name = "Windows Server 2016", StillSupported
        = true };
        context.OperatingSys.Add(os);
```

```
        os = new OperatingSys { Name = "Ubuntu Server 16.14.2 LTS",
        StillSupported = true };
        context.OperatingSys.Add(os);
        os = new OperatingSys { Name = "Ubuntu Server 17.04", StillSupported
        = true };
        context.OperatingSys.Add(os);
        context.SaveChanges();
    }
}
```

This is a little bit easier than entering everything in SSMS or using the interface for large amounts of additions (if you cut and paste a basic template that is). As you can see, we are adding each `OperatingSystem` object to the context each time, but we are only saving it once. There are a couple of ways you could have done this; can you figure out what they are? Take some time to play around with it and perhaps even add a check to see if they exist first. If you want to use the seed code, just add it to one of your menu items and run it one time. Just be sure to comment it out afterward, so you don't add the same information multiple times.

CHAPTER 2

Working with Multiple Tables

In Chapter 1 we created our application, set up our database and tables, and did some basic database operations with EF Core. While working with a single table is helpful and a good place to start, you'll be dealing with two or more tables for most things you do in your programming lives. We are going to cover the same operations that we did in Chapter 1 here, but using multiple tables. This chapter also explains how things are working in a little more detail, since you now have an understanding of the basics.

The first thing we need to be sure of is that we are starting with the same data in our `OperatingSystem` table. Figure 2-1 shows you the entries you should have in your table, although yours could be in a different order depending on what you did after you finished Chapter 1.

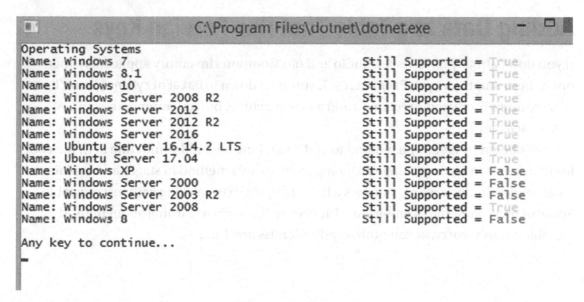

```
C:\Program Files\dotnet\dotnet.exe

Operating Systems
Name: Windows 7                      Still Supported = True
Name: Windows 8.1                    Still Supported = True
Name: Windows 10                     Still Supported = True
Name: Windows Server 2008 R2         Still Supported = True
Name: Windows Server 2012            Still Supported = True
Name: Windows Server 2012 R2         Still Supported = True
Name: Windows Server 2016            Still Supported = True
Name: Ubuntu Server 16.14.2 LTS      Still Supported = True
Name: Ubuntu Server 17.04            Still Supported = True
Name: Windows XP                     Still Supported = False
Name: Windows Server 2000            Still Supported = False
Name: Windows Server 2003 R2         Still Supported = False
Name: Windows Server 2008            Still Supported = True
Name: Windows 8                      Still Supported = False

Any key to continue...
```

Figure 2-1. *Table contents to start with*

49

© Derek J. Rouleau 2018
D. J. Rouleau, *Beginning Entity Framework Core 2.0*, https://doi.org/10.1007/978-1-4842-3375-7_2

If you are missing any of these entries, use your application to add them or modify them as needed. Sure, you could use SQL Server Management Studio, but what fun would that be?

The first thing we are going to do is add some machines to our database. If you look in SSMS at the Machines table, you should see Figure 2-2. As you can see, this table has two foreign keys—one we already populated with some data and the second one we'll take care of while we are creating our Machine object.

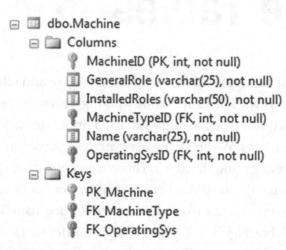

Figure 2-2. *Machines table in SSMS*

Adding Data to a Table That Has Foreign Keys

If you don't already have Visual Studio and our ComputerInventory application open, open them and then open Program.cs. If you scan down to DataEntryMenu(), you'll see that we already created a section to add a new machine, but it's commented out, //AddMachine();.

Let's begin by creating a method to add a machine and add some code to it; the code for this step is in Listing 2-1. We are going to create this method in stages and explain what we are doing as we go, since it's a little different than working with just one table. Some of these variables won't be used at first, so if you get a warning about unused variables, don't worry, as you probably didn't miss anything.

Listing 2-1. AddMachine() Initial Code

```
static void AddMachine() {
    Console.Clear();
    ConsoleKeyInfo cki;
    string result;
    bool cont = false;
    Machine machine = new Machine();
    WriteHeader("Add New Machine");
}
```

As you can see, this code looks like all of the other methods we have created up to this point. That's because the fundamentals are very similar. We need to figure out how we want to tackle the problem of adding a machine to our table. We know we need to add two foreign key entries—one for the machine type and one for the operating system. I think it makes the most sense to start off with what type of machine we are working with so we'll start there.

The first thing we need to do is get a list of the current choices for machine types. There is a very good chance that we may need to be able to do this later and someplace else in our code, so let's create a new method that returns a list of machines, as shown in Listing 2-2.

Listing 2-2. GetMachineTypes()

```
static List<MachineType> GetMachineTypes() {
    List<MachineType> lMachineType = new List<MachineType>();
    using(var context = new MachineContext()) {
        lMachineType = context.MachineType.ToList();
    }
    return lMachineType;
}
```

It's simple and gets the job done. We create the List<MachineType> named lMachineType. Yes, I'm in the habit of adding the variable type to the name for certain types (list being one of them), which I know many don't do any more.

We then create our using statement to access our DBContext object and then simply grab everything in the MachineType table and create a list with the results. We then return that to our calling method. You may wonder if this will throw an error because there is nothing in the table. You can test it or take my word for it, but at this point, it's not going to throw an error. It will simply return a empty list to the calling method.

51

If we have no machine types in our table, or if we don't have the right one, we need to add one. We'll take care of that right now. Listing 2-3 shows the code needed to add a machine type. As mentioned in Chapter 1, I'm a big fan of cutting and pasting code to make my life easier. Looking at what we have already created, I know that I have code that is similar to what I want to do, in AddOperatingSystem(). So we copy the first section and make changes to it so we can save a lot of typing and then grab some code from the bottom. You can also just type everything in; it's entirely up to you.

Listing 2-3. AddMachineType() and CheckForExistingMachineType()

```
static MachineType AddMachineType() {
    Console.Clear();
    ConsoleKeyInfo cki;
    string result;
    bool cont = false;
    MachineType mt = new MachineType();
    string mName = "";
    do {
        WriteHeader("Add New Machine Type");
        Console.WriteLine("Enter a Description for the Machine Type and hit Enter");
        mName = Console.ReadLine();
        if (mName.Length >= 6) {
            cont = true;
            mt.Description = mName;
        }
        else {
            Console.WriteLine("Please enter a valid Description of at least 6
            characters.\r\nPress and key to continue...");
            Console.ReadKey();
        }
    } while (!cont);

    cont = false;
    do {
        Console.Clear();
        Console.WriteLine($"You entered {mt.Description} as the
        Description.\r\nDo you wish to continue? [y or n]");
        cki = Console.ReadKey();
```

```
            result = cki.KeyChar.ToString();
            cont = ValidateYorN(result);
        } while (!cont);

        if (result.ToLower() == "y") {
            bool exists = CheckForExistingMachineType(mt.Description);
            if (exists) {
                Console.WriteLine("\r\nMachine Type already exists in the database\
                r\nPress any key to continue...");
                Console.ReadKey();
            }
            else {
                using (var context = new MachineContext()) {
                    Console.WriteLine("\r\nAttempting to save changes...");
                    context.MachineType.Add(mt);
                    int i = context.SaveChanges();
                    if (i == 1) {
                        Console.WriteLine("Contents Saved\r\nPress any key to
                        continue...");
                        Console.ReadKey();
                    }
                }
            }
        }
        return mt;
}

static bool CheckForExistingMachineType(string mtDesc) {
    bool exists = false;
    using (var context = new MachineContext()) {
        var mt = context.MachineType.Where(t => t.Description == mtDesc);
        if (mt.Count() > 0) {
            exists = true;
        }
    }
    return exists;
}
```

There is nothing new to this code that we haven't already seen. We are doing some basic checking and validation and then we ensure that the machine type hasn't already been added to the database while we are doing our work. When we add a new machine type, we verify that it is six or more characters and we then save it to our `MachineType` variable as the `Description`. As `CheckForExistingMachineType()` is basically the same code we used to check for an existing operating system.

The next possibility is that we have at least one record in our `MachineType` table, so we should display that output. Listing 2-4 shows a very short section of the code for this purpose.

Listing 2-4. DisplayMachineTypes

```
static void DisplayMachineTypes(List<MachineType> lMachineType) {
    foreach(MachineType mt in lMachineType) {
        Console.WriteLine($"ID: {mt.MachineTypeId} Description: {mt.
        Description}");
    }
}
```

We are passing along our list of `MachineType` to the method and looping through a list displaying the contents on the screen for the user. Let's update `AddMachine()`, a little bit of which you can see in Listing 2-5. We include everything this one last time. After this, we just show the additional code, plus more variables for future use.

Listing 2-5. AddMachine() Updated

```
static void AddMachine() {
    Console.Clear();
    ConsoleKeyInfo cki;
    string result;
    bool cont = false;
    Machine machine = new Machine();
    WriteHeader("Add New Machine");
    Console.WriteLine();
    List<MachineType> lMachineType = GetMachineTypes();
    MachineType machineType = new MachineType();
    Models.OperatingSys os = new Models.OperatingSys();
    if (lMachineType.Count == 0) {
```

```
        // No results so we need to add a machine type
        machineType = AddMachineType();
    }
    else {
        // We have at least one Result so we should display the results for
        the user to select from
        DisplayMachineTypes(lMachineType);
        Console.WriteLine("Enter the ID for the Machine Type you would like
        to use.");
        Console.WriteLine("To add a new Machine Type enter [a]");
        do {
            cki = Console.ReadKey(true);
            if (cki.Key == ConsoleKey.A) {
                machineType = AddMachineType();
                cont = true;
            }
            else {
                if (char.IsNumber(cki.KeyChar)) {
                    int idEntered = Convert.ToInt16(cki.KeyChar.ToString());
                    if (lMachineType.Exists(x => x.MachineTypeId == idEntered)) {
                        machineType = lMachineType.Find(x => x.MachineTypeId ==
                        idEntered);
                        cont = true;
                    }
                    else {
                        // No match, could add a counter here and after a certain
                        number of attempts
                        // Add in some error handling
                    }
                }
            }
        } while (!cont);
    }

    machine.MachineTypeId = machineType.MachineTypeId;
}
```

We should now have all the variables we need to complete this process. The first thing we are going to do is check to see if we have any `MachineType` entries in the database. If we do, we'll list them for the user to select. If there are no results returned, then the user is required to add one. Once the user adds the `MachineType` to the database, that object is saved in our `machineType` variable for future use.

If we do have results, we are presented with a list that users can either select from or add to. If they add a new type it's the same as if they are starting from the beginning with no entries. Once the `MachintType` is saved to our variable, we set our flag to `true` so we can continue.

If we have a result set and the type the user wants to use is in the list, we make sure that we are capturing and processing only numbers. After the users press a number key, we check the `List<MachineType>` variable we created earlier, called `lMachineType`, to see if the ID that the user entered exists. If it does exist, we save the `MachineType` to our variable and continue. If it doesn't exist, we keep in the loop.

Note   We are assuming that there will be nine or fewer `MachineTypes` in the database, which is why we are able to do this with a `Console.ReadKey()`. Normally, we'd have to allow for two digits to be entered.

As you have probably noticed, we are using a lot of LINQ and lambda expressions and we will continue to do so. If you are not familiar with either of them, I highly recommend doing some further reading on the subject, as it will make your life a lot easier once you move beyond this book.

However, I'll give you a quick explanation of how to read the expression, as that may make it a little easier to understand until you have time to do more reading on your own.

We have the following line of code `machineType = lMachineType.Find(x => x.MachineTypeId == idEntered);`. There is a bit of disagreement on the actual verbiage of this, but this is the one that I use, "x, such that `x.MachineTypeId` equals `idEntered`". The format is *input-parameters => expression or statement*. We'll be doing some more advanced ones shortly, which make it a little easier to understand.

The next part we'll add is pretty straightforward with nothing that should be new to you. As you'll see in Listing 2-6, we are getting information from the user and then displaying the list of operating systems that they can choose from.

Listing 2-6. AddMachine() Updated

```
...
machine.MachineTypeId = machineType.MachineTypeId;
// We have our machine type, now to get the machine info
Console.WriteLine("What is the name of the new machine?");
machine.Name = Console.ReadLine();

Console.WriteLine("What is the general role for this machine?");
Console.WriteLine("For example a server could be a Domain Controller or
Database Server.");
machine.GeneralRole = Console.ReadLine();

Console.WriteLine("What is the specific role of this machine? <separate
each with a comma>");
Console.WriteLine("For example a DC could have the following roles: DNS, DHCP");
machine.InstalledRoles = Console.ReadLine();

// Now we need to get the operating system
Console.WriteLine($"\r\n{"ID",-7}|{"Name",-50}|StillSupported");
Console.WriteLine("-----------------------------------------------------");
using (var context = new MachineContext()) {
   List<OperatingSys> lOperatingSys = context.OperatingSys.ToList();
   foreach (OperatingSys o in lOperatingSys) {
      Console.WriteLine($"{o.OperatingSysId,-7}|{o.Name,-50}|{o.
      StillSupported}");
   }
}
Console.WriteLine("\r\nEnter the ID of the Operating System you wish to use.");
Console.WriteLine("If you need to add an Operating System hit the 'a' key.");
Console.WriteLine("When you are done hit the Enter Key.");
```

Nothing new here. We reused our code to create our List< OperatingSys>, although we did make a slight change to the variable name in our foreach loop. At least we got to do a little bit of EF Core work to help reinforce what you have learned. The last thing we are going to do before we save our *machine* is add OperatingSys to our variable. Listing 2-7 shows that this is a modified version of what we have already done.

Listing 2-7. AddMachine() Updated

```
...
Console.WriteLine("When you are done hit the Enter Key.");

string id = string.Empty;
cont = false;
do {
   cki = Console.ReadKey(true);
   if (cki.Key == ConsoleKey.A) {
      cont = true;
      os = AddOperatingSystem();
   }
   else if (cki.Key == ConsoleKey.Enter) {
      if (id.Length > 0) {
         // Need to verify the OS is "good"
         os = GetOperatingSystemById(Convert.ToInt16(id));
         if (os == null) {
            Console.WriteLine("\r\nOperating System ID is not valid, please
            try again.");
            // Clear out the id so we can start over
            id = string.Empty;
         }
         else {
            cont = true;
         }
      }
      else {
         Console.WriteLine("Please enter an ID that is at least 1 digit.");
      }
   }
   else if (cki.Key == ConsoleKey.Backspace) {
      Console.Write("\b \b");
      try {
         id = id.Substring(0, id.Length - 1);
      }
```

```
        catch (System.ArgumentOutOfRangeException) {
          // at the 0 position, can't go any further back
        }
    }
    else {
        if (char.IsNumber(cki.KeyChar)) {
            id += cki.KeyChar.ToString();
            Console.Write(cki.KeyChar.ToString());
        }
    }
} while (!cont);

machine.OperatingSysId = os.OperatingSysId;
```

After you enter this, you should get an error indicating that you can't covert type `void` to `ComputerInventory.Models.OperatingSys`. That is because we have to change the `AddOperatingSystem()` method. You need to make the following two changes: change `static void AddOperatingSystem() {` to `static OperatingSys AddOperatingSystem() {`. And then right before the closing bracket, you need a `return` statement: `return os;`.

In the last line, we add our `OperatingSys` object to our `Machine` variable, which we'll use to display the information back to the user in the next step. We now have everything we need in order to add our machine to the database. Listing 2-8 shows the last part of the `AddMachine()` code that we are adding.

Listing 2-8. AddMachine() Last Section of Code

```
...
machine.OperatingSysId = os.OperatingSysId;

Console.Clear();
WriteHeader("Add New Machine");
Console.WriteLine("\r\nYou have entered the following:");
Console.WriteLine($"\tName: {machine.Name}");
Console.WriteLine($"\tType: {machineType.Description}");
Console.WriteLine($"\tOperating System: {os.Name}");
Console.WriteLine($"\tRole: {machine.GeneralRole}");
Console.WriteLine($"\tInstalled Roles: {machine.InstalledRoles}");
Console.WriteLine("Would you like to save your work? [y or n]");
```

```
cont = false;
do {
   cki = Console.ReadKey();
   result = cki.KeyChar.ToString();
   cont = ValidateYorN(result);
} while (!cont);

if(result.ToLower() == "y") {
   using(MachineContext context = new MachineContext()) {
      Console.WriteLine($"Saving {machine.Name} to the database");
      context.Machine.Add(machine);
      context.SaveChanges();
      Console.WriteLine("Done!");
   }
}
Console.WriteLine("\r\nHit any key to continue");
Console.ReadKey();
```

Finally, some multi-table data to display to the user. As you can see, we had to use our operating system and machine type variables in order to display certain data.

As you can see, displaying the `MachineType` or `OperatingSystem` values involves simple, standard dot notation. Because our `Machines` class contains an `OperatingSystem` and a `MachineType`. they are available to us as `.OperatingSys` or `.MachineType`. What's nice is that we didn't have to create anything extra to have this functionality.

Lastly, we gave the users the ability to choose if they want to save the machine or not and we use our handy `ValidateYorN()` method to validate their input. If they choose to save it, we create a new `DBContext`, add our machine to the context, and then save the changes.

For some extra credit, you could handle what happens when the users press n by giving them an option to fix whatever they don't like. However, because that would be 98% regular C# type programming, I'm not going to bore you with it. If you want extra credit, allow them to change the `MachineType` or `OperatingSystem` values.

Now let's add a couple of machines and make sure things work. Don't forget to uncomment out AddMachine() in DataEntryMenu().

When you get to the Data Entry menu and press 1 to get to the Add New Machine option, you are presented with adding a new machine type. We are going to add a server, so enter Server and press Enter. When you're prompted, press y to continue and save the changes. Call this machine DC1POR. The general role will be domain controller and for specific roles, add DNS, DHCP, and AD DS. For the operating system, choose Windows Server 2012 R2. After you have entered all this information, your console window should look like Figure 2-3.

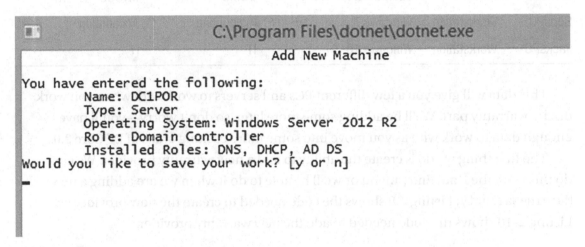

Figure 2-3. Entering the first machine

If everything looks good, press y to save the data to the table. We'll create a way to retrieve this in the next section. As long as you entered everything properly and didn't get an error, you should be good to continue. When we create the entry for the MachineWarranty and WarrantyProvider entities, we'll look at a different way to do this.

Let's add a couple more machines so we have something to work with. Table 2-1 lists the information you need.

Table 2-1. *Additional Machine Data*

Name	Type	OS	Role	Role Breakdown
DC2POR	Server	Windows Server 2012 R2	Domain Controller	AD DS, DNS, DHCP
RDS1POR	Server	Windows Server 2016	Remote Desktop	RDS
DB1SQL	Server	Windows Server 2008 R2	DBMS	SQL Server 2012
DB2SQL	Server	Ubuntu Server 17.04	DBMS	MySQL
BobsPC	Workstation	Windows 7	Accounting	Accounting
JacksPC	Workstation	Windows 10	IT	IT

This data will give you a few different PCs and servers to work with when you work on the warranty part. We'll be adding some more later, so don't worry—you'll have enough data to work with as you move into some more exciting areas of EF Core 2.0.

The first thing we do is create the ability to add a new warranty provider. We can do this from the Data Entry menu or we'll be able to do it when we are adding a new `MachineWarranty`. Listing 2-9 shows the code needed to create the new provider and Listing 2-10 shows the code needed to add the new warranty provider.

Listing 2-9. Creating a Warranty Provider

```
static WarrantyProvider CreateNewWarrantyProvider() {
    string provider = string.Empty;
    string phoneNumber = string.Empty;
    int? extension = null;
    ConsoleKeyInfo cki;
    bool cont = false;
    Console.Clear();
    WriteHeader("Add new Warranty Provider");
    Console.WriteLine("\r\n\r\nPlease enter the name of the Provider and
    then hit Enter.");
    provider = Console.ReadLine();

    Console.WriteLine("\r\nPlease enter the Providers phone number.");
    do {
        cki = Console.ReadKey(true);
```

```
   if (cki.Key == ConsoleKey.Enter) {
      if (phoneNumber.Length >= 7) {
         cont = true;
      }
      else {
         Console.WriteLine("Please enter a Phone number that is at least
         7 digits.");
      }
   }
   else if (cki.Key == ConsoleKey.Backspace) {
      Console.Write("\b \b");
      try {
         phoneNumber = phoneNumber.Substring(0, phoneNumber.Length - 1);
      }
         catch (System.ArgumentOutOfRangeException) {
         // at the 0 position, can't go any further back
      }
   }
   else {
      if (char.IsNumber(cki.KeyChar)) {
         phoneNumber += cki.KeyChar.ToString();
         Console.Write(cki.KeyChar.ToString());
      }
   }
} while (!cont);

cont = false;
Console.WriteLine("\r\nPlease enter the Providers extension.\r\nIf there
is no extension hit ESC or Enter to continue.");
string tempExt = string.Empty;
do {
   ck1 = Console.ReadKey(true);
   if (cki.Key == ConsoleKey.Escape) {
      cont = true;
      extension = null;
   }
```

```
    else if (cki.Key == ConsoleKey.Enter) {
        // can be any length or null
        if (tempExt.Length > 0)
            extension = Convert.ToInt32(tempExt);
        else
            extension = null;
        cont = true;
    }
    else if (cki.Key == ConsoleKey.Backspace) {
        Console.Write("\b \b");
        try {
            tempExt = tempExt.Substring(0, tempExt.Length - 1);
        }
        catch (System.ArgumentOutOfRangeException) {
            // at the 0 position, can't go any further back
        }
    }
    else {
        if (char.IsNumber(cki.KeyChar)) {
            tempExt += cki.KeyChar.ToString();
            Console.Write(cki.KeyChar.ToString());
        }
    }
} while (!cont);

WarrantyProvider wp = new WarrantyProvider() {
    ProviderName = provider,
    SupportNumber = phoneNumber,
    SupportExtension = extension
};
return wp;
}
```

We start by creating the variables we need as usual, although this time we had to create a nullable int for our extension variable, as the value can be null in the table. We are doing very little error handling for this, as the provider could be virtually anything and the same goes for the extension. We do make sure that the phone number is at least seven digits (for a country other than the United States or Canada, this may need to be changed).

We aren't checking for a upper limit to save some space and time, although it's something you should be able to easily add if you want. Finally, we create our WarrantyProvider object and return it to the calling method. We haven't added anything yet. All we are doing is creating the object, and you'll see why shortly.

Listing 2-10. Adding a Warranty Provider (Standalone)

```
static void AddNewWarrantyProvider(WarrantyProvider wp) {
   bool cont = false;
   ConsoleKeyInfo cki;
   string result = string.Empty;
   Console.WriteLine("\r\nYou have entered the following:");
   Console.WriteLine($"Provider Name: {wp.ProviderName}");
   Console.WriteLine($"Provider Number: {wp.SupportNumber}");
   Console.WriteLine($"Provider Extension: {wp.SupportExtension}");
   Console.WriteLine("\r\nIs this information correct? [y or n]");
   do {
      cki = Console.ReadKey(true);
      result = cki.KeyChar.ToString();
      cont = ValidateYorN(result);
   } while (!cont);

   if(result.ToLower() == "y") {
      using (MachineContext context = new MachineContext()) {
         var count = context.WarrantyProvider.Count(p => p.ProviderName ==
         wp.ProviderName);
         if (count == 0) {
            Console.WriteLine($"\r\nSaving {wp.ProviderName} to the
            database...");
            context.WarrantyProvider.Add(wp);
            context.SaveChanges();
            Console.WriteLine("Complete!");
         }
```

```
        else {
            Console.WriteLine(string.Format("\r\nWarranty Provider {0}
            already exists", wp.ProviderName));
        }
    }
}
else {
    Console.WriteLine("No changes have been made.");
}
Console.WriteLine("\r\nHit any key to continue...");
Console.ReadKey();
}
```

Not much new here, except we have changed the way that we determine if the record exists. Recall from Chapter 1 when we checked to see if an operating system existed, we did the following:

```
var os = context.OperatingSys.Where(o => o.Name == osName);
if (os.Count() > 0) {
    exists = true;
}
```

This is a fine way of checking to see if you have a value already in the database. However, there is another option, used in this example. By using the .Count in our LINQ expression, we are getting the count of results that match our condition, which in this case is the number of warranty providers that have a specific name. This is similar to doing a SqlCommand.ExecuteScalar, where you have a COUNT in your query.

Another line of code that we used again is cki = Console.ReadKey(true); which I hope you remember makes it so we aren't seeing any "invalid" characters cluttering up the console. In this case, we are keeping the y or n from displaying on the console.

Before we can test this, we need to make some changes to our DataEntry method so we can enter data. Add the following code for when the user enters a 3:

```
else if (result == 3) {
    WarrantyProvider wp = new WarrantyProvider();
    wp = CreateNewWarrantyProvider();
    AddNewWarrantyProvider(wp);
}
```

Once you are done, run the application and go to the Add Warranty Provider menu, which is CreateNewWarrantyProvider(). Figure 2-4 shows the screen with the entered data .

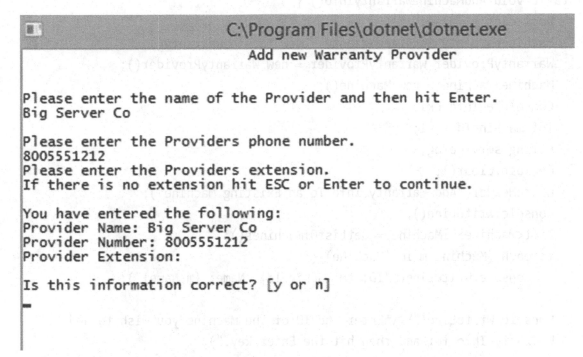

Figure 2-4. Adding a new warranty provider

If your information matches, press y and you should see the following:

```
Saving Big Server Co to the database... Complete!
Hit any key to continue...
```

If you look in SSMS, you should now see an entry in the WarrantyProvider table. If you don't see anything, verify that you have context.SaveChanges() in your code and didn't bypass it by accident. Also remember that we are only accepting up to 10 characters for the phone number, so if you enter 18005551212, it won't fit. We'll cover data validation a little bit later on in the book, but I want to bring this point up now in case you get an error.

Although we are working on multiple tables in this chapter, we need a way of adding our warranty provider as well. So let's now add our MachineWarranty. As I promised when we added the Machine, we are going to do something a little bit different this time. Listing 2-11 shows the code for adding a MachineWarranty and Listing 2-12 shows a helper method for retrieving a list of machines that you can use later.

Listing 2-11. AddMachineWarrantyInfo

```
static void AddMachineWarrantyInfo() {
    bool cont = false;
    MachineWarranty machineWarranty = new MachineWarranty();
    WarrantyProvider warrantyProvider = new WarrantyProvider();
    Machine machine = new Machine();
    ConsoleKeyInfo cki;
    int machineId = -1;
    string serviceTag;
    Console.Clear();
    WriteHeader("Add Warranty Info To an Existing Machine");
    Console.WriteLine();
    List<Machine> lMachine = GetListOfMachines();
    foreach (Machine m in lMachine) {
        Console.WriteLine($"ID: {m.MachineId}  Name: {m.Name}");
    }
    Console.WriteLine("\r\nEnter the ID of the Machine you wish to add
    Warranty Info for and then hit the Enter key.");

    string tempMachineId = string.Empty;
    do {
        cki = Console.ReadKey(true);
        if (cki.Key == ConsoleKey.Enter) {
            if (tempMachineId.Length > 0) {
                machineId = Convert.ToInt32(tempMachineId);
                machine = lMachine.Find(x => x.MachineId == machineId);
            }
            cont = true;
        }
        else if (cki.Key == ConsoleKey.Backspace) {
            Console.Write("\b \b");
            try {
                tempMachineId = tempMachineId.Substring(0, tempMachineId.
                Length - 1);
            }
```

```
        catch (System.ArgumentOutOfRangeException) {
            // at the 0 position, can't go any further back
        }
    }
    else {
        if (char.IsNumber(cki.KeyChar)) {
            tempMachineId += cki.KeyChar.ToString();
            Console.Write(cki.KeyChar.ToString());
        }
    }
} while (!cont);

Console.WriteLine("\r\nEnter the Service Tag of the machine and then hit
Enter.");
serviceTag = Console.ReadLine();

cont = false;
string tDate;
DateTime warrantyExp;
do {
    Console.WriteLine("Enter the date the warranty expires
    [mm/dd/yyyy].");
    tDate = Console.ReadLine();

    if (DateTime.TryParse(tDate, out warrantyExp)) {
        cont = true;
    }
    else {
        Console.WriteLine("\r\nNot a valid date, please try again.");
    }
} while (!cont);

List<WarrantyProvider> lWarrantyProvider = new List<WarrantyProvider>();
using (MachineContext context = new MachineContext()) {
    lWarrantyProvider = context.WarrantyProvider.ToList();
}
Console.WriteLine();
```

```csharp
foreach (WarrantyProvider wp in lWarrantyProvider) {
    Console.WriteLine($"ID: {wp.WarrantyProviderId}    Name: {wp.
    ProviderName}");
}

machineWarranty.ServiceTag = serviceTag;
machineWarranty.WarrantyExpiration = warrantyExp;
machineWarranty.MachineId = machineId;

Console.WriteLine("Enter the ID for the Warranty Provider you would like
to use.");
Console.WriteLine("To add a new Provider enter [a]");
string tempProviderId = string.Empty;
cont = false;
do {
    cki = Console.ReadKey(true);
    if (cki.Key == ConsoleKey.A) {
        cont = true;
        warrantyProvider = CreateNewWarrantyProvider();
        machineWarranty.WarrantyProvider = warrantyProvider;
    }
    else if (cki.Key == ConsoleKey.Enter) {
        if (tempProviderId.Length > 0) {
            int provID = Convert.ToInt32(tempProviderId);
            if (lWarrantyProvider.Exists(x => x.WarrantyProviderId ==
            provID)) {
                warrantyProvider = lWarrantyProvider.Find(x =>
                x.WarrantyProviderId == provID);
                machineWarranty.WarrantyProviderId = provID;
                cont = true;
            }
            else {
                Console.WriteLine("No match please verify your entry and try
                again!");
            }
        }
    }
```

```
      else {
         Console.WriteLine("Please enter an ID that is at least 1 digit.");
      }
   }
   else if (cki.Key == ConsoleKey.Backspace) {
      Console.Write("\b \b");
      try {
         tempProviderId = tempProviderId.Substring(0, tempProviderId.
         Length - 1);
      }
      catch (System.ArgumentOutOfRangeException) {
         // at the 0 position, can't go any further back
      }
   }
   else {
      if (char.IsNumber(cki.KeyChar)) {
         tempProviderId += cki.KeyChar.ToString();
         Console.Write(cki.KeyChar.ToString());
      }
   }
} while (!cont);

Console.Clear();
WriteHeader("Add Warranty Info To an Existing Machine");
Console.WriteLine("You have entered the following:");
Console.WriteLine($"Machine: {machine.Name}");
Console.WriteLine($"Service Tag: {machineWarranty.ServiceTag}");
Console.WriteLine($"Warranty Expiration: {machineWarranty.
WarrantyExpiration.ToShortDateString()}");
Console.WriteLine($"Warranty Provider: {warrantyProvider.
ProviderName}");

Console.WriteLine("\r\nIs this information correct? [y or n]");
string result;
do {
   cki = Console.ReadKey(true);
```

```
    result = cki.KeyChar.ToString();
    cont = ValidateYorN(result);
} while (!cont);
Console.WriteLine();

if (result.ToLower() == "y") {
    Console.WriteLine("Saving Machine Warranty Information");
    using (MachineContext context = new MachineContext()) {
        context.MachineWarranty.Add(machineWarranty);
        context.SaveChanges();
        Console.WriteLine("Save complete!");
    }
}
Console.WriteLine("Any key to continue...");
Console.ReadKey();
}
```

Phew, that was a lot! Let's add the helper method and then we'll explain a couple of things that are different in this one. See Listing 2-12.

Listing 2-12. Getting a List of Machines

```
static List<Machine> GetListOfMachines() {
    List<Machine> lmachine = new List<Machine>();
    MachineContext context = new MachineContext();
    lmachine = context.Machine.ToList();
    context.Dispose();
    return lmachine;
}
```

Let's discuss the simple one first. Hopefully, there is nothing new to you with GetListOfMachines(). I added the context.Dispose() mainly to show you that it's there, but you really don't need to use it. However, some would consider it good form to do so. Getting a list of machines or really any other entity can't be much easier than it is with Entity Framework.

Before we explain this, let's run it and be sure it works. However, before we can do that, we need to update our DataEntryMenu() a little bit. In this code snippet, the changes are in bold:

```
Console.WriteLine("3. Add a New Warranty Provider");
Console.WriteLine("4. Add New Machine Warranty Information");
Console.WriteLine("9. Exit Menu");
cki = Console.ReadKey();
try {
    result = Convert.ToInt16(cki.KeyChar.ToString());
    if (result == 1) {
        AddMachine();
    }
    else if (result == 2) {
        AddOperatingSystem();
    }
    else if (result == 3) {
        WarrantyProvider wp = new WarrantyProvider();
        wp = CreateNewWarrantyProvider();
        AddNewWarrantyProvider(wp);
    }
    else if (result == 4) {
        AddMachineWarrantyInfo();
    }
```

Let's add some warranty information for DC1POR. Figure 2-5 has our validation information. The information to enter is as follows:

- MachineId: 1 DC1POR

- Service Tag: 12DG3

- Warranty Expiration: 8/30/2020

- Warranty Provider: Add a new one

    a. Warranty Provider Name: Harvey Package Inc.

    b. Phone Number: 8665552323

    c. Provider Extension: 56

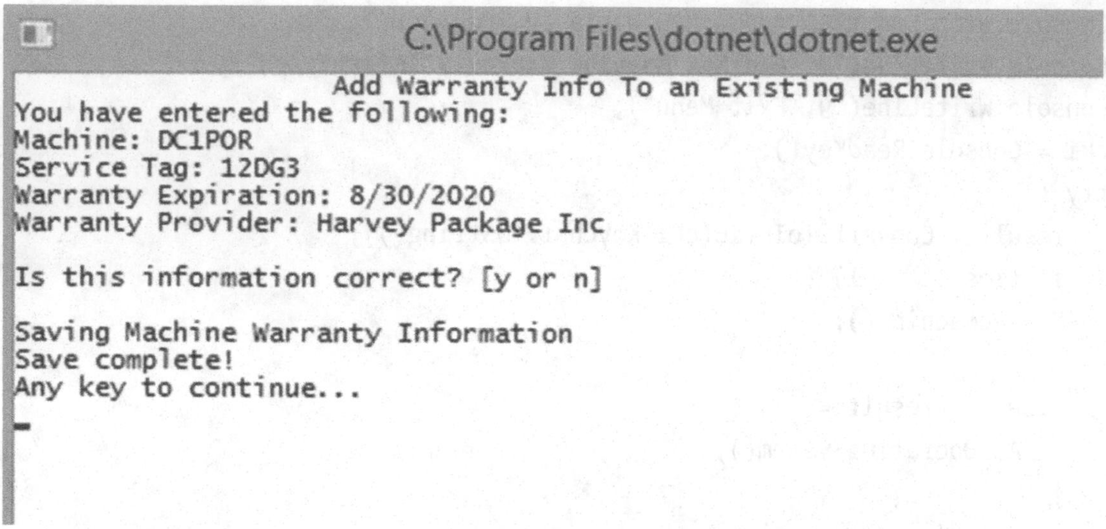

Figure 2-5. *Adding warranty information for DC1POR*

If you aren't relatively impressed with what you just did, you are forgetting
something. Note that there is only one DBContext.SaveChanges() in the code. But
we created a new warranty provider too, so we forgot to save that, right? If you look in
SSMS and at the WarrantyProvider table, you'll see that you now have two entries.
We handled adding our foreign key data a bit different for the Machine than we did for
the WarrantyProvider. If you look back, you'll see that we added the machineId to our
machineWarranty object: machineWarranty.MachineId = machineId;. Yet when we
added the WarrantyProvider, we added a WarrantyProvider object: machineWarranty.
WarrantyProvider = warrantyProvider; (but only if it was new). Had we added an
existing Machine or WarrantyProvider object to our machineWarranty object and saved,
we would get an SQL exception telling us that we cannot insert explicit values for identity
columns in "some table name". This is the reason we have different logic when we choose
an existing provider and why we only add the WarrantyProviderId:

```
warrantyProvider = lWarrantyProvider.Find(x => x.WarrantyProviderId == provID);
machineWarranty.WarrantyProviderId = provID;
```

Could we have created our warranty provider and saved it to the database and then
just added the ID to our machineWarranty object? Sure, why not. There is nothing wrong
with that. I just wanted to give you yet another way of handling things using Entity
Framework Core 2.0. You need to figure out which way you are most comfortable with
and which makes the most sense for what you are doing at the time.

74

Another thing that you'll want to consider when deciding on a strategy is how you are going to handle data integrity. In short, you'll want to be sure that the data you are referencing in another table is in that table before you add a reference to it.

Because this section of code is so long, there is a lot of error handling and validation that has been left out in the interest of not boring you with it. Feel free to go back through the code and add it, as it would be good practice. Just make sure that you are getting the desired results in the end.

Let's add a couple more `MachineWarranty` objects to Table 2-2 before we move on. For now, we'll stick with our two support folks, as they seem quite capable.

Table 2-2. *New Example Data*

Machine Name	Service Tag	Warranty Expiration	Service Provider
DC2POR	68987TYP	8/30/2020	Big Server Co
RDS1POR	HAR456	7/15/2019	Harvey Package Inc.
DB1SQL	YYM689	12/31/2017	Big Server Co
JacksPC	PWM207	2/15/2018	Big Server Co

Now we have a couple of entries in our `MachineWarranty` table to work with. I think that is good for now as far as entering data into our tables and what we need to do when we are working with tables that have relations. Let's now retrieve some data from our database from multiple tables, as we really should check to be sure what we think we entered is actually there.

Retrieving Data from Multiple Tables

Let's take a look at our machines that we have in inventory, as doing so will use most of the tables that we have in our database. We'll break this process down into smaller sections, as this is going to be quite lengthy but fairly straightforward. We are going to run our code a few times even before we complete the method to get a better look at what is going on.

If you have used Entity Framework 6.x, I apologize in advance for this section, as you aren't going to like it. If you are new to Entity Framework then this part won't bother you too much. I'll explain what I mean when we get there. Listing 2-13 shows the start of the code to retrieve information about our machines.

Listing 2-13. DisplayAllMachines

```
static void DisplayAllMachines() {
    Console.Clear();
    List<Machine> lMachine = GetListOfMachines();
    foreach(Machine m in lMachine) {
        Console.WriteLine($"{m.Name}  {m.OperatingSys.Name} {m.GeneralRole}");
    }
    Console.WriteLine("Hit any key to continue");
    Console.ReadKey();
}
```

If you were now to run your code, you would receive the error in Figure 2-6. If you have used EF 6.x in the past, you probably just had a few not-so-nice things to say about Entity Framework Core 2.0, just like I did. However if you are new you are probably thinking, "well, yeah, you never selected the operating system info from the database". In EF 6.x, you would have received all the information about your machine due to something called *lazy loading*. I'm not going to get into what it is, since it's not available to us right now, but it can be a good or a bad thing depending on how you use it.

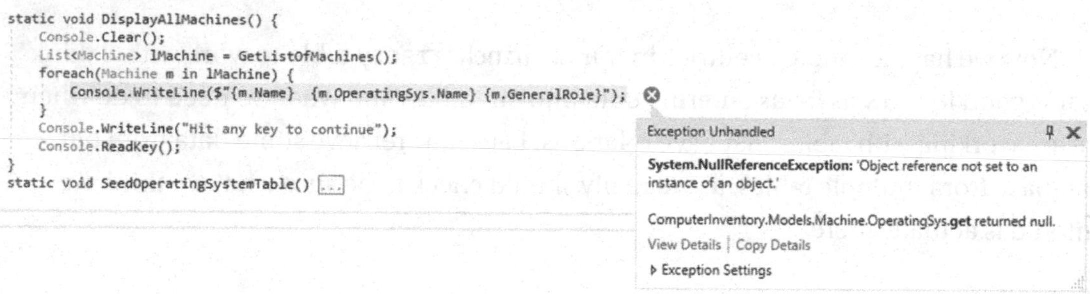

Figure 2-6. *This isn't EF 6.x*

We now need to make a decision about how our application is going to work. We have a couple of options. It comes down to how much information we are going to put on the screen. If this was a WinForms application or a web page, we would have a lot more space. However, since we are doing this on a Windows console, we are limited to the amount of horizontal space we have. For this first screen, let's stick with something simple and list the MachineID and the machine Name. The update to the extensive code that we have already written is shown in Listing 2-14.

Listing 2-14. Updated DisplayAllMachines

```
static void DisplayAllMachines() {
   Console.Clear();
   List<Machine> lMachine = GetListOfMachines();
   Console.WriteLine("Machine ID | Machine Name");
   foreach(Machine m in lMachine) {
      Console.WriteLine($"{m.MachineId,-11}| {m.Name}");
   }

   Console.WriteLine("\r\nEnter the MachineId followed by the Enter Key for
   more information.");
   Console.WriteLine("Hit the Esc key at anytime to exit the menu.");

   Console.WriteLine("Hit any key to continue");
   Console.ReadKey();
}
```

If you were to run your code now, you would get results you could read and not get an error. We are going to handle our data entry handling like we have in the past—we'll check for the Esc key, the Enter key, or any number, and handle it appropriately. I think it's time to create a helper method here, as we seem to be doing the same thing, over and over again, code-wise. Listing 2-15 shows a helper method that gets an ID value from the console.

Listing 2-15. GetNumbersFromConsole

```
static string GetNumbersFromConsole() {
   ConsoleKeyInfo cki;
   bool cont = false;
   string numbers = string.Empty;
   do {
      cki = Console.ReadKey(true);
      if (cki.Key == ConsoleKey.Escape) {
         cont = true;
         numbers = "";
      }
      else if (cki.Key == ConsoleKey.Enter) {
         if (numbers.Length > 0) {
            cont = true;
         }
```

77

```
        else {
            Console.WriteLine("Please enter an ID that is at least 1 digit.");
        }
    }
    else if (cki.Key == ConsoleKey.Backspace) {
        Console.Write("\b \b");
        try {
            numbers = numbers.Substring(0, numbers.Length - 1);
        }
        catch (System.ArgumentOutOfRangeException) {
            // at the 0 position, can't go any further back
        }
    }
    else {
        if (char.IsNumber(cki.KeyChar)) {
            numbers += cki.KeyChar.ToString();
            Console.Write(cki.KeyChar.ToString());
        }
    }
} while (!cont);
return numbers;
}
```

If you are feeling motivated, feel free to go back through your code and replace this code with a call to the method we just created. The following two methods show code that you can use to replace the code you have moved to the method. If you aren't sure, you can look at the code online for Chapter 2 and see the changes I made for these two cases.

```
SelectOperatingSystem
id = GetNumbersFromConsole();
CreateNewWarrantyProvider
tempExt = GetNumbersFromConsole();
if (tempExt.Length > 0) {
    extension = Convert.ToInt32(tempExt);
}
else {
    extension = null;
}
```

All righty then, on to retrieving some data from more than one table. Listing 2-16 shows one of the ways that we can do this. We are going to do this in two steps. First we'll list all of our machines and then we'll let the users choose which machine they want to get more information about (if any). In our first example, we do our SELECT with a "basic" LINQ query. It should will look somewhat familiar to you, as it's closer to a SQL Query.

Listing 2-16. Displaying Machine Detail to the User from Multiple Tables

```
static void DisplayMachineDetail(int machineId) {
    Console.Clear();
    Console.WriteLine("\r\nRetrieving information about our machine.");
    using (MachineContext context = new MachineContext()) {
        var mach = (from mac in context.Machine
            join mw in context.MachineWarranty on mac.MachineId equals
            mw.MachineId
            where mac.MachineId == machineId
            select new { mac.Name, MacType = mac.MachineType.Description,
            osName = mac.OperatingSys.Name, mac.OperatingSys.StillSupported,
            mw.WarrantyProvider, mw.WarrantyExpiration, mac.MachineType.
            Description }).FirstOrDefault();
        if(mach != null) {
            Console.WriteLine($"Machine: {mach.Name} is a {mach.Description}
            \r\nOS = {mach.osName}  Still Supported?: {mach.StillSupported}");
            Console.WriteLine($"Warranty Provider = {mach.WarrantyProvider.
            ProviderName}  Support Ends on: {mach.WarrantyExpiration.
            ToShortDateString()}");
        }
        else {
            Console.WriteLine($"No Machine Found with ID: {machineId}");
        }
    }
    Console.WriteLine("Hit any key to continue");
    Console.ReadKey();
}
```

We'll add the ability to get to this code in a moment. This method will give us the closest method to lazy loading that we have available. As normal, we have created our DBContext object with a using statement and within that we are doing our work. We create an anonymous type called mach and we populate that with our LINQ query. The only table we had to join on was the MachineWarranty table, because there is no direct relation from the Machine table to it.

As you can see, we can get our operating system information as well as our machine type without a join. If you are new to LINQ, then the last part of the query probably looks a little weird to you. That's because you have to end the queries with either a select or group by clause. The good thing is if you forget to do it, the error you get is helpful.

After we do our query, we check to see if mach is null or not. If it's not null, we display some information to the user. If it is null, we let the users know we didn't get any results. What's nice is we don't get an error if our result set is null, unless of course we try to display the information without the check, in which case we'd get a null reference exception. Listing 2-17 shows some of the code that makes it possible to get to the section of code we just wrote.

Listing 2-17. DisplayAllMachines, Code Update

```
static string DisplayAllMachines() {
    Console.Clear();
    List<Machine> lMachine = GetListOfMachines();
    Console.WriteLine("Machine ID | Machine Name");
    foreach(Machine m in lMachine) {
        Console.WriteLine($"{m.MachineId,-11}| {m.Name}");
    }

    Console.WriteLine("\r\nEnter the MachineId followed by the Enter Key for
    more information.");
    Console.WriteLine("Hit the Esc key at anytime to exit the menu.");

    string machineId = GetNumbersFromConsole();
    if(machineId.Length > 0) {
        int machId = Convert.ToInt32(machineId);
        DisplayMachineDetail(machId);
    }
    return machineId;
}
```

As with many of our other menus or sections of code, we are doing some basic error checking after we retrieve our the list of *machines*. If the length of the string is greater than zero, we call our new code. Because we know what the `MachineIds` are, we could run a quick check to see if they exist. However, I wanted to show you that getting a null return value is okay, so I have made it possible to do so. In your own applications going forward, you should do your checking here. *Don't forget to uncomment* `DisplayAllMachines();` *in* `MainMenu()` *so you can try it.*

When you run your code and choose `MachineID: 1 DC1POR`, your results should look like Figure 2-7.

```
C:\Program Files\dotnet\dotnet.exe

Retrieving information about our machine.
Machine: DC1POR is a Server
OS = Windows Server 2012 R2  Still Supported?: True
Warranty Provider = Harvey Package Inc  Support Ends on: 8/30/2020
Hit any key to continue
```

Figure 2-7. Results from multiple tables

As mentioned, there are multiple ways of running queries against multiple tables or entities. We will now take a look at doing so using a lambda expression. As you will see, other than the style being different, there are a couple of things you have to keep in mind.

Updating Tables

Listing 2-18 shows the start of the code to update a machine, including the operating system, machine type, and warranty information. If you are a LINQ expert, you'll be saying, "hey, there is a better way of doing this," and that is true. However, since this is a book on Entity Framework Core 2.0 and not LINQ, we'll stick with the easier way. As I have mentioned many times and will continue to do so, it behooves you to get comfortable with LINQ. I don't want to confuse you with a lot of really fancy LINQ syntax and take away from what you are trying to learn.

Listing 2-18. UpdateMachineDetails

```
static void UpdateMachineDetails() {
   Console.Clear();
   List<Machine> lMachine = GetListOfMachines();
   WriteHeader("Update Machine Details");

   string machineId = DisplayAllMachines();
   if (machineId.Length > 0) {
      int mId = Convert.ToInt32(machineId);
      Machine mach;
      MachineWarranty mWar;
      using (MachineContext context = new MachineContext()) {
         mach = context.Machine
            .Include(o => o.OperatingSys)
            .Include(t => t.MachineType)
            .Where(x => x.MachineId == mId).FirstOrDefault();

         mWar = context.MachineWarranty
            .Include(p => p.WarrantyProvider)
            .Where(x => x.MachineId == mach.MachineId).FirstOrDefault();
      }
      Console.Clear();
      Console.WriteLine("To Update the Machine Information Press 1");
      Console.WriteLine($"Name: {mach.Name}  General Role: { mach.
      GeneralRole}");
      Console.WriteLine($"Installed Role: {mach.InstalledRoles}");
      Console.WriteLine("\r\nTo Update the Operating System Information
      Press 2");
      Console.WriteLine($"OS Name: {mach.OperatingSys.Name}  Still
      Supported: {mach.OperatingSys.StillSupported}");
      Console.WriteLine($"\r\nTo Update the Machine Type Press 3");
      Console.WriteLine($"Machine Type: {mach.MachineType.Description}");
      Console.WriteLine($"\r\nTo Update the Warranty Information Press 4");
      Console.WriteLine($"Provider Name: {mWar.WarrantyProvider.
      ProviderName}");
```

```
    Console.WriteLine($"Expiration: {mWar.WarrantyExpiration.ToShort
    DateString()}");
  }
  Console.ReadKey();
}
```

As promised, we handled our queries in a different way than in the last example. As you can see, we created two objects this time. One is for our *machine* and the second is for the machine warranty information that we have in the database. The database was intentionally set up this way to show you how to handle a table that's added later and for some reason you can't update the table to add a foreign key field.

The Machine table doesn't know about the MachineWarranty table but the MachineWarranty table knows about the Machine table. At the end, we have a ReadKey() so we can view our code. We don't have a way of handling user input yet, so it will just run right past and out of the menu. In order to run our code, we need to make a quick change to DataModificationMenu(). You'll find that change in Listing 2-19.

Listing 2-19. DataModificationMenu with Changes

```
Console.WriteLine("2. Modify Operating System");
Console.WriteLine("3. Delete All Unsupported Operating Systems");
Console.WriteLine("4. Update Machine Information");
Console.WriteLine("9. Exit Menu");
cki = Console.ReadKey();
try {
    result = Convert.ToInt16(cki.KeyChar.ToString());
    if (result == 1) {
        SelectOperatingSystem("Delete");
    }
    else if (result == 2) {
        SelectOperatingSystem("Modify");
    }
    else if (result == 3) {
        DeleteAllUnsupportedOperatingSystems();
    }
```

```
else if (result == 4) {
    UpdateMachineDetails();
}
else if (result == 9) {
    // We are exiting so nothing to do
    cont = true;
}
```

When you run the code, choose Option 4 (the Data Modification menu), then choose Option 4 again (Update Machine Information). We'll go with the first machine, which is DC1POR, and you should see something similar to Figure 2-8 after you press Enter or any key.

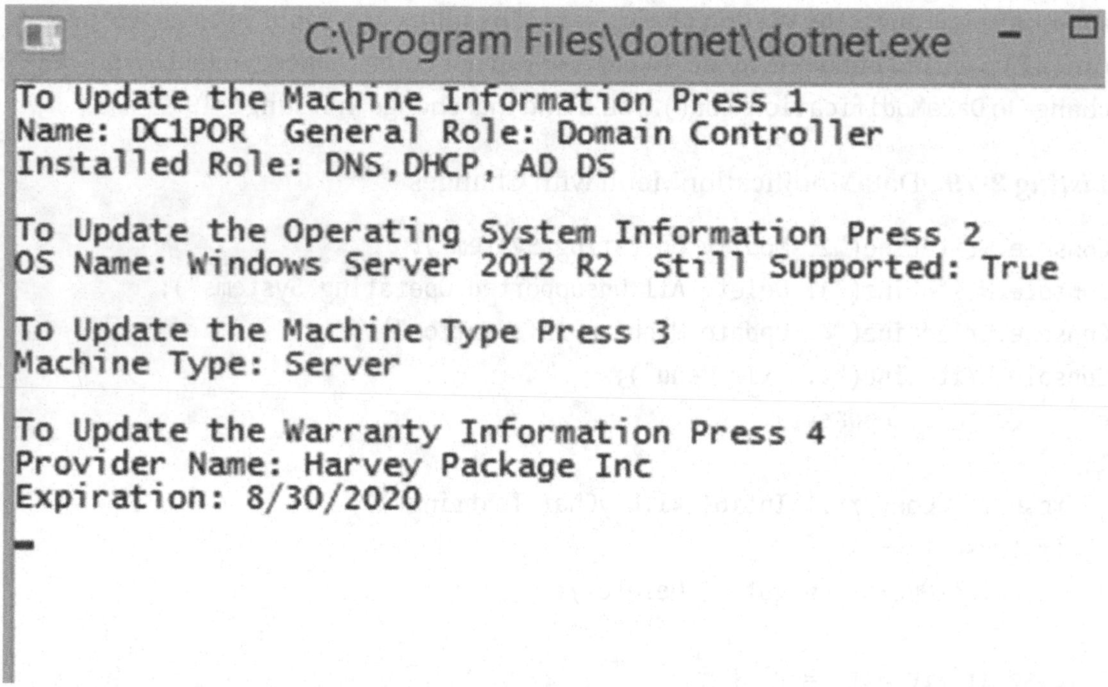

```
C:\Program Files\dotnet\dotnet.exe        _   □

To Update the Machine Information Press 1
Name: DC1POR  General Role: Domain Controller
Installed Role: DNS,DHCP, AD DS

To Update the Operating System Information Press 2
OS Name: Windows Server 2012 R2  Still Supported: True

To Update the Machine Type Press 3
Machine Type: Server

To Update the Warranty Information Press 4
Provider Name: Harvey Package Inc
Expiration: 8/30/2020
```

Figure 2-8. *UpdateMachineDetails output*

If we were doing a web page or some sort of form, we could handle this differently, but because we are using a console window, we need to go through a few extra steps. In the interest of not boring you, we are only going to update the Machine, OperatingSys, and MachineWarranty objects. You can add the other functionality later if you desire.

Let's start with Machine, as it's technically the easiest. Say that the list of servers you got from Bill is wrong. It shouldn't list DC1POR, but instead should list PORDC1. We'll take care of that starting with Listing 2-20, which includes a couple of helper methods.

Listing 2-20. Helper Methods

```
static char CheckForYorN(bool intercept) {
    ConsoleKeyInfo cki;
    char entry;
    bool cont = false;
    do {
        cki = Console.ReadKey(intercept);
        entry = cki.KeyChar;
        cont = ValidateYorN(entry.ToString());
    } while (!cont);
    return entry;
}

static string GetTextFromConsole(int minLength, bool allowEscape = false) {
    ConsoleKeyInfo cki;
    bool cont = false;
    string rtnValue = string.Empty;
    do {
        cki = Console.ReadKey(true);
        if (cki.Key == ConsoleKey.Escape) {
            if (allowEscape) {
                cont = true;
                rtnValue = "";
            }
        }
        else if (cki.Key == ConsoleKey.Enter) {
            if (rtnValue.Length >= minLength) {
                cont = true;
            }
            else {
                Console.WriteLine($"Please enter least {minLength} characters.");
            }
```

```
    }
    else if (cki.Key == ConsoleKey.Backspace) {
        Console.Write("\b \b");
        try {
            rtnValue = rtnValue.Substring(0, rtnValue.Length - 1);
        }
        catch (System.ArgumentOutOfRangeException) {
            // at the 0 position, can't go any further back
        }
    }
    else {
        rtnValue += cki.KeyChar.ToString();
        Console.Write(cki.KeyChar.ToString());
    }
  } while (!cont);
  return rtnValue;
}
```

No Entity Framework code here, but we did create a method with a default value, which we use in the next example. These two methods will save us a lot of typing later, as we'll be using this same code several times. See Listing 2-21.

Listing 2-21. UpdateMachine

```
static void UpdateMachine(int machineId) {
    Console.Clear();
    char response;
    using (MachineContext context = new MachineContext()) {
        Machine machine = context.Machine.Where(x => x.MachineId ==
        machineId).FirstOrDefault();
        if (machine != null) {
            Console.WriteLine($"Machine Name: {machine.Name}\r\nDo you wish to
            change it?");
            response = CheckForYorN(true);
            if (response == 'y') {
                Console.WriteLine("Enter a new Machine Name and then hit Enter
                to continue");
```

```
                machine.Name = GetTextFromConsole(3);
            }
            Console.WriteLine($"General Role: {machine.GeneralRole}\r\nDo you
            wish to change it?");
            response = CheckForYorN(true);
            if (response == 'y') {
                Console.WriteLine("Enter a new General Role For the Machine and
                then hit Enter to continue");
                machine.GeneralRole = GetTextFromConsole(5);
            }
            Console.WriteLine($"Installed Roles: {machine.InstalledRoles}\r\nDo
            you wish to change it?");
            response = CheckForYorN(true);
            if (response == 'y') {
                Console.WriteLine("Enter a new listing of Installed Roles For
                the Machine and then hit Enter to continue");
                Console.WriteLine("You can hit Esc to exit without making any
                changes");
                string result = GetTextFromConsole(5, true);
                if(result.Length >= 5) {
                    machine.InstalledRoles = result;
                }
            }
        }
        if (context.ChangeTracker.HasChanges()) {
            Console.WriteLine("\r\nSaving changes!");
            context.SaveChanges();
        }
        else {
            Console.WriteLine("\r\nNo Changes...");
        }
    }
    Console.WriteLine("Hit any key to continue...");
    Console.ReadKey();
}
```

We are going to make a change to UpdateMachineDetails to use the UpdateMachine method that we just created. If you want to use the menu-based method, you can, and it will be good practice if you are new to programming. I'm just going to comment it out in my code. Listing 2-22 shows the updated code for UpdateMachineDetails with the new call and the commented out section.

Listing 2-22. UpdateMachineDetails

```
static void UpdateMachineDetails() {
    Console.Clear();
    List<Machine> lMachine = GetListOfMachines();
    WriteHeader("Update Machine Details");

    string machineId = DisplayAllMachines();
    if (machineId.Length > 0) {
        int mId = Convert.ToInt32(machineId);
        Machine mach;
        MachineWarranty mWar;
        using (MachineContext context = new MachineContext()) {
            mach = context.Machine
                .Include(o => o.OperatingSys)
                .Include(t => t.MachineType)
                .Where(x => x.MachineId == mId).FirstOrDefault();

            mWar = context.MachineWarranty
                .Include(p => p.WarrantyProvider)
                .Where(x => x.MachineId == mach.MachineId).FirstOrDefault();
        }
        //Console.Clear();
        //Console.WriteLine("To Update the Machine Information Press 1");
        //Console.WriteLine($"Name: {mach.Name}  General Role: { mach.
        GeneralRole}");
        //Console.WriteLine($"Installed Role: {mach.InstalledRoles}");
        //Console.WriteLine("\r\nTo Update the Operating System Information
        Press 2");
        //Console.WriteLine($"OS Name: {mach.OperatingSys.Name}  Still
        Supported: {mach.OperatingSys.StillSupported}");
```

```
//Console.WriteLine($"\r\nTo Update the Machine Type Press 3");
//Console.WriteLine($"Machine Type: {mach.MachineType.Description}");
//Console.WriteLine($"\r\nTo Update the Warranty Information Press 4");
//Console.WriteLine($"Provider Name: {mWar.WarrantyProvider.
ProviderName}");
//Console.WriteLine($"Expiration: {mWar.WarrantyExpiration.
ToShortDateString()}");

    UpdateMachine(mach.MachineId);
    }
//Console.ReadKey();
}
```

We have a very simple way to update your *machine* here. I think it goes without saying, but I'm going to say it anyways—you should do a lot more validation in a production application than we are doing here. Let's take this for a test drive and see how it goes. Let's change DC1POR to PORDC1. Go to the Data Modification menu and choose Update Machine Information. After a couple of seconds, you should see something like Figure 2-9, although your IDs may be different.

```
C:\Program Files\dotnet\dotnet.exe                          —
Machine ID | Machine Name
5          | DC1POR
6          | DC2POR
7          | RDS1POR
8          | DB1SQL
9          | DB2SQL
10         | BobsPC
11         | JacksPC
12         | RDS1
13         | RDS2

Enter the MachineId followed by the Enter Key for more information.
Hit the Esc key at anytime to exit the menu.
```

Figure 2-9. Current list of machines

Choose the machine ID for DC1POR (in my case, it's 5) and press Enter. You should see something that looks like Figure 2-10. Figure 2-11 shows the prompt about changing the name of the machine.

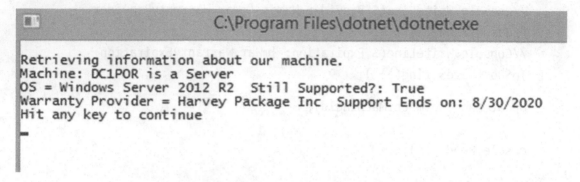

Figure 2-10. *Displaying the information about the machine prior to making changes*

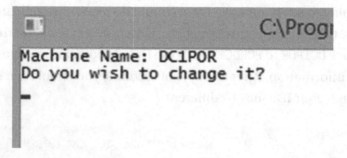

Figure 2-11. *Prompt for changing the machine name*

Figure 2-12 shows the remaining prompts. You should press N in each case and then save the changes.

```
C:\Program Files\dotnet\dotnet.exe
Machine Name: DC1POR
Do you wish to change it?
Enter a new Machine Name and then hit Enter to continue
PORDC1General Role: Domain Controller
Do you wish to change it?
Installed Roles: DNS,DHCP, AD DS
Do you wish to change it?

Saving changes!
Hit any key to continue...
```

Figure 2-12. *The rest of the choices and saving the machine*

As you can see, we need to clean up the console a bit. This is one downside to console applications and something you'll fix quite often in testing, which is why I left it here. As you can see, PORDC1 and the next prompt about the general role run together. Be sure that you add a carriage return and linefeed to your WriteLines or add a blank write line. Make the change to the two places that need it: Console.WriteLine($"\r\nGeneral Role: {machine.GeneralRole}\r\nDo you wish to change it?");. Do the same for the Installed Roles line. You could also add a [y or n] to your questions. I'll leave that up to you.

Before we go on to the next example, let's add two new servers to our database. We are going to add RDS1 and RDS2, which are Windows Server 2008. Both have a general role of terminal server and both have installed roles of RDS. To finish it off and make it official, we will add some warranty information. You can make up a service tag for each server (just make sure they are different), have them expire 2/1/2021, and indicate that are both serviced by Harvey Package, Inc.

This isn't something you would normally do, but since we are creating an example here, it'll be fine. We are going to create a way to upgrade all machines that have one operating system to another operating system.

Updating Multiple Records

In Chapter 1, we updated a single record. Now we are going to update multiple records at one time. For this example, let's pretend we just updated our Remote Desktop Servers and as a result they are going to be Windows Server 2016. Everything is going to stay the same except for the operating system, which is going to change. The first thing we need to do is add another item to the Main menu. We are going to add Option 5 (Update Operating Systems) and a call to UpdateOperatingSystems(). The following snippet shows what to add:

```
Console.WriteLine("4. Data Modification Menu");
Console.WriteLine("5. Update Operating Systems");
Console.WriteLine("9. Exit");
cki = Console.ReadKey();
try {
    result = Convert.ToInt16(cki.KeyChar.ToString());
    if (result == 1) {
        DisplayAllMachines();
```

```
    //SeedOperatingSystemTable();
  }
  else if (result == 2) {
    DisplayOperatingSystems();
  }
  else if (result == 3) {
    DataEntryMenu();
  }
  else if (result == 4) {
    DataModificationMenu();
  }
  else if(result == 5) {
    UpdateOperatingSystems();
  }
  else if (result == 9) {
    // We are exiting so nothing to do
    cont = true;
  }
}
```

Once you have added that option, you can start on the code. We are going to create a helper method called GetMachine() and our primary method called UpdateOperatingSystems(), which you probably already guessed. Listing 2-23 shows the code for both methods.

Listing 2-23. Updating Multiple Records

```
static Machine GetMachine() {
  Machine machine;
  List<Machine> lMachine = GetListOfMachines();
  Console.WriteLine("Machine ID | Machine Name");
  foreach (Machine m in lMachine) {
    Console.WriteLine($"{m.MachineId,-11}| {m.Name}");
  }
```

```
        Console.WriteLine("\r\nEnter the ID of the Machine you want then hit the
        Enter Key");
        int mId = Convert.ToInt16(GetNumbersFromConsole());
        machine = lMachine.Where(x => x.MachineId == mId).FirstOrDefault();
        return machine;
}

static void UpdateOperatingSystems() {
        ConsoleKeyInfo cki;
        string result;
        int newOsId = -1;
        bool valid = false;
        Console.Clear();
        WriteHeader($"Operating System Update");
        List<Machine> lMachines = new List<Machine>();
        bool cont = false;
        do {
            valid = false;
            lMachines.Add(GetMachine());
            Console.WriteLine("Do you want to add another Machine? [y or n]");
            do {
                cki = Console.ReadKey(true);
                result = cki.KeyChar.ToString();
                valid = ValidateYorN(result);
            } while (!valid);
            if(result.ToLower() == "n") {
                cont = true;
            }
        } while (!cont);

        Console.WriteLine($"{"ID",-7}|{"Name",-50}|Still Supported");
        Console.WriteLine("--------------------------------------------------------        ");
        using (var context = new MachineContext()) {
            List<OperatingSys> lOperatingSystems = context.OperatingSys.ToList();
            foreach (OperatingSys os in lOperatingSystems) {
```

```
        Console.WriteLine($"{os.OperatingSysId,-7}|{os.Name,-50}|
        {os.StillSupported}");
    }
}

Console.WriteLine("\r\nEnter the ID of the Operating System you want to
Update to.");
Console.WriteLine("Then hit the Enter Key");
string newOs = GetNumbersFromConsole();
newOsId = Convert.ToInt16(newOs);

using (MachineContext context = new MachineContext()) {
    foreach(Machine m in lMachines) {
        m.OperatingSysId = newOsId;
        context.Update(m);
    }
    context.SaveChanges();
}
}
```

Let's run the application. Choose Option 5 from the Main menu. When the list populates, we'll update RDS1 and RDS2 to Windows Server 2016. Figure 2-13 shows the change to RDS1. If you were to check RDS2, it would also show that it is now Windows Server 2016.

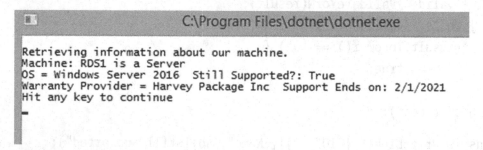

Figure 2-13. *Detailed information about the server we just updated*

The only thing that is new in this code is where we did `context.Update(m)`. When we get into programming for ASP, this method is generally used, because most everything is done outside of the `DBContext using` block. I cover this in greater detail later, but I thought this would be a good quick way to show you how to work outside of the block with data you retrieved from the database.

Summary

This chapter was very similar to Chapter 1, although we got information from multiple places to work with our objects and entities. We didn't cover deleting records, as we are going do that in the next chapter. I hope you are getting more comfortable getting data out of the database/entities and other objects using LINQ.

Before you go on to Chapter 3, you should be able to explain the following:

- How do you add data to a table with foreign keys?

- How can you retrieve data from multiple tables and display it?

- How do you update one or more records that have relationships to other tables?

Go back through the code and add some error handling or make it more aesthetically pleasing by adding carriage return/line feeds where we entered text and then had some text after it. You should be able to do this quite easily at this point and it will be good practice. This will help you think about where people could break your application, which is something that you need to be conscious of when you are building your own applications.

CHAPTER 3

Stepping Beyond the Basics

I think it's safe to say by this point that you are pretty comfortable with adding, retrieving, updating, and deleting records from a database using Entity Framework Core 2.0. Now it's time to do something that's a bit more exciting and slightly more difficult. We'll start off by selecting only the columns we want in our query, as we generally don't need every value in a table. In the example here, this might not seem like a big deal, but if you are working with a table that has 15+ columns and millions of rows, you can start to see why only getting the columns and rows that you need is important.

We are going to run these examples from a new menu item called `Testing` and change the method we call from there. Update `MainMenu()` to add the following lines:

```
Console.WriteLine("5. Update Operating Systems");
Console.WriteLine("6. Testing");
Console.WriteLine("9. Exit");
```

And then in the select section:

```
else if(result == 5) {
    UpdateOperatingSystems();
}
else if(result == 6) {

}
else if (result == 9) {
    // We are exiting so nothing to do
    cont = true;
}
```

© Derek J. Rouleau 2018
D. J. Rouleau, *Beginning Entity Framework Core 2.0*, https://doi.org/10.1007/978-1-4842-3375-7_3

As you can see, we left it empty so we can add our method once we are done. Note the variable cont. It is shorthand for continue. (Some people prefer to spell it out, but I've been in the habit of just using cont.) It basically answers the question, is it safe to continue?

Specifying Fields

Listing 3-1 creates a very simple example to show how you can select specific fields in your queries. As your tables get larger and larger, this will become more important to help increase the speed at which your queries run. Because we aren't going to be doing anything with our data, we are going to leave out the ID field. However, if you will later modify these tables based on your query, you should include it.

Listing 3-1. Specifying Fields

```
static void DisplaySpecificMachineData() {
    using(var context = new MachineContext()) {
        var machines = (from m in context.Machine
            join o in context.OperatingSys on m.OperatingSysId equals
            o.OperatingSysId
            where m.MachineTypeId == 1
            select new { MachineName = m.Name, Role = m.GeneralRole,
            OperatingSystem = o.Name });

        foreach(var m in machines) {
            Console.WriteLine($"{m.MachineName}  {m.OperatingSystem}
            {m.Role}");
        }
    }
}
```

That's all there is to it in this simple example, although to make it more interesting, we did use a join. Because we have two fields with the name (Name), we had to give our new fields different names. If you were to try to compile your program without doing that, you would receive the following error:

```
An anonymous type cannot have multiple properties with the same name
```

This makes sense, because how does the program know what Name you want? Listing 3-2 shows another short example.

Listing 3-2. Specifying Fields Example 2

```
static void DisplaySpecificMachineData2() {
    using (var context = new MachineContext()) {
        var machines = (from m in context.Machine
            join o in context.OperatingSys on m.OperatingSysId equals
            o.OperatingSysId
            where m.MachineTypeId == 1
            select new { m.Name, m.GeneralRole, OperatingSystem = o.Name });

        foreach (var m in machines) {
            Console.WriteLine($"{m.Name}   {m.OperatingSystem}
            {m.GeneralRole}");
        }
    }
}
```

As you can see, this is the same code except we changed the name of the operating system. Let's add a couple of lines to Option 6 in the Main menu and test this. The results are shown in Figure 3-1.

```
else if(result == 6) {
    Console.WriteLine();
    DisplaySpecificMachineData();
    Console.WriteLine();
    DisplaySpecificMachineData2();
    Console.ReadKey();
}
```

```
C:\Program Files\dotnet\dotnet.exe                                    —
Please select from the list below for what you would like to do today
1. List All Machines in Inventory
2. List All Operating Systems
3. Data Entry Menu
4. Data Modification Menu
5. Update Operating Systems
6. Testing
9. Exit
6
PORDC1   Windows Server 2012 R2   Domain Controller
DC2POR   Windows Server 2012 R2   Domain Controller
RDS1POR  Windows Server 2016   Remote Desktop
DB1SQL   Windows Server 2008 R2   DBMS
DB2SQL   Ubuntu Server 17.04   DBMS
RDS1  Windows Server 2016   Terminal Server
RDS2  Windows Server 2016   Terminal Server

PORDC1   Windows Server 2012 R2   Domain Controller
DC2POR   Windows Server 2012 R2   Domain Controller
RDS1POR  Windows Server 2016   Remote Desktop
DB1SQL   Windows Server 2008 R2   DBMS
DB2SQL   Ubuntu Server 17.04   DBMS
RDS1  Windows Server 2016   Terminal Server
RDS2  Windows Server 2016   Terminal Server
```

Figure 3-1. *Results from specifying fields*

As you can see, the loops produce the same results, which is what we expect to happen. This last quick example retrieves the MachineID and the Name of the code, as shown in Listing 3-3.

Listing 3-3. Retrieving the MachineID and the Code Name

```
static void DisplayMachineNameAndIdOnly() {
   using (var context = new MachineContext()) {
      var machines = (from m in context.Machine
         where m.MachineTypeId == 1
         select new { m.MachineId, m.Name });

      foreach (var m in machines) {
         Console.WriteLine($"{m.MachineId} {m.Name}");
      }
   }
}
```

This code is virtually identical; we just removed the join and retrieved only the two fields we needed. Make a change in Main menu so you call `DisplayMachineNameAndIdOnly()`. Your results should look similar to Figure 3-2. Don't forget that your IDs may be different.

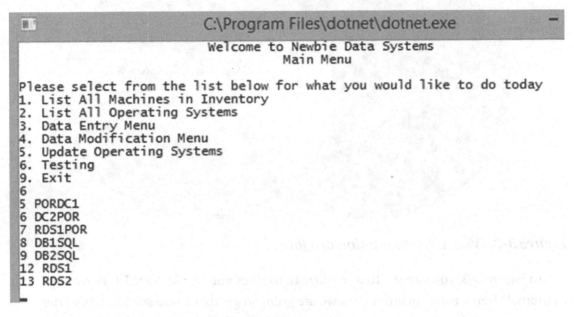

Figure 3-2. *Retrieving MachineId and Name only*

Now if you wanted to view workstations as well, you could change your where clause (or remove it entirely if you wanted to get all machines). The point here is to selectively retrieve what we want, which is why we are selecting only servers.

Joins

We already used joins in the previous example, so we aren't going to cover a lot that is new here. However, we'll explain the differences between the common types of joins and then look at a couple of examples. One will fix a bug that we currently have in our application (did you find it yet?). The most common joins are inner joins, outer joins, left and right outer joins, and cross joins. So far, you have seen inner joins in the examples. Figure 3-3 shows a visual representation of a join of the `Machine` and `WarrantyProvider` tables for a join on `MachineId`.

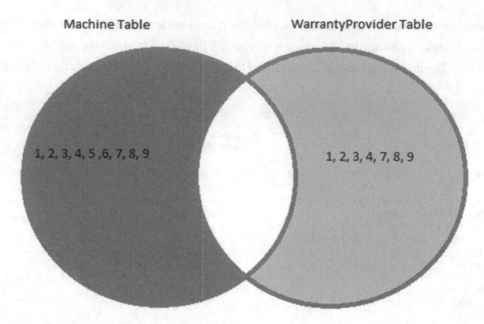

Figure 3-3. Visual representation of a join

In Figure 3-3, you can see that we have two tables and the MachineIds currently in them. When we use an inner join, we are going to get that white section where the tables have overlapping results. So that means that since MachineIds 1, 2, 3, 4, 7, 8, and 9 are in both tables, if we do an inner join we will get results that have those matching MachineIds. If we were to do a left outer join, we would get all the records (rows) in the machine table and from the right table. In this case, that's the WarrantyProvider table. If there are no matching columns in the right table, it will return a NULL value. You'll see an example of this in a moment.

A right outer join is the same as a left, just in the reverse order. A cross join produces a set that is the first table (total rows) multiplied by the number of rows in the second table if you don't use a where clause; if you use a where clause, then it's basically just an inner join. One of the main uses of cross joins is when you need to get a result set that includes every option. For instance, you are working with clothing and want to display every possible size and color combination that is possible. We'll take a look at the cross join in more detail in upcoming examples.

Left Outer Join

Let's take a look at using a left outer join with the two tables from Figure 3-3. Listing 3-4 shows the code to perform a left outer join.

Listing 3-4. Left Outer Join of Machine and MachineWarranty

```
static void LeftOuterJoin() {
    using (var context = new MachineContext()) {
        var leftJoin = from M in context.Machine
            join MW in context.MachineWarranty on M.MachineId equals
            MW.MachineId into lJoin
            from MW in lJoin.DefaultIfEmpty()
            select new {
                machineId = M.MachineId,
                machineName = M.Name,
                providerId = MW != null ? MW.WarrantyProviderId : (int?)null
            };

        foreach(var lj in leftJoin) {
            string pId;
            if (lj.providerId == null) { pId = "null"; }
            else { pId = lj.providerId.ToString(); }

            Console.WriteLine($"{lj.machineId} {lj.machineName}  {pId}");
        }
    }
}
```

You may have noticed that we didn't specify a left outer join, and that is because there isn't a way of doing that in C#. Instead, we had to use the `DefaultIfEmpty()` function to get that functionality. We also had to add *(int?)* before the null in the `providerId` line because we had to make our `int` value nullable. Otherwise, you would get an error telling you that there is no implicit conversion between `int` and `null`. To make the null value a bit more obvious than just a blank space in the output, we created a variable to display the value. We could have done this a different way, but I tried to keep it simple. Make the appropriate change to Option 6 of the Main menu. When you run your code, you should get a result similar to Figure 3-4.

```
┌─────────────────────────────────────────────────────────────────┐
│ ▦                  C:\Program Files\dotnet\dotnet.exe          ─  │
├─────────────────────────────────────────────────────────────────┤
│                   Welcome to Newbie Data Systems                  │
│                           Main Menu                              │
│ Please select from the list below for what you would like to do today │
│ 1. List All Machines in Inventory                                │
│ 2. List All Operating Systems                                    │
│ 3. Data Entry Menu                                               │
│ 4. Data Modification Menu                                        │
│ 5. Update Operating Systems                                      │
│ 6. Testing                                                       │
│ 9. Exit                                                          │
│ 6                                                                │
│ 5 PORDC1   2                                                     │
│ 6 DC2POR   1                                                     │
│ 7 RDS1POR  2                                                     │
│ 8 DB1SQL   1                                                     │
│ 9 DB2SQL   null                                                  │
│ 10 BobsPC  null                                                  │
│ 11 JacksPC  1                                                    │
│ 12 RDS1    2                                                     │
│ 13 RDS2    2                                                     │
│ ▄                                                                │
└─────────────────────────────────────────────────────────────────┘
```

Figure 3-4. *Results from a left outer join*

As you can see, we have values for everything but DB2SQL and BobsPC, which return a null value as expected.

Feel free to mess around a bit with this before moving on so you get a better idea of how it's working. One last thing—when you are pointing to your tables in your LINQ query, don't forget to specify the DBContext. Otherwise, you'll run into problems. I can't tell you how many times I sat for a minute or two trying to determine why I was getting an error before the light bulb turned on.

Right Outer Join

This section covers something new in order to show you how right outer joins can work in Entity Framework Core. Listing 3-5 shows the code to display right outer joins. Before you start, you need to add the following using statement to the top of the program:

```
using System.Data.Common;
```

You'll see why you need this using statement in a moment.

Listing 3-5. Right Outer Joins

```
static void RightOuterJoin() {
   using (var context = new MachineContext()) {
      var dataBaseConnection = context.Database.GetDbConnection();
      dataBaseConnection.Open();
      using(var cmd = dataBaseConnection.CreateCommand()) {
         string eSQL = "SELECT MW.MachineID, M.Name, MW.WarrantyProviderID,
         mw.WarrantyExpiration FROM MachineWarranty AS MW RIGHT OUTER JOIN
         Machine AS M ON MW.MachineID = M.MachineID";
         cmd.CommandText = eSQL;
         DbDataReader reader = cmd.ExecuteReader();

         if (reader.HasRows) {
            while (reader.Read()) {
               string mId;
               if (reader.IsDBNull(0)) { mId = "Null"; }
               else { mId = reader.GetInt32(0).ToString(); }

               string machineName = reader.GetString(1);

               string warrantyProviderId;
               if (reader.IsDBNull(2)) { warrantyProviderId = "Null"; }
               else { warrantyProviderId = reader.GetInt32(2).ToString(); }

               string warrantyExpiration;
               if (reader.IsDBNull(3)) { warrantyExpiration = "Null"; }
               else{ warrantyExpiration = reader.GetDateTime(3).
               ToShortDateString(); }
               Console.WriteLine($"{mId} {machineName} {warrantyProviderId}
               {warrantyExpiration}");
            }
         }
         dataBaseConnection.Close();
      }
      Console.WriteLine();
      var rightJoin = from mw in context.MachineWarranty
```

```
            join m in context.Machine on mw.MachineId equals m.MachineId into
            rJoin
            from m in rJoin.DefaultIfEmpty()
            select new {
                machineId = m != null ? m.MachineId : (int?)null,
                machineName = m.Name,
                warrantyProviderId = mw != null ? mw.WarrantyProviderId :
                (int?)null,
                warrantyExpiration = mw != null ? mw.WarrantyExpiration :
                (DateTime?)null
            };

        foreach (var rj in rightJoin) {
            string mId;
            string machineName;
            string warrProv;
            string warrExp;
            machineName = rj.machineName;
            if (rj.machineId == null) { mId = "null"; }
            else { mId = rj.machineId.ToString(); }
            if(rj.warrantyProviderId == null) { warrProv = "null"; }
            else { warrProv = rj.warrantyProviderId.ToString(); }
            if(rj.warrantyExpiration == null) { warrExp = "null"; }
            else { warrExp = rj.warrantyExpiration.ToString(); }

            Console.WriteLine(value: $"{mId} {machineName} {warrProv}
            {warrExp}");
        }
    }
}
```

I'll explain what's going on after you run the code. Now when you update Option 6 in the Main menu and run the code, you should see the results in Figure 3-5.

```
                        C:\Program Files\dotnet\dotnet.exe
2. List All Operating Systems
3. Data Entry Menu
4. Data Modification Menu
5. Update Operating Systems
6. Testing
9. Exit
6
5 PORDC1 2 8/30/2020
6 DC2POR 1 8/30/2020
7 RDS1POR 2 7/15/2019
8 DB1SQL 1 12/31/2017
Null DB2SQL Null Null
Null BobsPC Null Null
11 JacksPC 1 2/15/2017
12 RDS1 2 2/1/2021
13 RDS2 2 2/1/2021

6 DC2POR 1 8/30/2020 12:00:00 AM
7 RDS1POR 2 7/15/2019 12:00:00 AM
8 DB1SQL 1 12/31/2017 12:00:00 AM
11 JacksPC 1 2/15/2017 12:00:00 AM
12 RDS1 2 2/1/2021 12:00:00 AM
13 RDS2 2 2/1/2021 12:00:00 AM
5 PORDC1 2 8/30/2020 12:00:00 AM
```

Figure 3-5. *Right outer joins, kind of*

I know what you are thinking—hey our results are different. Yes, that's the great thing about using LINQ and Entity Framework for some queries. Without a ton of "mucking around," it's a bit hard to get things how you want them. The good news is you can just write a query like you normally would and off you go.

The good news is that you are learning something new and the better news is that it's pretty simple. As you can see, we still create the DBContext variable and do all of our work inside that using statement. We could have created two separate connections, but I didn't see the point in doing so.

Note   Remember that the DBContext creates a connection to the database.

We then create the dataBaseConnection variable, which gives us access to the database. We then create our DBCommand object and create a using block for it. Then we create our SQL string (called eSQL here, which is short for Entity SQL, because we are using what is called Entity SQL to retrieve our data from the database). I hope you are familiar with using a DataReader of some sort because that is what we are doing—creating a DbDataReader and executing our DBCommand.

This is where it gets a little tricky at first. Because I want to display a value of Null in the output, I convert the values to strings, but in order to avoid errors, I have to check if the value is null first. Otherwise, I will get an error when I run the code and hit a null value. We'll take a look at the first check in this code example, as the other two are virtually the same:

```
string mId;
if (reader.IsDBNull(0)) {
    mId = "Null";
}
else {
    mId = reader.GetInt32(0).ToString();
}
```

We expanded the code a bit to make it more readable instead of putting the if and else on a single line. We check to see if the value at position 0 of reader is null, and if it is, we set mId to a value of Null. Otherwise, we have to convert the integer value to a string and set that as the value of mId. You need to know what the expected value type is going to be when you are doing this, as you have to tell the reader what the data type is. We do this for all our types that aren't nullable by default, which is why we don't have to check first for a null value for the name.

As with all database applications, it's a good idea to close your connection, so we do that at the end. If you were going to do something with this data other than display it, you can create a struct or a class to hold the values in a list. But since we are just displaying the results, there isn't a reason to do that.

We ran our code and we got two results that have nulls in them like we would expect for a right outer join with the current state of our tables. Now we get to the LINQ part of our code, which is where this falls apart. As mentioned in the left outer join section, there isn't a way to specify what type of join you are using with LINQ that closely matches the phrasing you used with SQL, although we have the choice of Join and GroupJoin. With the exception of the extra fields, this should look exactly like the code used for the left outer join. The only other difference is the order of the tables. We then check for our null values like we did before making the types nullable where we need them to be. We run our code and there are no null values.

You want to take all of the records in the MachineWarranty table that have a MachineId of something and join them to the Machine table. Because it's not looking at the Machine table as well for MachineIds, it's only looking for those in the MachineWarranty table. This is why we aren't getting a true right outer join.

Cross Join

This section looks at a cross join so you can see what it looks like and see why for our purposes here, it's not overly helpful. Listing 3-6 shows the code for the cross join. After the last listing, I'm sure you're happy about how short it is.

Listing 3-6. Cross Join

```
static void CrossJoin() {
    using (var _context = new MachineContext()) {
        var crossJoin = from m in _context.Machine
            from mw in _context.MachineWarranty
            select new {
                m, mw
            };

        int counter = 1;
        foreach(var cj in crossJoin) {
            Console.WriteLine($"Row: {counter++}\t{cj.m.MachineId} {cj.m.Name}
            { cj.mw.WarrantyProviderId} {cj.mw.WarrantyExpiration}");
        }
    }
}
```

This is pretty simple. This time I changed the name of the DBContext variable to _context. I figured I'd mix it up a little bit. I also added a counter so you can see the number of rows at a quick glance. Update Option 6 in the Main menu and run your code. You should see results similar to Figure 3-6, which is only a small portion of the entire result set.

```
                                        C:\Program Files\dotnet\dotnet.exe
Row: 40 8 DB1SQL 2 2/1/2021 12:00:00 AM
Row: 41 9 DB2SQL 2 2/1/2021 12:00:00 AM
Row: 42 10 BobsPC 2 2/1/2021 12:00:00 AM
Row: 43 11 JacksPC 2 2/1/2021 12:00:00 AM
Row: 44 12 RDS1 2 2/1/2021 12:00:00 AM
Row: 45 13 RDS2 2 2/1/2021 12:00:00 AM
Row: 46 5 PORDC1 2 2/1/2021 12:00:00 AM
Row: 47 6 DC2POR 2 2/1/2021 12:00:00 AM
Row: 48 7 RDS1POR 2 2/1/2021 12:00:00 AM
Row: 49 8 DB1SQL 2 2/1/2021 12:00:00 AM
Row: 50 9 DB2SQL 2 2/1/2021 12:00:00 AM
Row: 51 10 BobsPC 2 2/1/2021 12:00:00 AM
Row: 52 11 JacksPC 2 2/1/2021 12:00:00 AM
Row: 53 12 RDS1 2 2/1/2021 12:00:00 AM
Row: 54 13 RDS2 2 2/1/2021 12:00:00 AM
Row: 55 5 PORDC1 2 8/30/2020 12:00:00 AM
Row: 56 6 DC2POR 2 8/30/2020 12:00:00 AM
Row: 57 7 RDS1POR 2 8/30/2020 12:00:00 AM
Row: 58 8 DB1SQL 2 8/30/2020 12:00:00 AM
Row: 59 9 DB2SQL 2 8/30/2020 12:00:00 AM
Row: 60 10 BobsPC 2 8/30/2020 12:00:00 AM
Row: 61 11 JacksPC 2 8/30/2020 12:00:00 AM
Row: 62 12 RDS1 2 8/30/2020 12:00:00 AM
Row: 63 13 RDS2 2 8/30/2020 12:00:00 AM
```

Figure 3-6. *Partial results of a cross join*

We have nine rows in the `Machine` table and seven rows in the `MachineWarranty` table, so if we multiply those, we get 63 rows. When we run our query, we get 63 rows so we know the math has worked out. In short, what this is saying is show me all possible combinations of `Table1` and `Table2`.

Inner Join: Method Syntax

Up until now, we have created all of our inner joins using query syntax because it's a lot easier and more straightforward. However, I wouldn't be doing my due diligence if I didn't show you how to do it using method syntax. As you will see, it's a bit harder. Listing 3-7 shows the code and Figure 3-7 shows the results.

Listing 3-7. Method Syntax for a Inner Join

```
static void InnerJoin() {
    using (var context = new MachineContext()) {
        var mw = context.MachineWarranty
            .Join(context.WarrantyProvider, m => m.WarrantyProviderId, p =>
            p.WarrantyProviderId, (m, p) => new {
```

```
                machineId = m.MachineId,
                warrantyProvider = p.ProviderName,
                warrantyExpiration = m.WarrantyExpiration,
                supportNumber = p.SupportNumber
            });

    foreach (var m in mw) {
        Console.WriteLine($"MachineID: {m.machineId} Warranty Provider:
        {m.warrantyProvider}");
        Console.WriteLine($"Warranty Expiration: {m.warrantyExpiration.
        ToShortDateString()} Support Number: {m.supportNumber}");
        Console.WriteLine("----------------------------------------");
        // 40 dashes
    }
  }
}
```

```
  C:\Program Files\dotnet\dotnet.exe

6. Testing
9. Exit
6
MachineID: 6 Warranty Provider: Big Server Co
Warranty Expiration: 8/30/2020 Support Number: 8005551212
----------------------------------------
MachineID: 7 Warranty Provider: Harvey Package Inc
Warranty Expiration: 7/15/2019 Support Number: 8665552323
----------------------------------------
MachineID: 8 Warranty Provider: Big Server Co
Warranty Expiration: 12/31/2017 Support Number: 8005551212
----------------------------------------
MachineID: 11 Warranty Provider: Big Server Co
Warranty Expiration: 2/15/2017 Support Number: 8005551212
----------------------------------------
MachineID: 12 Warranty Provider: Harvey Package Inc
Warranty Expiration: 2/1/2021 Support Number: 8665552323
----------------------------------------
MachineID: 13 Warranty Provider: Harvey Package Inc
Warranty Expiration: 2/1/2021 Support Number: 8665552323
----------------------------------------
MachineID: 5 Warranty Provider: Harvey Package Inc
Warranty Expiration: 8/30/2020 Support Number: 8665552323
----------------------------------------
```

Figure 3-7. *Results of the inner join using method syntax*

I think you can now see why I said creating joins using method syntax are a bit messy compared to query syntax. I have never created a group by join using method syntax, although if you want to become proficient at it then that's one more thing you can impress your friends with. So let's take a look at what we have and try to figure it out.

We create our anonymous type `mw`, which contains four anonymous types of its own—`machineId`, `warrantyProvider`, `warrantyExpiration`, and `supportNumber`. We did this when we declared them in the `new{}` block of the code. In this case, we are starting with the `MachineWarranty` model and we are going to join the `WarrantyProvider` model to it. The one part I usually forget here is that the code goes inside the parentheses when I first write these so try to remember that part.

The first parameter is `m`, which represents the `MachineWarranty` model. The second parameter is the table we are joining, which in this case is the `WarrantyProvider` model. In both of these cases, we are joining on the `WarrantyProviderId`, so that is why we have `m => m.WarrantyProviderId`, etc. The way that I understand the `(m, p)` to work is that we are saying that we want these two parameters available for the `new{}` block.

Now I hope you understand why I say it is a lot easier to use the query syntax when you are creating joins. However, knowing how to create them with method syntax is not a bad idea either.

Grouping

You should now have a better understanding of how you are going to handle joins as you progress in your Entity Framework Core career. Feel free to mess around a bit with what you have and create some other joins by building off what you already know. The next thing we are going to look at is grouping our results together. Sometimes we need to know how many of something is in our table. The first thing we'll do is figure out how many machines we have in each of our operating systems. First let's take a look at how we can do this using query syntax.

Query Syntax

Listing 3-8 shows the code for displaying a count of machines by operating system.

Listing 3-8. Grouping Machines by Operating System

```
static void GroupMachinesByOS() {
    using (var context = new MachineContext()) {
        var mli = (from m in context.Machine
            join o in context.OperatingSys on m.OperatingSysId equals
            o.OperatingSysId
            group new { m, o } by m.OperatingSysId into grouped
            select new { grouped.Key, count = grouped.Select(x=>x.m.Operating
            SysId).Count(), Name = grouped.Select(ma=>ma.o.Name) });

        foreach(var m in mli) {
            Console.WriteLine($"OS ID: {m.Key} Machine Count W/OS: {m.count}
            OS Name: {m.Name.ElementAt(0)}");
        }
    }
}
```

Like you saw in the last section, we created the query and used a join to bring in the OperatingSys model. The change here is where we have group new {} and, as you can probably guess by its name, this is what makes it a group by query. It groups m and o by a specified key, which in this case is m.OperatingSysId. We then select the values that we want to access. We have our range variable, which is grouped (you could have named this anything) and from that, we need the key, which is the OperatingSysId. We then want to get a count, which we do with an inline function (lambda).

From grouped, we are going to get a count of the OperatingSysId. Lastly, this example goes the extra mile and gets the name of the operating system as well. If you search online for group by for Entity Framework, you probably won't find one that includes this information. It's not very intuitive and Name = grouped. Select(ma=>ma.o.Name) is the easy part. The part that makes no sense at first is {m. Name.ElementAt(0)}. ElementAt returns the value from that index in sequence. Since we only have one element in our sequence, we want the first one, which is of course zero. Figure 3-8 shows the results.

```
■                    C:\Program Files\dotnet\dotnet.exe                    ─
                    Welcome to Newbie Data Systems
                               Main Menu
Please select from the list below for what you would like to do today
1. List All Machines in Inventory
2. List All Operating Systems
3. Data Entry Menu
4. Data Modification Menu
5. Update Operating Systems
6. Testing
9. Exit
6
OS ID: 16 Machine Count W/OS: 1 OS Name: Windows 7
OS ID: 19 Machine Count W/OS: 1 OS Name: Windows 10
OS ID: 22 Machine Count W/OS: 1 OS Name: Windows Server 2008 R2
OS ID: 24 Machine Count W/OS: 2 OS Name: Windows Server 2012 R2
OS ID: 25 Machine Count W/OS: 3 OS Name: Windows Server 2016
OS ID: 27 Machine Count W/OS: 1 OS Name: Ubuntu Server 17.04
■
```

Figure 3-8. *Grouping using query syntax*

Method Syntax

Just to show you how do it another way, let's figure out how many of each type of machine we have. Since we used query syntax to get our count for operating systems, we'll use method syntax this time for machine type. Listing 3-9 shows the code for doing this. Try to figure out how to do this without looking at Listing 3-9 first. Why not give it a try? Don't worry, we aren't going to be doing a join for this one, so it should be fairly easy.

Listing 3-9. Grouping Machines by Type Method Syntax

```csharp
static void GroupMachineByType() {
    using(var context = new MachineContext()) {
        var mType = context.Machine
            .GroupBy(m => m.MachineTypeId)
            .Select(g => new { id = g.Key, count = g.Count() });

        foreach (var m in mType) {
            Console.WriteLine($"{m.id}  {m.count}");
        }
    }
}
```

As you can see, when you don't do a join or anything it's pretty simple and straightforward. The results for this quick example are shown in Figure 3-9. We are grouping by MachineTypeId and we are passing along two anonymous types to mType, id, and count.

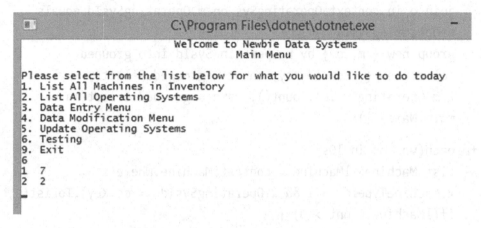

Figure 3-9. *Results from grouping by machine type*

The results show that for MachineType 1, we have seven machines and for MachineType 2, we have two machines. If you wanted a simple way to display the machine type description, you could have created a list that has the ID and description and within the loop. Then, when you display your output, you could quickly search the list and replace the output with the description.

Logical Operators

We are going to borrow a bit from one of the earlier examples and make a slight change to make it "new". What we are trying to do is get a list of machines grouped by operating system and then display the name as well as the role as a subgroup of the operating system. We have already done some of the work in GroupMachinesByOS(), so we can just copy that code for the query. Listing 3-10 shows all of the code for this example.

Listing 3-10. Logical AND Operator

```
static void LogicalAnd() {
    using (var context = new MachineContext()) {
        var lOs = (from m in context.Machine
            join o in context.OperatingSys on m.OperatingSysId equals
            o.OperatingSysId
            group new { m, o } by m.OperatingSysId into grouped
            select new { grouped.Key, count = grouped.Select(x =>
            x.m.OperatingSysId).Count(), Name = grouped.Select(ma =>
            ma.o.Name) });

        foreach(var os in lOs) {
            List<Machine> lMachine = context.Machine.Where(x =>
            x.MachineTypeId == 1 && x.OperatingSysId == os.Key).ToList();
            if(lMachine.Count > 0) {
                Console.WriteLine($"Servers Running {os.Name.ElementAt(0)}");
                foreach (Machine m in lMachine) {
                    Console.WriteLine($"\tName: {m.Name}\tRole: {m.GeneralRole}");
                }
                Console.WriteLine();
            }
        }
    }
}
```

The only change we made to our first query is to change the name to *lOs* since it is a list of operating systems. I'll be the first to admit that this isn't the most efficient way of getting results, but it's a decent example of how to use a logical AND. For each iteration, we check our model to see if we have any machines that have the OperatingSysId in our list and has a MachineTypeId of 1. If we have at least one result, we display the results to the user; otherwise, we go on to the next entry. Figure 3-10 shows the results of the query.

```
C:\Program Files\dotnet\dotnet.exe                        —
Please select from the list below for what you would like to do today
1. List All Machines in Inventory
2. List All Operating Systems
3. Data Entry Menu
4. Data Modification Menu
5. Update Operating Systems
6. Testing
9. Exit
6
Servers Running Windows Server 2008 R2
        Name: DB1SQL     Role: DBMS

Servers Running Windows Server 2012 R2
        Name: PORDC1     Role: Domain Controller
        Name: DC2POR     Role: Domain Controller

Servers Running Windows Server 2016
        Name: RDS1POR    Role: Remote Desktop
        Name: RDS1       Role: Terminal Server
        Name: RDS2       Role: Terminal Server

Servers Running Ubuntu Server 17.04
        Name: DB2SQL     Role: DBMS
```

Figure 3-10. *Results from the logical AND*

In a production example, you would more than likely have added a where clause to your initial query looking for MachineTypeId of 1, as that would have returned the set you were looking for. If you would like to test that, change LogicalAnd() to Listing 3-11. You will see that you get the same results.

Listing 3-11. Changes to the Method

```
static void LogicalAnd() {
    using (var context = new MachineContext()) {
        DateTime start = DateTime.Now;
        var lOs = (from m in context.Machine
            join o in context.OperatingSys on m.OperatingSysId equals
            o.OperatingSysId
            group new { m, o } by m.OperatingSysId into grouped
            select new { grouped.Key, count = grouped.Select(x =>
            x.m.OperatingSysId).Count(), Name = grouped.Select(ma =>
            ma.o.Name) });

        foreach(var os in lOs) {
            List<Machine> lMachine = context.Machine.Where(x =>
            x.MachineTypeId == 1 && x.OperatingSysId == os.Key).ToList();
```

```
        if(lMachine.Count > 0) {
            Console.WriteLine($"Servers Running {os.Name.ElementAt(0)}");
            foreach (Machine m in lMachine) {
                Console.WriteLine($"\tName: {m.Name}\tRole: {m.GeneralRole}");
            }
            Console.WriteLine();
        }
    }
    DateTime end = DateTime.Now;
    TimeSpan ts = end.Subtract(start);
    Console.WriteLine($"It took {ts.Milliseconds} ms to run");

    start = DateTime.Now;
    Console.WriteLine("Using a where clause for the same results...");
    var lOs2 = (from m in context.Machine
        join o in context.OperatingSys on m.OperatingSysId equals
        o.OperatingSysId
        where m.MachineTypeId == 1
        group new { m, o } by m.OperatingSysId into grouped
        select new { grouped.Key, count = grouped.Select(x =>
        x.m.OperatingSysId).Count(), Name = grouped.Select(ma =>
        ma.o.Name) });

    foreach (var os in lOs2) {
        List<Machine> lMachine = context.Machine.Where(x =>
        x.OperatingSysId == os.Key).ToList();
        if (lMachine.Count > 0) {
            Console.WriteLine($"Servers Running {os.Name.ElementAt(0)}");
            foreach (Machine m in lMachine) {
                Console.WriteLine($"\tName: {m.Name}\tRole:
                {m.GeneralRole}");
            }
            Console.WriteLine();
        }
    }
    end = DateTime.Now;
```

```
    ts = end.Subtract(start);
    Console.WriteLine($"It took {ts.Milliseconds} ms to run");
  }
}
```

We added the where clause and removed the && operator from the query, plus we added some DateTime variables to check for timing. If you run it again, you'll see that they produce identical results, but the second one is more efficient. Figure 3-11 shows part of the results but displays the timing results. Your times will be different, but this shows how a small change can make a big difference.

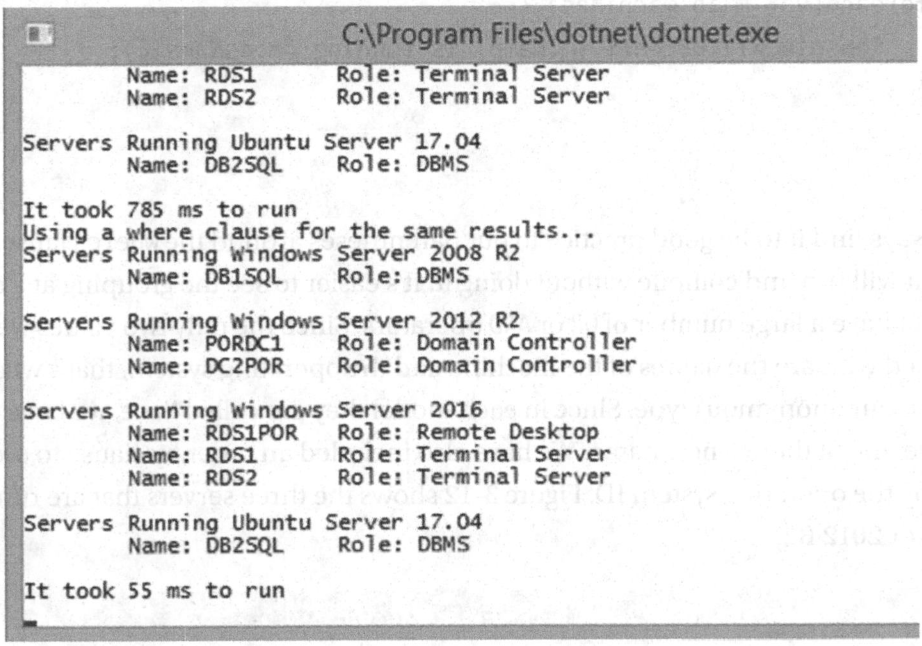

Figure 3-11. *Timing results*

Logical OR

The Logical OR (see Listing 3-12) works similarly to the AND with the exception that it looks to see if either operation is true. To show this, we are going to look for servers where the operating system is Server 2008 R2 or Server 2012 R2. This time, we'll just do it the more efficient way, which is how we'd likely do it in the real world.

Listing 3-12. Logical OR

```
static void LogicalOr() {
    using (var context = new MachineContext()) {
        var machines = from m in context.Machine
            join o in context.OperatingSys on m.OperatingSysId equals
            o.OperatingSysId into mj
            where (m.OperatingSysId == 22 || m.OperatingSysId == 24)
            orderby m.OperatingSysId
            select new { m.Name, osName = m.OperatingSys.Name };

        foreach(var m in machines) {
            Console.WriteLine($"{m.Name} is running {m.osName}");
        }
    }
}
```

I always find it to be good practice to put parentheses around the where clause, even though it will run and compile without doing it. It's easier to see the grouping at a quick glance if I have a large number of OR or AND operators. Since the only two values we are concerned with are the names of the machine and the operating system, that's what we create for our anonymous type. Since in each model they are called Name, we have to at least give one of them a new name. We have also included an order by clause to order the results by the operating system ID. Figure 3-12 shows the three servers that are running 2008 R2 or 2012 R2.

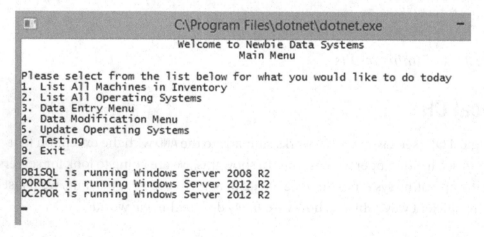

Figure 3-12. *Results from a logical OR*

Paging and Filtering Results

There are many times when you'll want to display only a certain amount of data on the screen. This is certainly the case when it comes to working with websites. Let's say you only have enough space to display five rows of data at a time on your page, but you have 200 rows in your database that meet the query's criteria. Do you want to retrieve all 200 rows and then have some sort of method for displaying the records in blocks? Like you saw in the logical AND example, that isn't always the best choice. When you run into this situation, you should use paging for your data results. Normally when you are paging, you are also filtering to keep your result set as small as possible. This will make it a more enjoyable experience for the end users.

Working with the data we currently have, let's say that we might want to page and filter our display of the operating systems. This will give the users a chance to select how they want to see the results. See Listing 3-13.

Listing 3-13. Paging and Filtering Results

```
static void PageAndFilterOperatingSystems() {
    ConsoleKeyInfo cki;
    string result;
    bool cont = false;
    System.Linq.Expressions.Expression<Func<OperatingSys, bool>> where
    Clause = o => o.StillSupported == true;
    string pageOptions = "";
    List<OperatingSys> lOperatingSys;
    Console.Clear();
    Console.WriteLine("Do you want to display all of the Operating Systems
    in one list? [y or n]");
    do {
        cki = Console.ReadKey(true);
        result = cki.KeyChar.ToString();
        cont = ValidateYorN(result);
    } while (!cont);

    if (result.ToLower() == "y") {
        DisplayOperatingSystems();
    }
    else {
```

```
Console.WriteLine("Do you want to view [a]ll, [s]upported operating
systems or [u]nsupported operating systems?");
cont = false;
do {
    cki = Console.ReadKey(true);
    if (cki.Key == ConsoleKey.A || cki.Key == ConsoleKey.S ||
    cki.Key == ConsoleKey.U) {
        result = cki.KeyChar.ToString();
        cont = true;
    }
} while (!cont);
if (result.ToLower() == "a") {
    whereClause = o => o.StillSupported == true || o.Still
    Supported == false;
}
else if (result.ToLower() == "s") {
    whereClause = o => o.StillSupported == true;
}
else if (result.ToLower() == "u") {
    whereClause = o => o.StillSupported == false;
}
int pageSize;
int pageIndex = 0;
Console.WriteLine("How many results do you want per page, enter a
number between 3 and 5");
cont = false;
do {
    cki = Console.ReadKey(true);
    if (cki.Key == ConsoleKey.D3 || cki.Key == ConsoleKey.D4 || cki.
    Key == ConsoleKey.D5) {
        result = cki.KeyChar.ToString();
        cont = true;
    }
} while (!cont);
pageSize = Convert.ToInt16(result);
cont = false;
```

```
do {
    Console.Clear();
    using (var context = new MachineContext()) {
        lOperatingSys = context.OperatingSys
            .Where(whereClause)
            .OrderBy(i => i.OperatingSysId)
            .Skip(pageIndex * pageSize)
            .Take(pageSize)
            .ToList();
    }
    foreach (OperatingSys os in lOperatingSys) {
        Console.Write($"Name: {os.Name,-39}\tStill Supported = ");
        if (os.StillSupported == true) {
            Console.ForegroundColor = ConsoleColor.Green;
        }
        else {
            Console.ForegroundColor = ConsoleColor.Red;
        }
        Console.WriteLine(os.StillSupported);
        Console.ForegroundColor = ConsoleColor.Black;
    }
    if(pageIndex == 0) {
        pageOptions = "Hit Esc to exit\tN for Next";
    }
    else {
    pageOptions = "Hit Esc to exit\tN for Next\tP for Previous";
    }
    Console.WriteLine($"Page: {pageIndex}\t{pageOptions}");
    cki = Console.ReadKey(true);
    if(cki.Key == ConsoleKey.Escape) {
        cont - true;
    }else if(cki.Key == ConsoleKey.N) {
        pageIndex++;
    }else if(cki.Key == ConsoleKey.P) {
        if(pageIndex > 0) {
            pageIndex--;
```

```
            }
        }
    } while (!cont);
    }
}
```

This is probably one of the most exciting and longest sections of code. Note that we reused the code for displaying the operating systems in a color-coded fashion. One of the most exciting parts of this comes early on:

```
System.Linq.Expressions.Expression<Func<OperatingSys, bool>> whereClause =
o => o.StillSupported == true;
```

We have just managed to make our where clause in our query a variable. We are replacing the where clause with the contents of the object, so it will read .Where(o => o.StillSupported == true) if we didn't have our variable.

This is something that you may find useful in the future. I had to give it a default value so the code could compile, so I decided to go with StillSupported = true. It was more so when you are looking at it and you have some idea what it is doing. We build our where clause based on what the user enters. We can have just one query that way. Toward the bottom of the code you'll see the paging and filtering.

```
using (var context = new MachineContext()) {
    lOperatingSys = context.OperatingSys
        .Where(whereClause)
        .OrderBy(i => i.OperatingSysId)
        .Skip(pageIndex * pageSize)
        .Take(pageSize)
        .ToList();
}
```

The Where clause produces the filtering. .Skip and .Take provide the paging ability. If you are using a version of SQL Server before 2012, this will not work (you'll have to do it the old fashioned way, sorry). For our skip argument, we are multiplying our page index variable by the page size. If our index is anything over zero, we will skip records in our query. The take argument tells SQL server how many records we want, or up to how many records we want. In the interest of making this slightly more compact, I haven't checked for a upper bound for moving onto the next page, so we can keep on going forever. Yes, EF Core will allow you to do that.

When we do something similar in our website, I'll show you how to check for the upper bound. When the users are tired of paging through the results, they can press the Esc key and leave the loop. Again, we couldn't keep loading the results again and again if they press the wrong keys like we are now, but I figured this example was long enough so I left that part out. You are welcome to alter your code and put in these fixes if you want.

Before you can test these changes, you need to update a few things. Make the following change in the Main menu:

```
Console.WriteLine("2. List Operating Systems");  // Changed from List All
Operating Systems
```

And then change Option 2:

```
else if (result == 2) {
    //DisplayOperatingSystems();
    PageAndFilterOperatingSystems();
}
```

When you run your code, you should see something similar to Figure 3-13. If you choose to view the supported operating systems, it lists four results per page. You can use Next to get to the second page. When we look at paging in the ASP .NET MVC Core application, we'll look at how to handle the upper bounds of a paged list. For now, we just keep it simple.

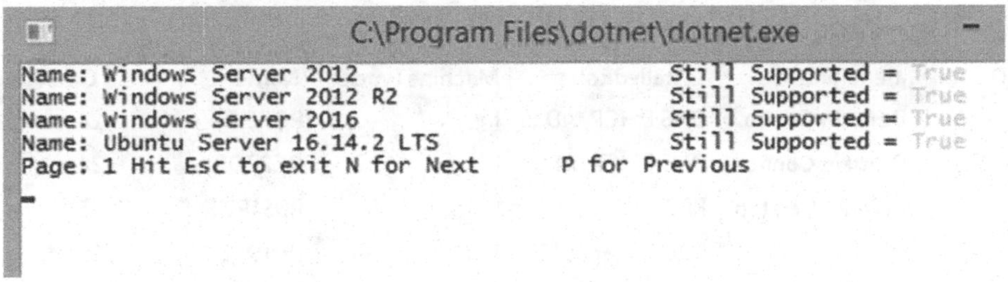

Figure 3-13. *Paging and filtering results*

Concurrency

I think it's pretty safe to say that we are the only ones using this application and the tables associated with it. However, when you are working on applications in a business environment or on a website, there is a very good chance that other people will modify the data the same time you are (hopefully not the same data). So let's test something.

Open SQL Server Management Studio to modify a table while we are in the process of modifying it from the application. Once you have done that, you need to make two more change to the application. Go to the `Machine` model, `Machine.cs`, and add the following `using` statement:

```
using System.ComponentModel.DataAnnotations;
```

Then make the following change in the class:

```
[ConcurrencyCheck]
public int OperatingSysId { get; set; }
```

By adding the [`ConcurrentyCheck`] to the `OperatingSysId` parameter, we tell Entity Framework Core that we want to check for concurrency conflicts. Back in `Program.cs`, find `UpdateOperatingSystems()` and, at the bottom of that method, put a breakpoint on the line that includes `context.SaveChanges();`.

There is no need to make any more changes, so run the application and choose Option 5 (Update Operating Systems). We are going to modify JacksPC, so choose the appropriate `MachineId` for that machine only. Pick any operating system from the list. When you hit the breakpoint, go to SSMS and edit the machine table by changing the value of `OperatingSysId` for JacksPC to some value other than what you selected. Figure 3-14 shows the table in SSMS and Figure 3-15 shows what happens when you continue the code.

MachineID	GeneralRole	InstalledRoles	MachineTypeID	Name	OperatingSysID
5	Domain Contro...	DNS,DHCP, AD ...	1	PORDC1	24
6	Domain Contro...	DNS,DHCP, AD ...	1	DC2POR	24
7	Remote Desktop	RDS	1	RDS1POR	25
8	DBMS	SQL Server 2012	1	DB1SQL	22
9	DBMS	MySQL	1	DB2SQL	27
10	Accounting	Accounting	2	BobsPC	16
11	IT	IT	2	JacksPC	22
12	Terminal Server	RDS	1	RDS1	25
13	Terminal Server	RDS	1	RDS2	25
NULL	NULL	NULL	NULL	NULL	NULL

Figure 3-14. *SSMS showing the change*

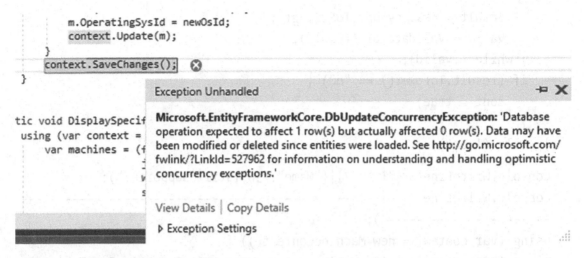

Figure 3-15. *Error in Visual Studio*

You have to admit it, the errors have gotten a lot better in the last couple of years. They aren't as vague as they used to be. We get the error that we thought we would get. So what are we going to do about it? Let's take care of the problem so we don't have to worry about it in the future. Listing 3-14 shows the changes added to UpdateOperatingSystems().

Listing 3-14. UpdateOperatingSystems() with Changes

```
static void UpdateOperatingSystems() {
   ConsoleKeyInfo cki;
   string result;
   int newOsId = -1;
   bool valid = false;
   Console.Clear();
   WriteHeader($"Operating System Update");
   List<Machine> lMachines = new List<Machine>();
   bool cont = false;
   do {
      valid = false;
      lMachines.Add(GetMachine());
      Console.WriteLine("Do you want to add another Machine? [y or n]");
      do {
         cki = Console.ReadKey(true);
```

```
      result = cki.KeyChar.ToString();
      valid = ValidateYorN(result);
   } while (!valid);
   if (result.ToLower() == "n") {
      cont = true;
   }
} while (!cont);

Console.WriteLine($"{"ID",-7}|{"Name",-50}|Still Supported");
Console.WriteLine("-----------------------------------------------------
----------- ----------");
using (var context = new MachineContext()) {
   List<OperatingSys> lOperatingSystems = context.OperatingSys.ToList();
   foreach (OperatingSys os in lOperatingSystems) {
      Console.WriteLine($"{os.OperatingSysId,-7}|{os.Name,-50}|
      {os.StillSupported}");
   }
}

Console.WriteLine("\r\nEnter the ID of the Operating System you want to
Update to.");
Console.WriteLine("Then hit the Enter Key");
string newOs = GetNumbersFromConsole();
newOsId = Convert.ToInt16(newOs);

using (MachineContext context = new MachineContext()) {
   foreach (Machine m in lMachines) {
      var mach = context.Machine.Single(x => x.MachineId ==
      m.MachineId);
      mach.OperatingSysId = newOsId;
      context.Update(mach);
      try {
         context.SaveChanges();
      }
      catch (DbUpdateConcurrencyException ex) {
         foreach (var e in ex.Entries) {
            if (e.Entity is Machine) {
```

```
        var dbEntity = context.Machine.AsNoTracking().Single
        (m1 => m1.MachineId == ((Machine)e.Entity).MachineId);
        var dbEntry = context.Entry(dbEntity);

        foreach (var property in e.Metadata.GetProperties()) {
            if (property.Name == "OperatingSysId") {
                var proposedValue = e.Property(property.Name).
                CurrentValue;
                var dbValue = dbEntry.Property(property.Name).
                CurrentValue;
                Console.WriteLine("The value has been changed
                outside of the program.");
                OperatingSys osN = GetOperatingSystemById(Convert.
                ToInt32(dbValue));
                Console.WriteLine($"The new value is {osN.Name}");
                osN = GetOperatingSystemById(Convert.
                ToInt32(proposedValue));
                Console.WriteLine($"You entered {osN.Name}");
                Console.WriteLine("Do you want to overwrite this
                change? [y or n]");
                cki = Console.ReadKey(true);
                result = cki.KeyChar.ToString();
                if (result.ToLower() == "y") {

                    e.Property(property.Name).OriginalValue =
                    dbEntry.Property(property.Name).CurrentValue;
                    //try again
                    context.SaveChanges();
                }
            }
        }
    }
}
```

This listing has a lot going on and we have done a little bit of hard coding to make it easier to explain what we are doing. We made all of the changes around `context.SaveChanges();`, staring with a `try catch` and looking for a `DbUpdateConcurrencyException`. When we set up `dbEntity`, we do so with `.AsNoTracking()`, so that the changes won't be tracked by the change tracker.

`ProposedValue` is the value that we said we wanted to change to. We are proposing to change the value in the database to `x`. `DbValue`, on the other hand, is the current value in the database. We got our proposed value from our error via the Entity entry and we go to the database value from the database, which in this case originated from `dbEntity`. Once we have that straight, we check to see which value the user wants to use. If they decide they want to use theirs or what is in the database, we have to change the Entity Entry Original Value to the value that we entered. Sometimes it gets confusing as to which value is which. While you are setting this up, try using breakpoints, as they are a great way to get it all straight and to verify that you are using the right values.

Summary

This chapter expanded your abilities to retrieve one or more records based on multiple criteria. You no longer have to retrieve all the columns from an entity, but can retrieve just the ones you want in an effort to increase efficiency. You can now perform different types of joins and use regular SQL in your applications if you need it. After all, Entity Framework Core 2.0 is just another tool in your toolbox and there isn't one tool that does every job well. Can you use a crescent wrench to hammer in a nail? Sure, but a hammer does a much better job, just like you learned with the right outer join.

You should be able to group your results together in logical ways as well as use logical operators. If you are using SQL Server 2012 or newer, you will be able to page your results in a much simpler way that results in retrieving fewer records at a time. Lastly, we solved the issue of someone else updating records.

What does all this mean? Before moving on to the next chapter, you should be able to explain and do the following:

- Write a query and retrieve only the fields you want

- Perform different types of joins on entities

- Group results together using both query and method syntax

- Perform operations using logical AND and logical OR statements

- Page and filter results

- Handle concurrency issues with your tables

If any of these are still a bit fuzzy, don't worry. As with learning anything new, it takes time and practice. Fortunately, as you continue on in this book, we'll be hitting a lot of these subjects again to give you more practice.

CHAPTER 4

Data Validation and POCOs

One of the most important things to remember when working with a database is to sure that the data you are putting into the database is as clean as possible. Let's say you are a customer service rep and you get a call from John Smith. One of the first things you are supposed to do is verify his information. Now I'm not putting down CSRs, as they have a tough job, but some of them are like *Anchorman* and will just read what is in front of them. So let's go to the wonderful world of make believe and see how this could go with bad data in the database:

Caller: "Good morning, this is John Smith and my account number is JSmith1234". (He calls in a lot and knows the drill.)

CSR: "Good morning Mr. Smith and thank you for calling. Is your phone number still 123AJK5678?"

Now I know what you are thinking—that never happens. Well, like with *Dragnet*, the names have been changed for protect the innocent but I have seen/heard this happen. Other than the CSR not paying attention to what they were reading, the problem was the software in place to load data into the system was only set up to look for 10 characters, not even digits, but characters. The person who was loading the data wasn't paying close attention when they loaded it and didn't notice the alpha characters in the telephone number field. Now we have a situation.

Other than making sure that this doesn't happen again by paying better attention to what is loaded by bulk processing, how can avoid such issues?

If you have access to the source code you can be sure to validate your data before you put it into the database in the first place. There are two ways you can do this (actually there are more, but we'll stick with two in this example).

© Derek J. Rouleau 2018
D. J. Rouleau, *Beginning Entity Framework Core 2.0*, https://doi.org/10.1007/978-1-4842-3375-7_4

You could have a process that scrubs your data files prior to getting them to the loading stage. Let's say your application is called Data Loader and it loads the data into some form that you can view to check for glaring errors. If you created a scrubber type application, you would run that application by reading the file you were going to load. Your scrubber application would then make sure that all the phone numbers are valid, perhaps fix any formatting issues that are in the file, and output a cleaner version of the original file.

If you don't have access to the source code because your application that loads data is off-the-shelf software, that could be your only choice. But you are running two applications instead of one and perhaps at some point after getting clean files for 6 or 9 months, your data entry person might start skipping the scrubbing step.

Validation Using DataAnnotations

One good thing about Entity Framework Core 2.0, and eventually if you go that route, MVC, is that it encourages you to keep your code as centralized as possible and not repeat code in multiple places. One of the ways we can use it is via the `DataAnnotations` namespace. What's nice is if you go through the class listing, you'll see things like `CreditCardAttribute`, `EmailAddressAttribute`, and `PhoneAttribute`. Since we have been discussing phone numbers, we'll pick that out of the list. Through the use of regular expressions, this class will validate phone numbers without you having to write a regular expression to do so. It's very easy to use, although it is geared more toward MVC type applications. You can still use it. Look back at `Program.cs` in the ComputerInventory application and you'll see that we already did some basic validation. Take a look at Listing 4-1 to see what we already did.

Listing 4-1. Validation in CreateNewWarrantyProvider()

```
Console.WriteLine("\r\nPlease enter the Providers phone number.");
do {
    cki = Console.ReadKey(true);
    if (cki.Key == ConsoleKey.Enter) {
        if (phoneNumber.Length >= 7) {
            cont = true;
        }
        else {
```

```
        Console.WriteLine("Please enter a Phone number that is at least
            7 digits.");
        }
    }
    else if (cki.Key == ConsoleKey.Backspace) {
        Console.Write("\b \b");
        try {
            phoneNumber = phoneNumber.Substring(0, phoneNumber.Length - 1);
        }
        catch (System.ArgumentOutOfRangeException) {
            // at the 0 position, can't go any further back
        }
    }
    else {
        if (char.IsNumber(cki.KeyChar)) {
            phoneNumber += cki.KeyChar.ToString();
            Console.Write(cki.KeyChar.ToString());
        }
    }
} while (!cont);
```

Keep in mind, if you look in WarrantyProvider.cs, you'll see that the SupportNumber property is a string. This was done so we would have better control over the actual variable, which may sound strange as we are storing a number, but you'll see why in a moment. Back to Listing 4-1. As you might recall, we did some basic error checking to get a number that is at least seven characters and we checked to make sure that users are only entering digits. This will alleviate our problem of having a number such as 123AGB5678. Since I'm writing this book in the United States, I'm going to base the logic on phone numbers that are valid in the US and Canada.

Using the Phone attribute is a quick check, but unfortunately it doesn't work very well. Let's say you entered 123AGB5678 and validated against that. You would get an error, which you would expect. However, if you were to enter 12345678, it will validate as a properly formatted number. For that reason I'm going to recommend that you use caution when using the built-in validation and do a lot of testing to be sure it works for your needs.

But don't fret, there is still a way. We need to think about what we are trying to accomplish, which is to validate North American based phone numbers (US and Canada). We know that the phone numbers can be 7 or 10 digits long, so that is a good start. To do this, we are going to use a regular expression since we are using the DataAnnotations namespace. Listing 4-2 shows an updated version of WarrantyProvider.cs with the new code in it.

Listing 4-2. WarrantyProvider.cs

```csharp
using System;
using System.Collections.Generic;
using System.ComponentModel.DataAnnotations;

namespace ComputerInventory.Models {
    public partial class WarrantyProvider {
        public WarrantyProvider() {
            MachineWarranty = new HashSet<MachineWarranty>();
        }

        public int WarrantyProviderId { get; set; }
        public string ProviderName { get; set; }
        public int? SupportExtension { get; set; }

        [RegularExpression("^(?=(?:.{7}|.{10})$)[0-9]*$", ErrorMessage =
        "Must be 7 or 10 digits")]
        public string SupportNumber { get; set; }

        public ICollection<MachineWarranty> MachineWarranty { get; set; }
    }
}
```

The two additions are the using statement for DataAnnotations and the RegularExpression attribute that we are assigning to our SupportNumber property. Let's look at the regular expression, as that part can be a little confusing if you aren't used to using it. The hat symbol (^) denotes that we are starting with the beginning of the string or line and the dollar sign is used for end of string. The ?= is a lookahead that isn't captured but must be followed by parentheses. In the parentheses we have ?:, which matches the following expression but doesn't capture it. In our case, those expressions are .{7}|.{10}, which you can read as any character exactly 7 repetitions or any character exactly 10 repetitions through the end of the string. That covers the first part of the statement: ^(?=(?:.{7}|.{10})$).

The end of the statement is pretty straightforward. We are looking for any character between 0 and 9, with any number of repetitions (remember that the repetitions were taken care of in the first part of the statement) and we end with the end of the line or a string character. If this doesn't make a ton of sense to you, don't worry, as it took me a while to get the hang of it. I still use a Regular Expression Editor for anything that's complex, like this one.

Now that we have added some validation to our model, we need a way of knowing if we have a valid property or not. To do this, we will go back to `Program.cs` and `CreateNewWarrantyProvider()`. Right now we are concerned with the end of the method, which you'll see in Listing 4-3. I removed the other code from the listing to make it easier to see the changes. We aren't doing anything other than checking to see if our value is valid. We'll add some more code for that shortly.

Listing 4-3. Validating the Warranty Provider Support Number

```
WarrantyProvider wp = new WarrantyProvider() {
    ProviderName = provider,
    SupportNumber = phoneNumber,
    SupportExtension = extension
};

var vResults = new List<ValidationResult>();
var vContext = new ValidationContext(wp);
bool isValid = Validator.TryValidateObject(wp, vContext, vResults, true);

return wp;
```

We haven't made any changes to the creation of our `WarrantyProvider` variable, but the magic starts on the following line where we create our `List<ValidationResult>` variable. You could have declared it specifically rather than using the generic, but I think it's a lot neater and shorter to use the `var`:

```
List<ValidationResult> vResults = new List<ValidationResult>();
var vResults = new List<ValidationResult>();
```

Whichever method you choose is entirely up to you. Just try to be consistent. Now you may have noticed that you got some errors when you added this code. That's because you need to add the following using statement:

```
using System.ComponentModel.DataAnnotations;
```

You have created a list of validation results, but what does that mean? When we check to see if we have any errors/validation results, we need a place to put them, and since we need to have a ICollection<ValidationResult> to pass them to, it seems like a pretty good idea to create one.

We then need to create our ValidationContext variable, which is what we use so our validator knows what class or type our validation is going to be performed on.

Lastly, we have our bool value, which tells us if our validation is valid. This is done by using the Validator class and TryValidateObject. The part that people tend to have the most problem with when it comes to doing this is that last argument (true), as the default is false. What does that mean? The default is not to check any of the properties other than the "required" attribute (which we didn't use yet so don't panic if you aren't finding it in the code), so it wouldn't check our regular expression and would validate as true no matter what value we put in there. I like to think of that as a feature, not a very good one, but a feature of the language.

I'm going to add a breakpoint to the return statement so we can check to see if our validation is working. The good thing is, even if it's not, we have built in a check to ask the user if the information is correct and we will press n for no. Feel free to run your code along with me, so you can be sure yours is working.

Navigate to the Data Entry menu and add a new warranty provider. The name doesn't matter as we aren't going to save it, but I'm going to enter Will's Discount Servers as the provider. For the phone number, I'm going to enter 12345678, which is eight digits. Remember, we are looking for seven or 10 digits and our method code will catch anything under seven. I skip the extension by pressing the Esc key. If all goes right, we will be at our breakpoint, which you can see in Figure 4-1.

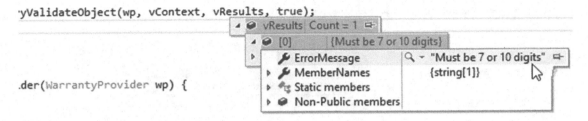

Figure 4-1. *vResult value*

If you hover over isValid, you will see that the value is false, which is good, as that is what we expect. I expanded the results for vResults and as you can see the Count = 1 and we have our custom error message that we created. There are default error messages that you could use, but they aren't the best. Had we not created a custom message our error message would have been: "The field SupportNumber must match the regular expression '^(?=(?:.{7}|.{10})$)[0-9]*$'.". If you are the only one using this application, then by all means have at it, but the custom one is more helpful.

We are going to validate one more field before we point out an issue. If you haven't done so already, exit the application without saving the data. If you did save it, it's not the end of the world and I'm pretty sure I saved one by accident while testing.

Looking at our model, the only other field that makes sense right away to validate is the ProviderName property. This will give me a chance to show you how *not* to validate the phone number field at the same time without you needing to type any extra code to later delete, as it's wrong. We need to think about how we want to validate this property. We know it can only be a total of 50 characters, so that's a good place to start. Do we want to have a minimum number of characters? I think we should have at least two characters in this property, so we will do the following code right above the ProviderName property just like you did for the SupportNumber.

```
[StringLength(50, MinimumLength = 2, ErrorMessage = "You must have between
2 and 50 characters for the Provider Name")]
public string ProviderName { get; set; }
```

We are now checking to be sure that we have at least two characters and no more than 50. If we re-run the application and this time enter A as the provider name and 12345678 as the phone number, we should have two validation errors. Let's try it. Figure 4-2 shows the results.

```
TryValidateObject(wp, vContext, vResults, true);
```

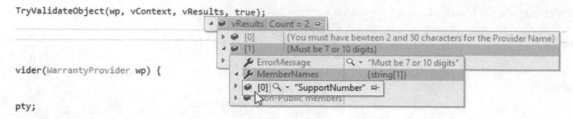

```
vider(WarrantyProvider wp) {
```

```
pty;
```

Figure 4-2. *Two validation errors*

So that you can see it better, I expanded the second value, which is our
SupportNumber property, but as you can see both of the validation errors are there. We
could have done something similar for our phone number and searched for numbers
between seven and 10 digits, but if you entered eight digits, it would be a valid number,
which isn't what we wanted. That's why we had to use the regular expression. I also
added an attribute to ProviderName, the Required attribute. Since this is a required
field, we need to add that attribute. Look in SQL Server Management Studio or in
MachineContext.cs and you'll find the code in Listing 4-4.

Listing 4-4. MachineContext.cs, WarrantyProvider

```
modelBuilder.Entity<WarrantyProvider>(entity => {
    entity.Property(e => e.WarrantyProviderId).HasColumnName("Warranty
    ProviderID");

    entity.Property(e => e.ProviderName)
        .IsRequired()
        .HasMaxLength(50)
        .IsUnicode(false);

    entity.Property(e => e.SupportNumber)
        .IsRequired()
        .HasMaxLength(10)
        .IsUnicode(false);
});
```

To fix this, all we do is add the Required attribute to the code:

```
[Required]
[StringLength(50, MinimumLength = 2, ErrorMessage = "You must have between
2 and 50 characters for the Provider Name")]
public string ProviderName { get; set; }
```

Now if we run our application and don't enter anything for the provider name we get the following error: "The `ProviderName field is required`".

The good news is the default error message for this one is actually helpful, so we don't need to change it.

Note   One thing to keep in mind if you are writing an application that will be in multiple languages. You'll need to localize your custom error messages for the proper language.

Why have we done this even though it's not technically Entity Framework Core 2.0 code? Because if we didn't, we'd get an error message when we try to save (in the case of our provider name, we would). Since we are forcing a minimum number of seven characters to our `SupportNumber` field, it will not throw an error unless you try to enter too many numbers. I commented out my `Validation` code and tried to save the changes in Figure 4-3.

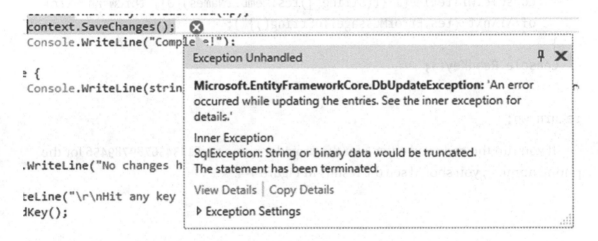

Figure 4-3. *Entity Framework Core error*

In this case, it's throwing an exception because I entered a value for `SupportNumber` that was 17 characters. As a result, we haven't done any Entity Framework Code per se, but we have saved ourselves from getting an Entity Framework Core error, so we'll go with close enough. I now put the validation back in place and enter the same information; we are back to having some values in `vResults`.

In an effort to make our lives a little bit easier, we aren't going to change a lot of code from what we already have. Although we are going to do this in two steps as we have an option.

Go back to the CreateWarrantyProvider method in Program.cs. We are going to add a check to see if our model is valid. If it's not, then we are going to loop through the list of VResults and display them to the user. Listing 4-5 shows the bottom section of the code that we will be changing.

Listing 4-5. CreateWarrantyProvider()

```
var vResults = new List<ValidationResult>();
var vContext = new ValidationContext(wp);
bool isValid = Validator.TryValidateObject(wp, vContext, vResults, true);

if (!isValid) {
  Console.WriteLine();
  foreach (var res in vResults) {
      Console.WriteLine($"{((string[])res.MemberNames)[0]} threw an error
      of:\r\n\t {res.ErrorMessage.ToString()}");
  }
  Console.ReadKey();
}

return wp;
```

If you run the code and enter A for the provider name and 123456789789456 for the phone number, you should see the results in Figure 4-4.

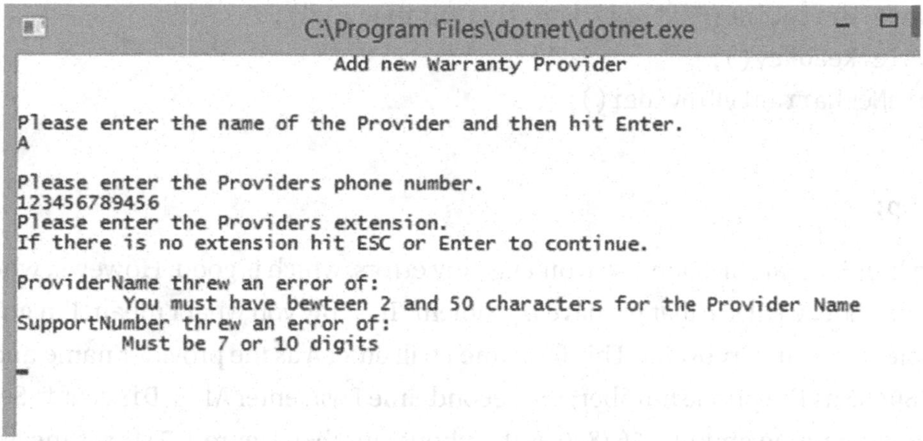

Figure 4-4. *Displaying the error to the user*

Using Recursion

You need to make a decision—how are you going to get from this error to having a good well formed WarrantyProvider object? You could wrap the code in a loop and check to see if isValid is true at the end. If it's not, then you'd loop through the code again. Or you could use everyone's favorite thing, *recursion*. A couple of things about recursion— you need to have a way to exit the loop, because otherwise you will end up in an infinite loop, which no one wants. Secondly, you have to be sure it's actually doing what you want it to do. Fortunately, I can show you a broken recursive call without you needing to type anything extra. Listing 4-6 shows the code we just entered with the recursive call added.

Listing 4-6. Adding a Recursive Call

```
var vResults = new List<ValidationResult>();
var vContext = new ValidationContext(wp);
bool isValid = Validator.TryValidateObject(wp, vContext, vResults, true);

if (!isValid) {
   Console.WriteLine();
   foreach (var res in vResults) {
      Console.WriteLine($"{((string[])res.MemberNames)[0]} threw an error
      of:\r\n\t {res.ErrorMessage.ToString()}");
   }
```

143

```
    Console.WriteLine("Hit any key to continue...");
    Console.ReadKey();
    CreateNewWarrantyProvider();
}

return wp;
```

If we build our application, we won't get any errors, which is good. However, when we run our code, we'll see that we have a problem. To show you what I mean, I'm going to add a new warranty provider. This first time I will enter A as the provider name and 123456789456 as the phone number; the second time I will enter Al's Discount Servers as the provider name and 1234567890 as the phone number. Figure 4-5 shows the issue.

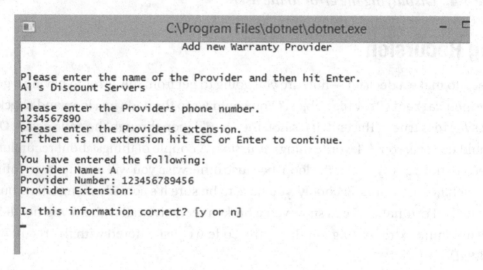

Figure 4-5. *Wait, what happened to our values?*

As you can see, the correct information was entered the second time and was validated, but when we exit the method and display our data for the user to also validate, we see the original data. What's going on? Even though we did get valid data in our second call to CreateNewWarrantyProvider(), the original value of wp is returned by the method. However, we just need to press a few keys and our problems are solved. Change your recursive call to:

```
wp = CreateNewWarrantyProvider();
```

Now when we do the exact same thing, we get the results shown in Figure 4-6.

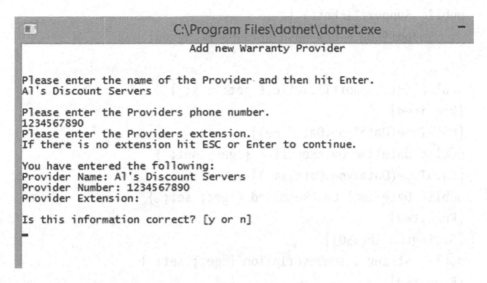

Figure 4-6. Recursion is now successfully implemented

There we have it; we have successfully entered the wrong data and then entered the correct data. Our application is moving forward with that correct data. There are some other things you can do in order to save the user some work if you want to. You could have some argument with default values that you could pass back to CreateNewWarrantyProvider if they are valid. Something like:

```
static WarrantyProvider CreateNewWarrantyProvider(string pName = "",
string pNumber = "", string pExt = "")
```

You could then do some checking to see if each of them has a value before prompting the user to enter the same information again. Feel free to do that as some extra practice.

Let's practice some more with using the DataAnnotations class. We will do some work with the support log and support tickets that we haven't touched yet. We will start with the ticket, as you can't have a log without a ticket. See Listing 4-7.

Listing 4-7. SupportTicket.cs

```
using System;
using System.Collections.Generic;
using System.ComponentModel.DataAnnotations;
```

```
namespace ComputerInventory.Models {
    public partial class SupportTicket {
        public SupportTicket() {
            SupportLog = new HashSet<SupportLog>();
        }

        public int SupportTicketId { get; set; }
        [Required]
        [DataType(DataType.DateTime)]
        public DateTime DateReported { get; set; }
        [DataType(DataType.DateTime)]
        public DateTime? DateResolved { get; set; }
        [Required]
        [StringLength(150)]
        public string IssueDescription { get; set; }
        [Required]
        public string IssueDetail { get; set; }
        [Required, StringLength(50)]
        public string TicketOpenedBy { get; set; }
        public int MachineId { get; set; }

        public Machine Machine { get; set; }
        public ICollection<SupportLog> SupportLog { get; set; }
    }
}
```

We added our validation to our model and there are two new things for us to look at. The first is that we are able to specify that DateReported is a DateTime data type. The good news is that DateTime isn't our only choice. If you look at Figure 4-7, you'll see a couple of choices that you could have made.

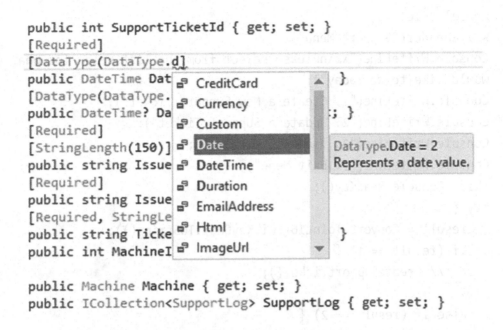

```
public int SupportTicketId { get; set; }
[Required]
[DataType(DataType.d]
public DateTime Dat                        }
[DataType(DataType.     CreditCard   ▲
public DateTime? Da     Currency          ; }
[Required]                Custom
[StringLength(150)]       Date          DataType.Date = 2
public string Issue       DateTime      Represents a date value.
[Required]                Duration
public string Issue       EmailAddress
[Required, StringLe       Html
public string Ticke                        }
public int MachineI     ImageUrl   ▼


public Machine Machine { get; set; }
public ICollection<SupportLog> SupportLog { get; set; }
```

Figure 4-7. *Just a few of our choices for data types*

The second thing that is new is that we combined our attributes on one line for
TicketOpenedBy. You can chain together a whole bunch of attributes if you want,
although keep in mind at some point you'll probably have to come back and look at it
again. If you want to set up error messages for your attributes, feel free to do that. For the
interest and readability of the readers, I'm going to leave them out in this example.

We are going to create a way to add support tickets, so let's create a quick menu.
Since we have done this many times before, I'm going to create a basic one with
very little error checking. If you were going to use this application, you would want
to put a little more effort into it. Back in Program.cs, we'll add a new method called
SupportMenu(), as shown in Listing 4-8.

Listing 4-8. SupportMenu()

```
static void SupportMenu() {
    ConsoleKeyInfo cki;
    int result = -1;
    bool cont = false;
    do {
```

```
    Console.Clear();
    WriteHeader("Support Menu");
    Console.WriteLine("\r\nPlease select from the list below for what you
    would like to do today");
    Console.WriteLine("1. Create a New Support Ticket");
    Console.WriteLine("2. Update a Support Ticket");
    Console.WriteLine("3. View All Tickets");
    Console.WriteLine("9. Exit Menu");
    cki = Console.ReadKey();
    try {
        result = Convert.ToInt16(cki.KeyChar.ToString());
        if (result == 1) {
            // CreateSupportTicket();
        }
        else if (result == 2) {
            //UpdateSupportTicket();
        }
        else if (result == 3) {
            //DisplaySupportTickets();
        }
        else if (result == 9) {
            // We are exiting so nothing to do
            cont = true;
        }
    }
    catch (System.FormatException) {
        // a key that wasn't a number
    }
} while (!cont);
}
```

Just a little tip—I copied the body of the code from DataEntryMenu and replaced or deleted what I needed. There is absolutely nothing new here, so we aren't even going to go through the code. When you run it, you'll know if you missed anything.

Before we create our method, we should think about what values we need to get from our users. Since we are creating a ticket, we can assume that the `DateReported` should be today, unless you are using yellow sticky notes to keep track of them before you log them so we can get that for the user. We should be able to retrieve the username ourselves, though we could double check that just to be sure it's the right user.

Perhaps it will be used where everyone logs in as `SupportAgent` on this particular PC. We'll ask the user to verify that the name is correct but save them from typing if it is. They will need to pick a machine and then we simply need a description and some detail. Let's get some basic functionality so we can get data into the table.

The first thing we need to do is modify `DisplayAllMachines()` to adjust the text that doesn't work. Listing 4-9 shows the updated method.

Listing 4-9. DisplayAllMachines()

```
static string DisplayAllMachines(string textToDisplay) {
    Console.Clear();
    List<Machine> lMachine = GetListOfMachines();
    Console.WriteLine("Machine ID | Machine Name");
    foreach (Machine m in lMachine) {
        Console.WriteLine($"{m.MachineId,-11}| {m.Name}");
    }
    Console.WriteLine();
    Console.WriteLine(textToDisplay);
    Console.WriteLine("Hit the Esc key at anytime to exit the menu.");

    string machineId = GetNumbersFromConsole();
    if (machineId.Length > 0) {
        int machId = Convert.ToInt32(machineId);
        DisplayMachineDetail(machId);
    }
    return machineId;
}
```

149

Once you have made the changes, you should get the error: There is no argument given that corresponds to the required formal parameter 'textToDisplay' of 'Program.DisplayAllMachines(string)'. You have two options. You can go to those two locations and add an argument of "Enter the MachineId followed by the Enter Key for more information" or you can add a default value for textToDisplay. If you choose to go the default value route, your declaration will look like the following:

```
static string DisplayAllMachines(string textToDisplay = "Enter the
MachineId followed by the Enter Key for more information") {
```

It will still list the machine details, but the text makes a little bit more sense when we get to running our code. Listing 4-10 shows the start of the code. After we have entered the following code we will have all the data we need in order to create our support ticket, just no way to save the data yet.

Listing 4-10. CreateSupportTicket()

```
static void CreateSupportTicket() {
    string ticketOpenedBy = Environment.UserName;
    DateTime dateReported = DateTime.Now;
    int machineId;
    string issueDescription;
    string issueDetail;

    string tempMachineId = DisplayAllMachines("Enter the MachineId followed
    by the Enter Key for our Support Ticket.");
    bool machineIdReturned = Int32.TryParse(tempMachineId, out machineId);
    if (machineIdReturned) {
        Console.WriteLine("\r\nEnter a brief description of the issue:");
        issueDescription = GetTextFromConsole(5, false);
        Console.WriteLine("\r\nEnter a detailed description of the issue:");
        issueDetail = GetTextFromConsole(5, false);
    }
}
```

Because we have created a lot of our data entry methods, we don't need to do a lot here to get the information from the user. The next part of code we add will be in the if block after issueDetail = GetTextFromConsole(5, false);, as shown in Listing 4-11.

Listing 4-11. Validating the Support Ticket

```
SupportTicket _supportTicket = new SupportTicket {
MachineId = machineId,
    TicketOpenedBy = ticketOpenedBy,
    DateReported = dateReported,
    IssueDescription = issueDescription,
    IssueDetail = issueDetail
};

var vResults = new List<ValidationResult>();
var vContext = new ValidationContext(_supportTicket);
bool isValid = Validator.TryValidateObject(_supportTicket, vContext,
vResults, true);

if (!isValid) {
    Console.WriteLine();
    foreach (var res in vResults) {
        Console.WriteLine($"{((string[])res.MemberNames)[0]} threw an error
        of:\r\n\t {res.ErrorMessage.ToString()}");
    }
    Console.WriteLine("Hit any key to continue...");
    Console.ReadKey();
}
```

Not very different from what we did before. The only interesting part here is the only value that can be wrong is the description. Everything else is either handled by us through code or the value can be any length string. So the only validation error we have to worry about is that one, so we will check to see if we have that error. If we do, we'll give them a chance to fix it, update the value, and then we can save it (see Listing 4-12).

Listing 4-12. Fixing the Error and Saving

```
if (!isValid) {
Console.WriteLine();
    foreach (var res in vResults) {
        Console.WriteLine($"{((string[])res.MemberNames)[0]} threw an error
        of:\r\n\t {res.ErrorMessage.ToString()}");
```

```
    if(((string[])res.MemberNames)[0] == "IssueDescription") {
        Console.WriteLine("Please enter a description that is 50
        characters or less.");
        do {
            issueDescription = GetTextFromConsole(5, false);
        } while (issueDescription.Count() <= 50);
        _supportTicket.IssueDescription = issueDescription;
    }
  }
Console.WriteLine("Hit any key to continue...");
Console.ReadKey();
}
Console.WriteLine("Saving new Support Ticket");
using (MachineContext context = new MachineContext()) {
    context.SupportTicket.Add(_supportTicket);
    context.SaveChanges();
    Console.WriteLine("Save complete!");
}
```

Would I do something like this in production code? Probably not. However, it does show you some different ways of handing your errors. If you wanted to, you could create a way of checking for all the possible error types and handle each one as they arise. This is easier than killing the entire thing and starting over like we did in the first example.

We could run our code and test it, but we don't have a way to view our results yet. That's okay because we have SQL Server Management Studio for that. Before you can run your code, you'll need to make sure you can get to it. In the Main menu, you need to add Option 6, which will call the SupportMenu() method. Add the following code in the appropriate location (if you aren't sure where, just take a stab at it or download the code online). One thing to note, I'm using Option 6 here, which we used for testing earlier. You can move testing to Option 7 or just update the code like I have.

```
Console.WriteLine("6. Support Tickets and Log");
```

And then

```
else if (result == 6) {
    SupportMenu();
}
```

Lastly, if you haven't already done so, uncomment `CreateSupportTicket()` in `SupportMenu()`. I'm going to add the following record:

```
MachineId = 5
IssueDescription = Stuck at login screen
 = Server froze and Bob did a hard boot, now stuck at the log in screen.
Can't enter any information nor is there any movement of the mouse.
```

When you run your code, it should be pretty unremarkable. The only thing you should see is the following two lines—"Saving new Support Ticket" and "Save complete!"—going by very fast. Figure 4-8 is a view from the SQL Server Management Studio showing the record in the table.

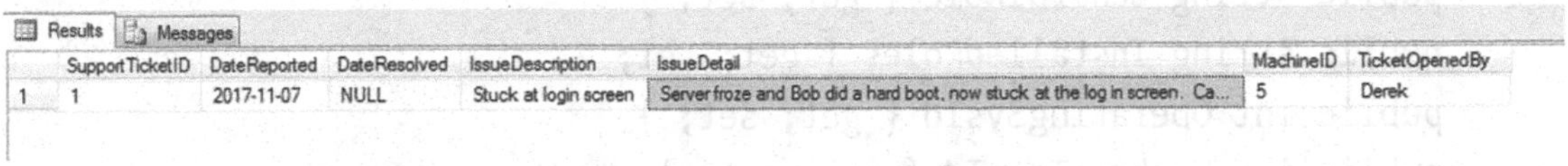

	SupportTicketID	DateReported	DateResolved	IssueDescription	IssueDetail	MachineID	TicketOpenedBy
1	1	2017-11-07	NULL	Stuck at login screen	Server froze and Bob did a hard boot, now stuck at the log in screen. Ca...	5	Derek

Figure 4-8. *Results in SQL Server Management Studio*

As you can see, it's very hard to read and we didn't even try to display the full message in `IssueDetail`. Obviously, this isn't the way that we want our users to be getting this information. Don't worry, we'll take care of that in a little while. For now we can be satisfied in knowing that we are able to create support tickets.

I hope by now you have a better understanding of one of the ways of validating your data. When we work on the MVC application in Chapters 6 and 7, you'll see where this method of validation really shines. It works pretty well in a WinForms application, but there is of course another way you can validate your data.

POCOs

If you haven't done much reading on Entity Framework or Entity Framework Core, you may not know what a POCO is. What can I say, we computer types (and people in general) love acronyms. POCO stands for Plain Old CLR Objects, which is just a class that isn't directly tied to any framework-specific base class. So what does that mean? Let's look at a simple example, shown in Listing 4-13.

Listing 4-13. POCO, Machine.cs

```
using System;
using System.Collections.Generic;

namespace ComputerInventory.Models {
   public partial class Machine {
      public Machine() {
         SupportTicket = new HashSet<SupportTicket>();
      }

      public int MachineId { get; set; }
      public string Name { get; set; }
      public string GeneralRole { get; set; }
      public string InstalledRoles { get; set; }
      public int OperatingSysId { get; set; }
      public int MachineTypeId { get; set; }

      public MachineType MachineType { get; set; }
      public OperatingSys OperatingSys { get; set; }
      public ICollection<SupportTicket> SupportTicket { get; set; }
   }
}
```

There you go, that is a POCO, and you've been using it all along. I know some of you are thinking, "no, that is our Entity Framework Core code, it's not a POCO". But a POCO is a class that isn't directly tied to any framework-specific base class. So take a look again, is this class tied to any specific base class, in our case, Entity Framework Core 2.0?

Let's talk a little bit in theory here before we do something with some regular plain old classes. If you are new to Entity Framework, you probably didn't know what lazy loading was until I mentioned it because we can't do it yet in Entity Framework Core. That being said, maybe you still want to be able to do it even though it's not natively available in EF Core. You could create a class that would do all the work for you. It's not "true" lazy loading, but it would behave the same way. Let's use our machine from Listing 4-13 as an example. If we retrieve a machine record from the database, what do we get in return if we want to retrieve the record that has a MachineId of 5?

- MachineId = 5

- Name = PORDC1

- GeneralRole = Domain Controller

- InstalledRoles = DNS, DHCP, AD DS

- OperatingSystemId = 24

- MachineTypeID = 1

- MachineType = Empty

- OperatingSys = Empty

Since we want to use lazy loading, we need a way of also retrieving a MachineType and OperatingSys that is also populated. We have done this to an extent but we did it in Program.cs. Let's look at some code that we wrote for UpdateMachineDetails(), shown in Listing 4-14.

Listing 4-14. Using an include Statement to Get Related Data

```
using (MachineContext context = new MachineContext()) {
    mach = context.Machine
        .Include(o => o.OperatingSys)
        .Include(t => t.MachineType)
        .Where(x => x.MachineId == mId).FirstOrDefault();

    mWar = context.MachineWarranty
    .Include(p => p.WarrantyProvider)
    .Where(x => x.MachineId == mach.MachineId).FirstOrDefault();
}
```

Those include statements give us the equivalent of lazy loading and, as you can see, if you wanted to do a large set of data, it would be a little bit more complicated to the extent that you would need to do it in a loop and store your results in some sort of list object. Keep in mind that Entity Framework Core is somewhat more geared toward web development, so you wouldn't want to be retrieving large amounts of data each time. To be honest, even in desktop type applications, you don't want to be pulling large amounts of data every time if you can help it.

CHAPTER 4   DATA VALIDATION AND POCOS

So what can we do with classes that we haven't already done? Well, if you are asking that question, then you are one of those people who the rest of us love that puts everything or just about everything in `Program.cs` or on the Form code page. Adding classes to your application will help make it easier to follow and easier to maintain and reduce code duplication. We already did that in our current application, although we didn't put it in a separate class. The simplest example I could find for this is the `ValidateYorN()` method, shown in Listing 4-15.

Listing 4-15. Helper Method

```
static bool ValidateYorN(string entry) {
    bool result = false;
    if (entry.ToLower() == "y" || entry.ToLower() == "n") {
        result = true;
    }
    return result;
}
```

There is something that I usually create called *helper classes.* I'm going to create a new class to show how this could work. If you don't want to and are quite comfortable doing this, you can skip this section, as we aren't going to add anything new. However, if you are new to programming and don't use classes a lot or at all, you'll want to pay attention.

Helper Classes

We start off by creating a new class file. From the menu bar, choose Project and then Add Class. A type of class should be selected. If not, click on it and change the name to `BasicValidation.cs`. Once it's created it should open. Then all you need to do is make sure it looks like Listing 4-16.

Listing 4-16. BasicValidation(), a Helper Class

```
using System;
using System.Collections.Generic;
using System.Text;
```

```
namespace ComputerInventory {
  public class BasicValidation {
    public static bool ValidateYorN(string entry) {
      bool result = false;
      if (entry.ToLower() == "y" || entry.ToLower() == "n") {
        result = true;
      }
      return result;
    }
  }
}
```

We have made the class public so it will be accessible from anywhere in the application. If you aren't familiar with creating classes, you should look into it. After this, you'll be able to fake it relatively well, but you'll have a pretty large hole in your class knowledge. To use this, it will be quite similar to what you have already been doing. After doing a quick scan, I found that we are using this method in AddNewWarrantyProvider(), so that is where I'm going to make my change. Since we aren't going to be using this method multiple times, I'm not going to bother creating a BasicValidation object, plus I made the method static. For that reason, we don't need it. Let's take a look at part of our code and find the needed changes, as shown in Listing 4-17.

Listing 4-17. Calling the Method from the Helper Class

```
static void AddNewWarrantyProvider(WarrantyProvider wp) {
    bool cont = false;
    ConsoleKeyInfo cki;
    string result = string.Empty;
    Console.WriteLine("\r\nYou have entered the following:");
    Console.WriteLine($"Provider Name: {wp.ProviderName}");
    Console.WriteLine($"Provider Number: {wp.SupportNumber}");
    Console.WriteLine($"Provider Extension: {wp.SupportExtension}");
    Console.WriteLine("\r\nIs this information correct? [y or n]");
    do {
        cki = Console.ReadKey(true);
        result = cki.KeyChar.ToString();
```

```
        cont = BasicValidation.ValidateYorN(result);
    } while (!cont);
...

}
```

The functionality will be the same, but you can feel free to test it if you want. So obviously we are going to do a little bit more than just create a helper class to check for a Y or N character. You may be wondering why I keep referring to them as helper classes and methods, well to be honest I forget who got me saying that but I remember the reason. It's because the class really doesn't do anything on its own, but it helps to get something done.

Another concept that is big and if you get into MVC even more so is separation of concerns (SOC). So what does that mean? The concept is pretty simple but if you aren't careful you'll find yourself breaking it a lot. The idea is that when you create a class that it will specifically do that one thing and nothing else. Obviously, we haven't done a good job of that thus far, as we have pretty much put all of our code in `Program.cs`. However, if we go with what we have, we have at least put all of our models into their own classes and they do nothing else but give us a place to get our entity data. In the next example, we are going to break free from our current model and create a class that will handle our "business logic". As a good rule of thumb, all of your business logic for you application should be done outside of the model. It shouldn't be on your form or in the case of a console application, in the `Program.cs` (if you didn't rename it) file.

Let's create two new classes called `SupportTicketLogEntry.cs` and `ConsoleHelper.cs`. The good news is that `ConsoleHelper` will pretty much be all copy and paste so the hard part will be finding what you are looking for. We will populate `ConsoleHelper.cs` first to help reduce the number of errors we get in our code while typing. One last thing before we get to some more code. Something that I usually do is leave the initial three `using` statements in my classes until I'm done with them and then if I don't use them, I will remove them. There are cases where I know that I won't be using `System.Collections.Generic` so I may delete that one right off, but I generally don't delete any of them until I'm ready to send my application to the world just in case. See Listing 4-18.

Listing 4-18. ConsoleHelper.cs

```csharp
using System;
using System.Collections.Generic;
using System.Text;

namespace ComputerInventory {
    public class ConsoleHelper {
        public void WriteHeader(string headerText) => Console.
        WriteLine(string.Format("{0," + ((Console.WindowWidth / 2) +
        headerText.Length / 2) + "}", headerText));

        public char CheckForYorN(bool intercept) {
            ConsoleKeyInfo cki;
            char entry;
            bool cont = false;
            do {
                cki = Console.ReadKey(intercept);
                entry = cki.KeyChar;
                cont = BasicValidation.ValidateYorN(entry.ToString());
            } while (!cont);
            return entry;
        }

        public int GetNumbersFromConsole() {
            ConsoleKeyInfo cki;
            bool cont = false;
            string numbers = string.Empty;
            int rtnVal = -1;
            do {
                cki = Console.ReadKey(true);
                if (cki.Key == ConsoleKey.Escape) {
                    cont = true;
                    numbers = "";
                }
```

```csharp
        else if (cki.Key == ConsoleKey.Enter) {
            if (numbers.Length > 0) {
                cont = true;
            }
            else {
            Console.WriteLine("Please enter an ID that is at least 1 digit.");
            }
        }
        else if (cki.Key == ConsoleKey.Backspace) {
            Console.Write("\b \b");
            try {
                numbers = numbers.Substring(0, numbers.Length - 1);
            }
            catch (System.ArgumentOutOfRangeException) {
                // at the 0 position, can't go any further back
            }
        }
        else {
            if (char.IsNumber(cki.KeyChar)) {
                numbers += cki.KeyChar.ToString();
                Console.Write(cki.KeyChar.ToString());
            }
        }
    } while (!cont);
    rtnVal = Convert.ToInt32(numbers);
    return rtnVal;
}

public string GetTextFromConsole(int minLength, bool allowEscape =
false) {
    ConsoleKeyInfo cki;
    bool cont = false;
    string rtnValue = string.Empty;
    do {
```

```
            cki = Console.ReadKey(true);
            if (cki.Key == ConsoleKey.Escape) {
                if (allowEscape) {
                    cont = true;
                    rtnValue = "";
                }
            }
            else if (cki.Key == ConsoleKey.Enter) {
                if (rtnValue.Length >= minLength) {
                    cont = true;
                }
                else {
                    Console.WriteLine($"Please enter least {minLength}
                    characters.");
                }
            }
            else if (cki.Key == ConsoleKey.Backspace) {
                Console.Write("\b \b");
                try {
                    rtnValue = rtnValue.Substring(0, rtnValue.Length - 1);
                }
                catch (System.ArgumentOutOfRangeException) {
                    // at the 0 position, can't go any further back
                }
            }
            else {
                rtnValue += cki.KeyChar.ToString();
                Console.Write(cki.KeyChar.ToString());
            }
        } while (!cont);
        return rtnValue;
    }
  }
}
```

Expression-Bodied Members

All of the methods except for WriteHeader are copies of the versions from Program.cs. You do need to change them to public and remove the static. WriteHeader was a great example of a different way that you can write what is called expression-bodied members. You can use this form when your method or property consists of a single expression. Some people claim they are easier to read; perhaps after I get used to it and use them more I'll agree, but for now I'll probably stick with the older version. This feature was introduced in C# 6 and was expanded in C# 7, so if you haven't seen it before, that is probably why. So there we have it, we now have a bunch of duplicated code. If you want to clean up Program.cs, just search for the methods that we added in ConsoleHelper.cs and delete them from Program.cs. Wherever you get an error, reference the new method. If you aren't used to using classes, the next example will show you how.

The new class for handling support ticket log entries will look pretty similar to what you have done in the past, although it will be all grouped together in one place as opposed to being littered throughout Program.cs. See Listing 4-19.

Listing 4-19. SupportTicketLogEntry.cs

```
using System;
using System.Collections.Generic;

using ComputerInventory.Models;
using Microsoft.EntityFrameworkCore;
using ComputerInventory.Data;
using System.Linq;

namespace ComputerInventory {
    public class SupportTicketLogEntry {
        private ConsoleHelper cHelper = new ConsoleHelper();

        public SupportTicketLogEntry() {
        }

        public List<SupportLog> RetreiveLogEntries(int ticketId) {
            List<SupportLog> logEntries = new List<SupportLog>();
            using(MachineContext context = new MachineContext()) {
                logEntries = context.SupportLog
```

```
            .Where(x => x.SupportTicketId == ticketId)
            .OrderBy(x => x.SupportTicket).ToList();
        }
        return logEntries;
    }

public List<SupportTicket> RetreiveOpenTickets() {
    List<SupportTicket> openTickets = new List<SupportTicket>();
    using (MachineContext context = new MachineContext()) {
    openTickets = context.SupportTicket
        .Include(m => m.Machine)
        .Where(x => x.DateResolved == null).ToList();
    }
    return openTickets;
}

public void UpdateSupportTicket() {
    Console.Clear();
    cHelper.WriteHeader("Update Support Ticket");
    Console.WriteLine("\r\nPlease Select an Open Support Ticket from
    the List\r\n");
    List<SupportTicket> openTickets = RetreiveOpenTickets();
    string logEntry;
    foreach (var ticket in openTickets) {
        Console.WriteLine($"Ticket Number: {ticket.SupportTicketId}
        Machine Name: {ticket.Machine.Name}\r\n    Description:
        {ticket.IssueDescription}");
    }
    int ticketId = cHelper.GetNumbersFromConsole();
    Console.WriteLine();
    bool validEntry = false;
    int errorCount = 0;
    do {
        if (openTickets.Exists(x => x.SupportTicketId == ticketId)) {
            validEntry = true;
        }
```

163

```
        else {
            Console.WriteLine($"{ticketId} is not a valid SupportId,
            please try again");
            ticketId = cHelper.GetNumbersFromConsole();
            Console.WriteLine();
            errorCount++;
        }
        if (errorCount > 2) {
            // 4 times should be enough, initial try plus 3
            break;
        }
    } while (!validEntry);

    if (validEntry) {
        List<SupportLog> logEntries = RetreiveLogEntries(ticketId);
        Console.Clear();
        cHelper.WriteHeader("Update Support Ticket");
        Console.WriteLine("\r\n");
        if (logEntries.Count > 0) {
            foreach(var log in logEntries) {
                Console.WriteLine($"{log.SupportLogEntryDate}: {log.
                SupportLogEntry}");
                Console.WriteLine($"  Entered By: {log.SupportLogUpdatedBy}");
                Console.WriteLine("================================");
            }
        }
        else {
            Console.WriteLine("There are currently no Log Entries");
        }
        Console.WriteLine("Please enter your notes, when you are done
        hit the Enter Key");
        logEntry = cHelper.GetTextFromConsole(10);
        Console.WriteLine("\r\nIs this ticket now closed? Y or N");
        bool closeTicket = false;
        char yOrN = cHelper.CheckForYOrN(true);
        if (yOrN == 'y' | yOrN == 'Y') {
```

```
        closeTicket = true;
      }
      AddSupportLogEntry(logEntry, closeTicket, ticketId);
    }
    else {
      Console.WriteLine("I'm sorry it looks like you are having
      trouble, please try again later.");
    }
    Console.WriteLine("Hit any key to continue...");
    Console.ReadKey();
  }
  private void AddSupportLogEntry(string entry, bool close, int ticketId) {
    Console.WriteLine("Saving new log entry");
    using(MachineContext context = new MachineContext()) {
        SupportLog sLogEntry = new SupportLog() {
            SupportTicketId = ticketId,
            SupportLogEntry = entry,
            SupportLogUpdatedBy = Environment.UserName,
            SupportLogEntryDate = DateTime.Now
        };
        context.SupportLog.Add(sLogEntry);
        int res = context.SaveChanges();
        Console.WriteLine($"{res} record saved");
    }
    if (close) {
        CloseTicket(ticketId);
    }
  }

    private void CloseTicket(int ticketId) {
      Console.WriteLine("Closing ticket...");
      using(MachineContext context = new MachineContext()) {
        SupportTicket sTicket = context.SupportTicket.Where(x =>
        x.SupportTicketId == ticketId).FirstOrDefault();
        sTicket.DateResolved = DateTime.Now;
```

165

```
        context.Update(sTicket);
        context.SaveChanges();
        Console.WriteLine("Ticket is closed");
    }
  }
 }
}
```

We'll just work our way down the class file from top to bottom since there is quite a bit there, although the good thing is by this point you should have seen everything that is in here. It's just more practice to help it sink in a little better.

We start by adding three using statements. This is another habit I got into, which for some reason I put a space between what I added and what the system added for me. The one upside is at a quick glance, I can tell what I needed in order to do what I did with the class. If I'm looking for borrow some code from another project, I can get a pretty good idea what namespaces I'm going to need.

I made the class public, but for what we are doing we really don't need to, so if you missed that you will still be okay. We are going to be using our ConsoleHelper class throughout this class so I created a private field (variable) to handle it. That way, I don't have to keep recreating it throughout the class. I also only want it to be accessible from within this class, which is why it's private. Lastly before we get into the methods, I have created a default constructor for our class. This is one of those things that object oriented programming says is a good thing and it really doesn't take up much space, so why not?

RetreiveLogEntries() is pretty straightforward. We are going to return a List<SupportLog> to whatever calls it. We use a using statement to encapsulate our LINQ query, and we use a where clause as we are only looking for log entries for one ticket. We need to do an OrderBy so we can be sure they are in the order we want. Hopefully you are now able to write this type of query in your sleep, but if not, don't worry about it. With practice, you will be able to.

RetreiveOpenTickets() is virtually the same as RetreiveLogEntries(), except we needed to do an include and well as our Where. Since we are looking for open tickets, it would make sense that DateResolved would be null for these tickets. We could have also created a field in our table that would act as a flag to tell us if the ticket was still open or not.

UpdateSupportTicket() by far caused the most stress on our fingers. We are doing a lot of the same steps we have done in the past. We clear the console window and add a title (header) by using the method from our ConsoleHelper class. We get our list of open tickets and display them to the user. If you had a lot of tickets, your window would fill up pretty quickly, although you could page your results if you needed to since you now know how to do that. Once the user selects a ticket, which we do by again calling one of our helper methods, we display any log entries for that ticket. If there aren't any entries, we tell the user that. The user then updates the ticket with the new information, lets us know if it's closed or not, and then saves their work.

AddSupportLogEntry() does what it says. This is where we add the entry to our DBContext and save it to the database. Once that is done if the ticket is to be closed we call CloseTicket(). Close ticket retrieves the SupportTicket we are working with and updates DateResolved to the current date and time. It then updates DBContext and saves it to the database. Figure 4-9 shows all of this in action.

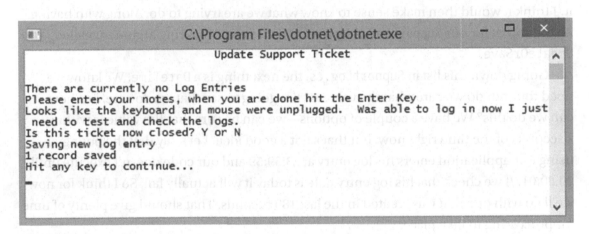

Figure 4-9. *Using our new classes*

I chose to leave the ticket open at this stage so we'll have an open ticket for our next part. Hopefully by now, you know how to get this working. If not, compare your code to the chapter code on the website.

Validating Using a Class

Let's say that we want to validate our data, but we don't want to use the DataAnnotations namespace for some reason, or we just want to have more control over what we are doing. The obvious choice is to do it ourselves since we are the ones who want the control. We will do this by creating a new class called ModelValidation. Why not put our model validation with our regular validation (remember we created BasicValidation.cs)? If we are using SOC as our guideline, we would want to keep them separated, as they are doing two different things. That is why we are going to have two separate classes.

We will first do a simple validation for SupportLog. We will pass a SupportLog object to our method and return a bool letting us know if the SupportLog object has valid data in it and it's safe to save or update. We could call this method before we try to save or update our object.

Let's think about what we need to do. If we are updating our object when we need to have a SupportLogId, but if we are doing an initial save, then we don't need to have it. I think it would then make sense to know what we are trying to do. Along with having an argument for our SupportLog object, we will also create a string argument called UpdateOrSave.

Going down this list in SupportLog.cs, the next thing is a DateTime. We know we need this, but do we care what the value is? I'm going to say that we do care, but how can we do this? We have a couple of options—we can be sure that the value is within x seconds of the time right now, but that's not a good idea. Let's say that the poor guy using our application enters his log entry at 23:59:59 and our code doesn't execute until 00:00:01. If we check that his log entry date is today it will actually fail. So I think for now we'll go with one that was created in the last 180 seconds. That should give plenty of time for processing to take place.

The next is our actual log entry. We obviously want something here—the question is how much of that something do we want? To make life easier, let's go with a length of at least 10. This way you can enter "It's fixed" and be okay. SupportLogUpdated is similar, although we are just looking for a name, so let's say 2 is a good number. This way, Al can do his job.

Now for the last one, SupportTicketId. This one is technically tricky. Do we just care that we have a SupportTicketId (option 1) or do we want to see if that SupportTicketId is valid (option 2)? If you answered option 1, then you like to live life on the edge. Right now it's pretty safe to say that our SupportTicketId is going to be valid, but what about in the future if your program is expanded to where the user could just enter all the information manually for a "quick update" and the `SupportTicketId` is 8675309 and they enter 8679309? Well, there is a chance that the second ticket hasn't actually been created yet and thus is not a valid ticket number. Now that we have some working notes, let's create our class to see how it could be implemented. The same could have been argued for `SupportLogId`. Perhaps if we decide to let users modify support log entries, we can add the validation then. See Listing 4-20.

Listing 4-20. ModelValidation.cs

```
using System;
using System.Collections.Generic;
using System.Text;

using ComputerInventory.Models;
using ComputerInventory.Data;
using System.Linq;

namespace ComputerInventory {
    public class ModelValidation {
        public ModelValidation() {
        }

        public bool ValidateSupportLog(SupportLog supportLog, string
        updateOrSave) {
            bool valid = true;
            if(updateOrSave.ToLower() == "update") {
                valid = SupportTicketIdExists(supportLog.SupportTicketId);
            }

            if (supportLog.SupportLogEntryDate < DateTime.Now.AddSeconds(-180)) {
                valid = false;
            }
            if (supportLog.SupportLogEntry.Length < 10) {
                valid = false;
            }
            if (supportLog.SupportLogUpdatedBy.Length < 2) {
                valid = false;
            }
```

```
        return valid;
    }

    public bool SupportTicketIdExists(int supportTicketId) {
        bool exists = false;
        using (MachineContext context = new MachineContext()) {
            exists = context.SupportTicket.Any(x => x.SupportTicketId.
            Equals(supportTicketId));
        }
        return exists;
    }
  }
}
```

LINQ Using .Any to Check for Existing Records

Let's start by looking at SupportTicketIdExists(). You may recall that we checked
to see if a record existed in the database. This was at the same time we were checking
to see if the operating system or machine type existed. In those instances, we used a
pretty simple query where we checked to see if the IQueryable<T> had a count that was
greater than zero. That is fine and does work, but there is another way to get the same
functionality and will less overhead. By using .Any, we check to see if there is a record
that meets our criteria, and if so, let us know. If you hover over .Any, you will see that it
returns a type of bool, which is all we are looking for in this case. We just want a simple
yes or no.

The rest of the error checking for ValidateSupportLog is pretty rudimentary and I'm
sure if you put some thought into it, you could probably do a slightly better job. However,
what we are interested in is checking to see if our DateTime value is the value we want
versus just a DateTime. If we look at WarrantyProvider.cs, we see that we used a regular
expression to check SupportNumber. We could use the same regular expression in our
class as well, although we would need to make the appropriate reference in order to use
regular expressions in our class.

I guess we are going to need to test this. The simplest test we can do is to change our
SupportLogEntryDate to 2000 seconds before right now. Add a really short log entry
and change the SupportTicketId to a number you know doesn't exist. We will start by
making the time 2000 seconds before right now, as shown in Listing 4-21.

Listing 4-21. Updates to AddSupportLogEntry()

```
private void AddSupportLogEntry(string entry, bool close, int ticketId) {
    bool modelIsValid = false;
    ModelValidation mv = new ModelValidation();
    Console.WriteLine("Saving new log entry");
    using(MachineContext context = new MachineContext()) {
        SupportLog sLogEntry = new SupportLog() {
            SupportTicketId = ticketId,
            SupportLogEntry = entry,
            SupportLogUpdatedBy = Environment.UserName,
            SupportLogEntryDate = DateTime.Now.AddSeconds(-2000)
        };
        modelIsValid = mv.ValidateSupportLog(sLogEntry, "save");
        if (modelIsValid) {
            context.SupportLog.Add(sLogEntry);
            int res = context.SaveChanges();
            Console.WriteLine($"{res} record saved");
        }
    }
    if (modelIsValid) {
        if (close) {
            CloseTicket(ticketId);
        }
    }
    else {
        Console.WriteLine("There is a problem with your Entry, please try
        again");
        Console.Write("Hit any key to continue...");
        Console.ReadKey();
    }
}
```

We added a `bool` called `modelIsValid` so we would have a way of knowing if we have a valid object. Then we created our `ModelValidation` object so we can check our model against the method we created in that class. We check to see if our model is valid. It's not valid, as we subtract 2000 seconds (you have to add a negative number to subtract). Since our model isn't valid, we tell the users that there is a problem. They are left wondering what is wrong (see Figure 4-10).

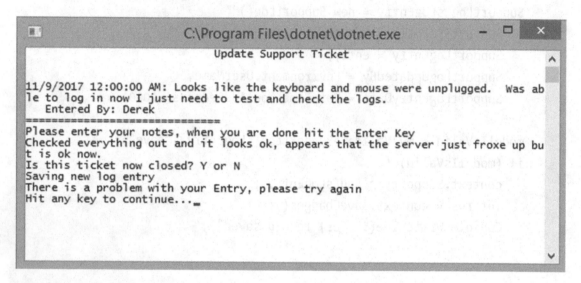

Figure 4-10. *Testing our new code*

As you can see, we didn't try to save the invalid data back to the database. The bad news is we have no idea what is wrong. You may have also noticed that the time is 12:00:00 AM. That is because in the database, our field type is `Date` and not `DateTime`. Oops. Don't worry, we planned that and are going to fix it in Chapter 5.

Adding a Class to a Class File

Let's fix the current issue. Right now we know we have an error, but we don't know what it is. To find it, we will add a class to `ModelValidation.cs` called `ErrorList`. Now you could create an entirely new class file if you wanted, but since we are only going to use `ErrorList` from within `ModelValidation` and with the object reference to `ModelValidation`, we'll put it in that file. Adding a class to an existing class file is quite simple. Take a look at Listing 4-22 and you'll see what we are adding and where.

Listing 4-22. Adding a Class to a Class

```
namespace ComputerInventory {
    public class Errors {
        public int Position { get; set; }
        public string FieldName { get; set; }
        public string Error { get; set; }
    }

    public class ModelValidation {
        public List<Errors> errorList;
        public ModelValidation() {
            errorList = new List<Errors>();
        }

        public bool ValidateSupportLog(SupportLog supportLog, string
        updateOrSave) {
            . . .
```

See, that was quite simple, wasn't it? Now we have a way to track our errors
and we even created a List<Errors> to keep track of them. We created a position
variable when we validate against a list of objects. We added to our default
constructor an initialization of the errorList variable so it will be ready to go if we
need it. These default constructors can come in handy. Lastly, we added the start of
ValidateSupportLog so you know where you are in our code of ModelValidation.cs.

Now that you have a way of knowing where the issue is, let's make some changes so
you can use it. The changes will be pretty simple and since we are not working against a
list, we will have our value of position be zero. See Listing 4-23.

Listing 4-23. Updates to ValidateSupportLog()

```
public bool ValidateSupportLog(SupportLog supportLog, string updateOrSave) {
    bool valid = true;
    Errors error;
    if (updateOrSave.ToLower() == "update") {
        valid = SupportTicketIdExists(supportLog.SupportTicketId);
        error = new Errors {
            Position = 0,
```

```
      FieldName = "SupportTicketId",
      Error = "Not a valid SupportTicketId"
   };
   errorList.Add(error);
}

if (supportLog.SupportLogEntryDate < DateTime.Now.AddSeconds(-180)) {
   valid = false;
   error = new Errors {
      Position = 0,
      FieldName = "SupportLogEntryDate",
      Error = "Date is not valid"
   };
   errorList.Add(error);
}
if (supportLog.SupportLogEntry.Length < 10) {
   valid = false;
   error = new Errors {
      Position = 0,
      FieldName = "SupportLogEntry",
      Error = "Enter at least 10 characters."
   };
   errorList.Add(error);
}
if (supportLog.SupportLogUpdatedBy.Length < 2) {
   valid = false;
   error = new Errors {
      Position = 0,
      FieldName = "SupportLogUpdatedBy",
      Error = "Enter at least 2 characters"
   };
   errorList.Add(error);
}
return valid;
}
```

One thing that could be new to some is the following code:

```
error = new Errors {
    Position = 0,
    FieldName = "SupportLogUpdatedBy",
    Error = "Enter at least 2 characters"
};
```

It is a somewhat simpler version of this code:

```
error = new Errors();
error.Position = 0;
error.FieldName = "SupportLogEntryDate";
error.Error = "Date is not valid";
```

In the grand scheme of things, it really doesn't save you a lot. However, I thought I would bring it up in case you have been looking for a different way of handling that with slightly fewer keystrokes.

Now we just need to make the changes to AddSupportLogEntry(). I include the entire method, as I also "broke" SupportLogEntry and want to show you how I did that. See Listing 4-24.

Listing 4-24. AddSupportLogEntry() Updates

```
private void AddSupportLogEntry(string entry, bool close, int ticketId) {
    bool modelIsValid = false;
    ModelValidation mv = new ModelValidation();
    Console.WriteLine("Saving new log entry");
    using (MachineContext context = new MachineContext()) {
        SupportLog sLogEntry = new SupportLog() {
            SupportTicketId = ticketId,
            SupportLogEntry = "broke",
            SupportLogUpdatedBy = Environment.UserName,
            SupportLogEntryDate = DateTime.Now.AddSeconds(-2000)
        };
        modelIsValid = mv.ValidateSupportLog(sLogEntry, "save");
        if (modelIsValid) {
            context.SupportLog.Add(sLogEntry);
```

```
        int res = context.SaveChanges();
        Console.WriteLine($"{res} record saved");
    }
}
if (modelIsValid) {
    if (close) {
        CloseTicket(ticketId);
    }
}
else {
    Console.WriteLine("There is a problem with your Entry");
    foreach(var error in mv.errorList) {
        Console.WriteLine($"{error.FieldName} {error.Error}");
    }
}
}
```

Even though I typed more than 10 characters, the value I passed to the validator was not more than 10, and as a result it is now displaying two helpful error messages. Figure 4-11 shows both errors. Before you forget, go back and change your code so it passes the proper values.

```
SupportLog sLogEntry = new SupportLog() {
    SupportTicketId = ticketId,
    SupportLogEntry = entry,
    SupportLogUpdatedBy = Environment.UserName,
    SupportLogEntryDate = DateTime.Now
};
```

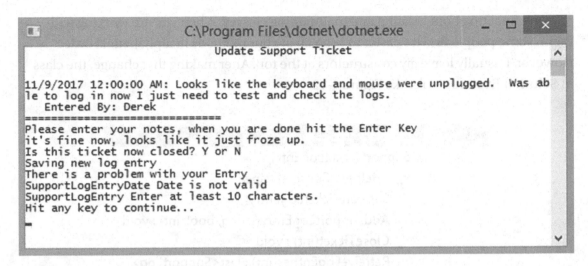

Figure 4-11. *Displaying both errors*

Summary

If you are currently not using multiple classes in your applications, I hope that this has helped to show you why it's a good thing to do so. Just think if you have 150 different methods in your application all in the class file and let's say the average number of lines per method was 30. That would mean that you would have around 4,500 lines of code in that one file. I'm not saying that is a lot or a little, but if you can group them a little better and put those 150 methods into five different classes, for example, you are only talking about 900 or so lines of code for each. It would be a lot easier to sift through 900 lines than 4,500 lines.

You should also have a better understanding of how to do some different types of data validation in your application. When you do the ASP.NET MVC Core Application starting in Chapter 6, you will see where using the DataAnnotations namespace is really helpful and shines. We also added a new LINQ tool to our toolbox that I think some of you will find useful in your daily programming.

At this point, you could go back through your code in Program.cs and start to move things out to BasicValidation.cs and to ConsoleHelper.cs to see just how much of a difference it makes. You could also create some other classes to hold the business logic for the manipulation of your models, like we did with SupportTicketLogEntry.cs.

One final tip about creating and maintaining classes. When you are working with them, some people find it's easier to keep all of your methods in alphabetical order. However, I usually leave my constructors at the top. After making that change, the class in Solution Explorer looks like Figure 4-12.

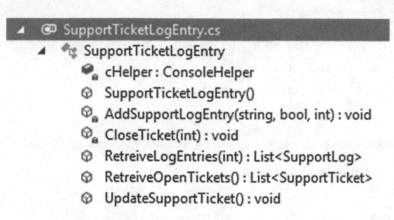

Figure 4-12. *Class viewed in Solution Explorer*

This is just a small class but because of that it makes it easier to see the benefit. If I want to go to my code for RetreiveOpenTickets(), I can just double-click on it in the list and it will bring me to that section of code. I can also find it quicker, as I know that my list is in alphabetical order, so I can quickly scan past all the letters I don't need to find the Rs.

One more thing we covered rather quickly was the use of expression-bodied members. If this is something that interests you because you just love the look of lambda expressions, then take some time to do some research on it. Also remember that you can do this with more than just methods; you can also do this with property get and set statements, constructors, finalizers, and indexers. Since it's new, I'm sure some of you may not have even known that it existed.

CHAPTER 5

Stored Procedures, Table Design, and Modifications

Although it might sound like this is going to be a horribly long and tedious chapter, I'm hopeful that you will find it to be the opposite. We aren't going to dive deeply into theory, as that would require an entire other book. What we are going to talk about is how to use stored procedures and how you should try to structure your tables and thoughts about them when working with Entity Framework Core 2.0.

Stored Procedures

The first thing we cover is the use of stored procedures in Entity Framework Core 2.0. If you aren't familiar with stored procedures, they can be quite helpful. DBAs love them because they give them a chance to be programmers. Stored procedures are groups of one or more Transact-SQL statements that are saved and run on the database server. Like the methods that we have been writing, stored procedures will accept input parameters and return multiple values to the calling program, which are in the form of output parameters.

It's pretty simple when you think about it—input parameters for inputting data and output parameters for returning or outputting data. Stored procedures can also have programming statements that perform operations on the database or calls to other stored procedures. What's nice is that they will let you know if the procedure completed successfully or not and can report why the procedure failed. One of the benefits of using stored procedures is that they reduce the amount of network IO, as there is less traffic

© Derek J. Rouleau 2018
D. J. Rouleau, *Beginning Entity Framework Core 2.0*, https://doi.org/10.1007/978-1-4842-3375-7_5

going between the DBMS (Database Management System) and the client. If you have been doing this long enough, you can probably think of a few processes that are IO intensive and on a web application that is really frowned upon.

Another benefit is code reuse. Let's say you have a couple of applications that all do something similar but different, but there are a handful of operations that are the same for each application. Instead of having to write the same code multiple times or having DLL files and remembering to maintain them, you can store the code in a stored procedure. This also makes code maintenance easier, as you make changes in only one place. Although you do need to be sure that it doesn't break one of those many places.

We start with a simple stored procedure that mimics some code that we have already written. The procedure returns a list of SupportLog entries based on the SupportTicketId. Granted, this is something you can do with a class, but if you are new to stored procedures, it's helpful to start with something that is simple and easy to wrap your head around. If you are a stored procedure guru, you'll probably not find this overly helpful.

One way you can create a stored procedure is to open SQL Server Management Studio, navigate to your database (in our case, BegEfCore2), and then look for the Programmability folder. Within that, find the Stored Procedures folder. Right-click it and choose New ➤ Stored Procedure. See Figure 5-1.

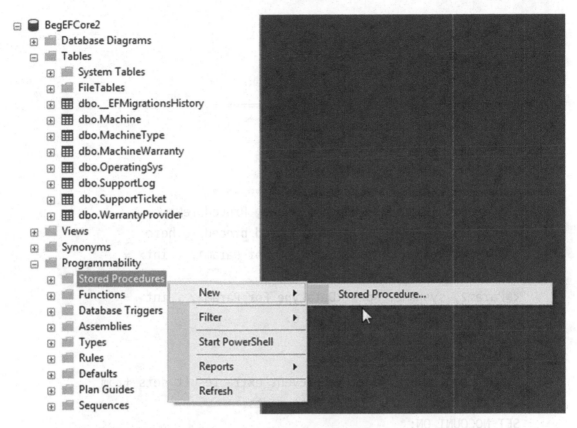

Figure 5-1. *SQL Server Management Studio*

When you create your new stored procedure, you should see something similar to Listing 5-1.

Listing 5-1. Stored Procedure Template

```
-- =================================================
-- Template generated from Template Explorer using:
-- Create Procedure (New Menu).SQL
--
-- Use the Specify Values for Template Parameters
-- command (Ctrl-Shift-M) to fill in the parameter
-- values below.
--
-- This block of comments will not be included in
-- the definition of the procedure.
-- =================================================
```

```
SET ANSI_NULLS ON
GO
SET QUOTED_IDENTIFIER ON
GO
-- ===============================================
-- Author:        <Author,,Name>
-- Create date:   <Create Date,,>
-- Description:   <Description,,>
-- ===============================================
CREATE PROCEDURE <Procedure_Name, sysname, ProcedureName>
      -- Add the parameters for the stored procedure here
      <@Param1, sysname, @p1> <Datatype_For_Param1, , int> =
       <Default_Value_For_Param1, , 0>,
      <@Param2, sysname, @p2> <Datatype_For_Param2, , int> =
       <Default_Value_For_Param2, , 0>
AS
BEGIN
      -- SET NOCOUNT ON added to prevent extra result sets from
      -- interfering with SELECT statements.
      SET NOCOUNT ON;

    -- Insert statements for procedure here
      SELECT <@Param1, sysname, @p1>, <@Param2, sysname, @p2>
END
GO
```

The first thing to note here is we have the SET ANSI_NULLS ON line, which may be a bit confusing. What this is saying is that we are going to handle the equals (=) and not equal to (<>) operators in an ISO-compliant way. There is a very good write up on the Microsoft website if you search for SET ANSI_NULLS that explains just what that means.

The next line is SET QUOTED_IDENTIFIER ON, which is very similar to ANSI_NULLS in that by setting it to on, you will be using quotation marks in an ISO-compliant manner.

We then come to the CREATE PROCEDURE line. I think the template is a bit confusing the first time you look at it. All it's saying is what are you going to name your procedure. I generally add sp_ to the front of my stored procedure names so they jump out a little bit more when I'm looking at my code.

The great thing about stored procedures is you can use parameters to pass values into the stored procedure to make them a bit more useful. Since the point of stored procedures is reusability, that makes a lot of sense. In this example, we aren't using a default value, but if you were, you would assign that value when you create the parameter.

The template explains what `SET NOCOUNT ON` means, but if you want more of a description, feel free to look it up. Lastly is the statement, which as you can see from the example, isn't too exciting.

If you use the Ctrl+Shift+M command, you can fill in the parameter values of the procedure. Figure 5-2 shows the procedure all filled out. Of course, you can just enter the same information manually.

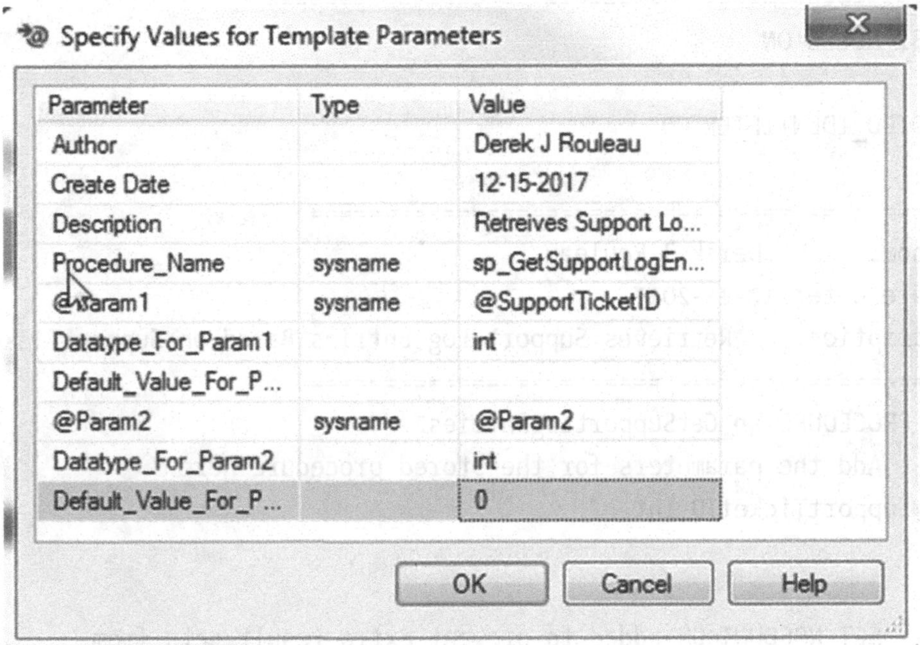
Specify Values for Template Parameters
Parameter
Type
Value
Author
Derek J Rouleau
Create Date
12-15-2017
Description
Retreives Support Lo...
Procedure_Name
sysname
sp_GetSupportLogEn...
@Param1
sysname
@SupportTicketID
Datatype_For_Param1
int
Default_Value_For_P...
@Param2
sysname
@Param2
Datatype_For_Param2
int
Default_Value_For_P...
0
OK
Cancel
Help

Figure 5-2. *Stored procedure template parameters*

This makes it a bit easier, but you still have to edit a few things or add them if you need more parameters. Either way, just make sure your stored procedure looks like Listing 5-1a before continuing.

Listing 5-1a. Creating the Stored Procedure

```
-- ====================================================
-- Template generated from Template Explorer using:
-- Create Procedure (New Menu).SQL
--
-- Use the Specify Values for Template Parameters
-- command (Ctrl-Shift-M) to fill in the parameter
-- values below.
--
-- This block of comments will not be included in
-- the definition of the procedure.
-- ====================================================
SET ANSI_NULLS ON
GO
SET QUOTED_IDENTIFIER ON
GO
-- =============================================
-- Author:        Derek J Rouleau
-- Create date: 12-15-2017
-- Description:    Retrieves Support Log Entries Based on SupportTicketID
-- =============================================
CREATE PROCEDURE sp_GetSupportLogEntries2
      -- Add the parameters for the stored procedure here
      @SupportTicketID int
AS
BEGIN
      -- SET NOCOUNT ON added to prevent extra result sets from
      -- interfering with SELECT statements.
      SET NOCOUNT ON;

    -- Insert statements for procedure here
      SELECT
            SupportLogID,
            SupportLogEntry,
            SupportLogEntryDate,
```

```
        SupportLogUpdatedBy,
        SupportTicketID
    FROM SupportLog
    WHERE SupportTicketID = @SupportTicketID

END
GO
```

I left some of the default text in there so you can see it. If you want to, you could fill in the Author, Create Date, and Description. That is always a good idea in a production environment or even a test environment so if you have any questions you know who to blame (I mean go to). When you are ready, click Execute. It will create your stored procedure and add it to your `Stored Procedures` folder.

As you can see, stored procedures are nothing more than SQL queries or statements that are saved on the server that you can pass parameters to. In this case, we are passing in one parameter called `@SupportTicketID` and it's of type `int`. We then can use it in our query like we would any other value or variable.

Calling a Stored Procedure with One Parameter

Now that you have a stored procedure, what can you do with it? In this example, I'm going to create a hidden menu item on the Main menu for testing. This way, we can just do a quick test without having to dive into the menu. The key is remembering to remove it when you get beyond the testing stage. Within our `MainMenu()` method, I added the following, which is essentially a hidden menu for doing more testing:

```
else if(result == 7) {
    using(MachineContext context = new MachineContext()) {
        context.Database.OpenConnection();
        List<SupportLog> lst = context.SupportLog.FromSql
        ("sp_GetSupportLogEntries @p0", 1).ToList();
    }
}
```

I put a breakpoint on the List line so that I can easily test it without having to output anything to the console (although writing a simple loop would be fairly easy). Figure 5-3 shows you how I tested the code to be sure that the stored procedure and call are working.

```
else if(result == 7) {
    using(MachineContext context = new MachineContext()) {
        context.Database.OpenConnection();
        List<SupportLog> lst = context.SupportLog.FromSql("sp_GetSupportLogEntries @p0", 1).ToList();
    } ≤634ms elapsed
}
else if (result == 9) {
    // We are exiting so nothing
    cont = true;
}

atch (System.FormatException) {
    // a key that wasn't a number
```

| lst Count = 1 |
| [0]   (ComputerInventory.Models.SupportLog) |

SupportLogEntry	"Looks like the keyboard and mouse were unplugged. Wa
SupportLogEntryDate	{11/9/2017 12:00:00 AM}
SupportLogId	1
SupportLogUpdatedBy	"Derek"
SupportTicket	null
SupportTicketId	1

Figure 5-3. Testing the stored procedure

It looks like it's working, as we have one record in the table for SupportTicketId 1 and the data looks correct. I think we can call that a good first test and can assume that our stored procedure is working correctly.

In Entity Framework Core, we have to use FromSQL in order to execute stored procedures to get data and then use ExecuteSqlCommand for CRUD operations. In our example, we have a parameter even though you could have a stored procedure that doesn't have parameters. In the first example (there will be more), we called our parameter @p0. This is because we want to work the parameter at position 0 in the list of parameters. If we had more parameters, they would be @p1, @p2, etc.

Let's say you don't like to use @p0, @p1, etc., and you want to use something a bit more familiar. The good news is you can do that too.

```
else if(result == 7) {
    using(MachineContext context = new MachineContext()) {
        context.Database.OpenConnection();
        List<SupportLog> lst = context.SupportLog.FromSql
        ("sp_GetSupportLogEntries {0}", 1).ToList();
    }
}
```

As you can see, we replaced @p0 with {0}, which will be familiar to most people who have been programming in C# for any length of time. If you rerun the application and choose the hidden/testing option, you should get the same results shown in Figure 5-2.

Using Parameter Names

Both of these ways are great, but let's say that for some reason, you need to pass your parameter by name because you were told you have to, which is always a good reason. In order to pass the parameter by parameter name, you have to create a `DbParameter` or in this case a `SqlParameter` that inherits from `DbParameter`.

```
else if(result == 7) {
    using(MachineContext context = new MachineContext()) {
        context.Database.OpenConnection();
        var sTicketIdParam = new SqlParameter("@SupportTicketID", 1);
        List<SupportLog> lst = context.SupportLog.FromSql("sp_
        GetSupportLogEntries @SupportTicketID", sTicketIdParam).ToList();
    }
}
```

In order to do this, you either have to use the fully qualified name for `SqlParameter` like this:

```
var sTicketIdParam = new System.Data.SqlClient.SqlParameter("@Support
TicketID", 1);
```

Or you can just add `using System.Data.SqlClient;` to your class file. If I'm going to use something only one time in a class, I often just use the fully qualified name and don't add the namespace. Whichever method you use, try to be consistent. Figure 5-4 shows that we are using our parameter and that we have received the same output.

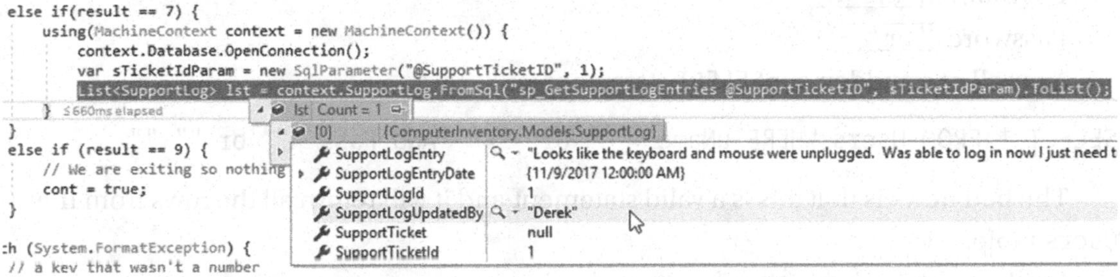

Figure 5-4. *Output using parameters*

One nice thing about using SQL parameters is that they help to shield you from SQL Injection. DBContext is supposed to help protect us from SQL Injection attacks, but if you are looking for that extra layer of protection, SQL parameters are the way to go.

SQL Injection

If your job requires you to work with outside-facing databases or if you are just worried that you may eventually have an employee who wants to cause harm to your business, you should understand what SQL Injection is. This section explains one of the most commonly given examples for SQL Injection and from there you can do some more reading on your own (if it scares you enough).

Let's say you have a simple login window for your application or website, whereby the user enters their credentials. Your form or website may have something that looks like the following:

Username: John Smith

Password: Password123

In your code, you would see something similar to this:

```
userName = username.Text();
userPassword = password.Text();
string sqlString = string.Format("SELECT * FROM Users WHERE uName = '{0}'
AND Pass = '{1}'", userName, password);
```

This would result in a query string that looks like this:

```
SELECT * FROM Users WHERE uName = "John Smith" AND Pass = "Password123"
```

Okay, everything looks good, right?

Now let's say the person doesn't enter their username or password, but enters the following:

Username: " or ""="

Password: " or ""="

Now all of a sudden our SELECT statement is:

```
SELECT * FROM Users WHERE uName = "" or ""="" AND Pass ="" or ""=""
```

The bad news is that this is a valid statement and it will return all the rows from the Users table.

Lastly, everyone's favorite:

Username: John Smith

Password: Password123; DROP TABLE Accounts

```
SELECT * FROM Users WHERE uName = "John Smith" AND Pass = "Password123";
DROP TABLE Accounts
```

This will do the SELECT as normal, but it will also drop the table after the SELECT query. That is going to result in you or someone else having a really bad day!

There are lots more fun and exciting ways for someone to perform SQL Injection. These are just two of the most popular examples that are out there.

DBContext is supposed to provide a layer of protection as well as using SQL parameters. When you are using stored procedures with Entity Framework Core, it's a good idea to use the parameters if you are concerned with these types of attacks. Because you aren't using DBContext directly to access the database, you are instead interacting directly with the database. When in doubt, better safe than sorry.

Inserting Into Multiple Tables

This next example is something that you are more likely to see in a database of stored procedures. We are going to create a stored procedure to add a new support ticket and a new log entry that simply says "Ticket Created". Ticketing software often requires the first log entry to indicate that the ticket was created by a certain user, for some reason. This is also a great way to show you how this process works. See Listing 5-2.

Listing 5-2. Sp_AddNewSupportTicket

```
USE [BegEFCore2]
GO
/****** Object:  StoredProcedure sp_AddNewSupportTicket
        Script Date: 11/3/2017 10:19:04 PM ******/
SET ANSI_NULLS ON
GO
SET QUOTED_IDENTIFIER ON
GO

CREATE PROCEDURE sp_AddNewSupportTicket
    -- parameters for the stored procedure
    @UserName varchar(50),
    @EnteredOn date,
    @IssueDescription varchar(150),
    @IssueDetail varchar(MAX),
    @MachineId int,
```

```
     @NewSupportTicktId int = NULL Output
AS
BEGIN
    -- SET NOCOUNT ON added to prevent extra result sets from
    -- interfering with SELECT statements.
    SET NOCOUNT ON;

    -- Insert statements for procedure here
    INSERT INTO dbo.SupportTicket (DateReported, IssueDescription,
    IssueDetail, MachineId, TicketOpenedBy)
        VALUES (@EnteredOn, @IssueDescription, @IssueDetail, @MachineId,
        @UserName)
    SET @NewSupportTicktId = SCOPE_IDENTITY()

    INSERT INTO dbo.SupportLog (SupportLogEntry, SupportLogEntryDate,
    SupportLogUpdatedBy, SupportTicketID)
        VALUES ('Ticket Created', @EnteredOn, @UserName, @NewSupportTicktId)
END
```

Just like before, we create the parameters to use in our statements that are to follow. As you can see, I gave them names in some cases that don't match the field names in the tables. The parameter names don't need to be the same as the fields. The last one, called @NewSupportTicketId, is used in our second statement and is one that your application can get in return. SCOPE_IDENTITY gets the value that is inserted into an identity column in the current session and within the current scope. So, when we do our INSERT, even though someone else could be doing one at the same time, we should get the identity value that we created by doing the INSERT and not someone else's.

The two INSERT INTO statements are fairly straightforward, although keep in mind that order is important, since you can't insert your log entry before you create your ticket.

If you are new to working with SQL Server or any other DBMS, this is a good place to mention that what we are doing here is something called a *transaction*. What that means is that we have a group of one or more statements that we want to either work in their entirety or fail and have no data written to the database. The great thing is you can set up error checking and if you do get errors, you can roll back your transactions like they never happened. If you'll be doing a lot of work with databases, it will behoove you to look into transactions.

Multiple Properties

Just like with a single property, using multiple properties is pretty straightforward (see Listing 5-3). The key is making sure that your properties and values match. Nine out of ten times, if you're going to have a problem when using multiple properties, it's because you messed up the order of your properties and values.

Listing 5-3. Adding Multiple Properties

```
else if(result == 7) {
    using(MachineContext context = new MachineContext()) {
        context.Database.OpenConnection();
        var userNameParam = new SqlParameter("@UserName", "Derek");
        var enteredOnParam = new SqlParameter("@EnteredOn", DateTime.Now);
        var issueDescriptionParam = new SqlParameter("@IssueDescription",
        "Needs Office 2016");
        var issueDetailParam = new SqlParameter("@IssueDetail", "Bob needs
        Office 2016 installed so he can do his job.");
        var machineIdParam = new SqlParameter("@MachineId", 10);
        context.Database.ExecuteSqlCommand("sp_AddNewSupportTicket @UserName,
        @EnteredOn, @IssueDescription, @IssueDetail, @MachineId", userNameParam,
        enteredOnParam, issueDescriptionParam, issueDetailParam, machineIdParam);
    }
}
```

Obviously, everything here is hardcoded to show how it works in a quick example. However, you could do all of your work by validating your model and then use the model values as your variable values. If you run your code, there isn't a whole lot to look at, but if you open SQL Server Management Studio, you can see that you have two new records (see Figure 5-5).

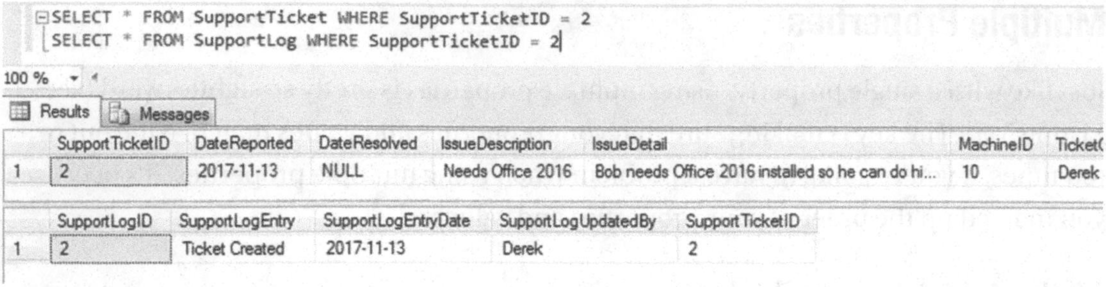

```
SELECT * FROM SupportTicket WHERE SupportTicketID = 2
SELECT * FROM SupportLog WHERE SupportTicketID = 2
```

100 %   ▼ ◄

Results | Messages

	SupportTicketID	DateReported	DateResolved	IssueDescription	IssueDetail	MachineID	Ticket(
1	2	2017-11-13	NULL	Needs Office 2016	Bob needs Office 2016 installed so he can do hi...	10	Derek

	SupportLogID	SupportLogEntry	SupportLogEntryDate	SupportLogUpdatedBy	SupportTicketID
1	2	Ticket Created	2017-11-13	Derek	2

Figure 5-5. *Results from sp_AddNewSupportTicket*

In my case, the next SupportTicketID was 2. In one call, we have managed to update two tables with similar data from property names that didn't match either table's field names. I think it's safe to say that the second stored procedure is slightly more helpful than the first, although in both cases, you could have just as easily done the same thing in your code.

If you can do this with code in your classes, why bother with stored procedures? Years ago, stored procedures were a lot more useful, as there was a huge boost in query performance when running large queries that way. But with improvements in networking, server, and workstation performance and the database engines themselves, a lot of these performance benefits aren't as significant as they once were.

Recall that stored procedures do help keep your code centrally located, which makes it easier to maintain. They also keep code more secure, as fewer users tend to have access to the database than to file shares or other network locations. Essentially, how much you use stored procedures has a lot to do with your work environment.

Table and Entity Design

Up to this point, all of our models have a one-to-one mapping with data tables in the database, but the beauty of Entity Framework Core is that you don't need to follow that design. As you learned in Chapter 4, when it comes down to it, we are basically working with classes, so there is no reason that we can't inherit from our "model" and handle it in a different way for multiple classes.

Let's say you have a table called Account that holds all of your account information. You have business and personal accounts, but all of the data is stored in one table. You can set it up so you have one class that handles business accounts and one that handles personal accounts. Why have two classes? Generally, databases are designed with performance, scalability, and maintainability in mind, but not with what developers may need or have in mind. Sticking with our account example, a personal account may use different fields than a business account, yet they are in the same table. By using different classes, we can set it up so that we have access only to applicable fields.

We can also do the reverse with our entity classes. We could have one class that maps to multiple tables. For example, we could have an Employee class that maps to an Employee table, a Machine table (like in our Computer Inventory application), and perhaps a Workgroup table. These are more advanced topics and if it's something that you would like to learn more about, there are resources out there for you.

Using the current application as an example, how could we create an entity that is based on multiple tables? The first table that comes to mind is the Machine table, so let's use that for our fictitious entity. Think about what fields or properties you would have in that entity:

- MachineID

- GeneralRole

- InstalledRoles

- Name

- MachineType/Description

- OperatingSystemName

- StillSupported

Because we still need access to them, we also need the ID fields for our joined tables, so we still need OperatingSysID and MachineTypeID. As a good mental exercise, try to implement the new class. Do you need to have interfaces to your existing models in order to get this to work? Can you create a new machine successfully? What about adding a new machine that has a new operating system?

If you get stuck on this, don't worry, as it's a bit more advanced than anything we have looked at so far. Keep at it and you should be able to work through it. I can tell you that you will have a slightly easier time doing it in Entity Framework 6.x than in Entity Framework Core 2.0, so that might be a good place to start. Since EF Core 2.0 is a lightweight version of EF 6.x, there is some functionality that you don't have access to. Sometimes doing something in EF 6.x and reverse-engineering it in EF Core 2.0 is helpful if you get stuck.

Making Changes to the Table

What happens if we have everything created and we need to make a change to the database? As mentioned, we created our SupportTicket and SupportLog tables with date fields instead of using datetime. I think it may be a good idea to change that. But how do you do it?

Take a look at MachineContext.cs and specifically at the code for SupportLog, shown in Listing 5-4.

Listing 5-4. SupportLog in MachineContext.cs

```
modelBuilder.Entity<SupportLog>(entity => {
    entity.Property(e => e.SupportLogId).HasColumnName("SupportLogID");

    entity.Property(e => e.SupportLogEntry)
        .IsRequired()
        .IsUnicode(false);

    entity.Property(e => e.SupportLogEntryDate).HasColumnType("date");

    entity.Property(e => e.SupportLogUpdatedBy)
        .IsRequired()
        .HasMaxLength(50)
        .IsUnicode(false);

    entity.Property(e => e.SupportTicketId).HasColumnName("SupportTicketID");

    entity.HasOne(d => d.SupportTicket)
        .WithMany(p => p.SupportLog)
        .HasForeignKey(d => d.SupportTicketId)
        .OnDelete(DeleteBehavior.ClientSetNull)
        .HasConstraintName("FK_SupportTicket");
});
```

We need to change entity.Property(e => e.SupportLogEntryDate). HasColumnType("date"); to entity.Property(e => e.SupportLogEntryDate). HasColumnType("datetime");. Basically we are changing the type from date to datetime.

Once we have done that, we need to open our pal, the Package Manager console. Go to Tools ➤ NuGet Package Manager ➤ Package Manager Console to do so. From there, type Add-Migration, as shown here.

```
PM> Add-Migration
cmdlet Add-Migration at command pipeline position 1
Supply values for the following parameters:
Name: SupportLogUpdate
```

You could also type this in one line, which would be Add-Migration SupportLogUpdate. After you do this and press Enter, it should begin the scaffolding process and you should get a warning message that says:

```
An operation was scaffolded that may result in the loss of data. Please
review the migration for accuracy.
```

To undo this action, use Remove-Migration.

If you look at the Solution Explorer, you should see a folder that is called Migrations, and in it should be a file that starts off with the date followed by _SupportLogUpdate.cs. My version looks like Listing 5-5, although yours could look a little different. If you get an error telling you that "Add-Migration: the term Add-Migration is not recognized as the name of a cmdlet, function, script file, or operable program," then you probably didn't add the Microsoft.EntityFrameworkCore.Tools package when you set up your application.

Listing 5-5. 20171113193945-SupportLogUpdate.cs

```
using Microsoft.EntityFrameworkCore.Migrations;
using System;
using System.Collections.Generic;

namespace ComputerInventory.Migrations
{
    public partial class SupportLogUpdate : Migration
    {
        protected override void Up(MigrationBuilder migrationBuilder)
        {
            migrationBuilder.AlterColumn<string>(
                name: "IssueDetail",
```

195

```
            table: "SupportTicket",
            type: "varchar(max)",
            unicode: false,
            nullable: false,
            oldClrType: typeof(string),
            oldUnicode: false,
            oldNullable: true);

        migrationBuilder.AlterColumn<DateTime>(
            name: "SupportLogEntryDate",
            table: "SupportLog",
            type: "datetime",
            nullable: false,
            oldClrType: typeof(DateTime),
            oldType: "date");
    }
    protected override void Down(MigrationBuilder migrationBuilder)
    {
        migrationBuilder.AlterColumn<string>(
            name: "IssueDetail",
            table: "SupportTicket",
            unicode: false,
            nullable: true,
            oldClrType: typeof(string),
            oldType: "varchar(max)",
            oldUnicode: false);

        migrationBuilder.AlterColumn<DateTime>(
            name: "SupportLogEntryDate",
            table: "SupportLog",
            type: "date",
            nullable: false,
            oldClrType: typeof(DateTime),
            oldType: "datetime");
    }
}
```

Wait a minute, I thought we were changing from date to date time, but here it says the old type was `DateTime`? That's because there is no "date" data type in the C# language, only `DateTime` and `DateTimeOffset`. Once you are happy that you aren't going to destroy your database, type `Update-Database` and press Enter.

Note   If you aren't sure and you are doing this in a test environment or in production, back it up first!

My results will be slightly different from yours due to the date and time, but you should see something like the following:

```
PM> Update-Database
Applying migration '20171113193945_SupportLogUpdate'.
Done.
```

If you open SQL Server Management Studio and refresh your connection, you should see that the table has been updated (see Figures 5-6 and 5-7).

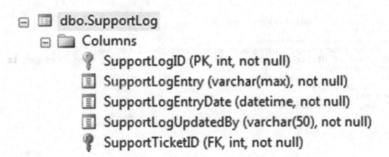

Figure 5-6.   *The table in SQL Server Management Studio*

	SupportLogID	SupportLogEntry	SupportLogEntryDate	SupportLogUpdatedBy	SupportTicketID
1	1	Looks like the keyboard and mouse were unplugge...	2017-11-09 00:00:00.000	Derek	1
2	2	Ticket Created	2017-11-13 00:00:00.000	Derek	2

Figure 5-7.   *New values in the table*

As you would expect, the date portion of the SupportLogEntryDate value hasn't changed and it now has a time portion of 00:00:00.000. If you run the application and want to update ticket number 2, which is Bob Needing Office Installed, you would see something similar to Figures 5-8 and 5-9.

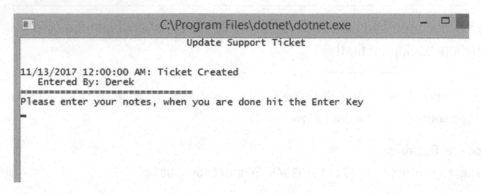

Figure 5-8. *Information displayed in the application*

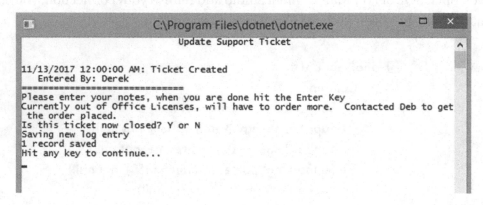

Figure 5-9. *Ticket updated*

Currently, we don't have a way to view our open tickets, so let's take care of that so we can view our changes.

Before we do anything, we are going to make a change to GetNumbersFromConsole() in ConsoleHelper.cs. We need to catch what happens if someone presses the Esc key. Right now, we are looking for positive numbers, so we will make the value -5 if they press Esc. The end of that method should look like the following code, which is the addition of the try/catch block.

```
try {
   rtnVal = Convert.ToInt32(numbers);
}

   catch (System.FormatException) {
      rtnVal = -5;
   }
return rtnVal;
```

You can now add the code to SupportTicketLogEntry.cs. We are going to add two small methods, so I just add them both at one time, as shown in Listing 5-6.

Listing 5-6. Updates to SupportTicketLogEntry.cs

```
public void ViewSupportTickets() {
   Console.Clear();
   cHelper.WriteHeader("Open Support Tickets");
   List<SupportTicket> openTickets = RetreiveOpenTickets();
   foreach(var ticket in openTickets) {
      Console.WriteLine($"Ticket Number: {ticket.SupportTicketId}
      Machine Name: {ticket.Machine.Name}\r\n    Description: {ticket.
      IssueDescription}");
   }
   Console.WriteLine("\r\nPlease Select an Open Support Ticket from the
   List\r\nOtherwise hit the ESC key to exit");
   int ticketId = cHelper.GetNumbersFromConsole();
   if (ticketId > 0) {
      ViewTicketLog(ticketId);
   }
}

public void ViewTicketLog(int supportTicketId) {
   List<SupportLog> logEntries = RetreiveLogEntries(supportTicketId);
   Console.Clear();
   cHelper.WriteHeader("Support Ticket Log");
   foreach(var log in logEntries) {
      Console.WriteLine($"{log.SupportLogEntryDate}: {log.SupportLogEntry}");
      Console.WriteLine($"    Entered By: {log.SupportLogUpdatedBy}");
      Console.WriteLine("==============================");
```

```
   }
   Console.WriteLine("Hit any key to continue...");
   Console.ReadKey();
}
```

Both methods are fairly straightforward. We are going to call ViewSupportTickets() from Program.cs, so we have to add that code. ViewTicketLog() is very similar to the code we wrote before, but this way it's contained in its own method in case we need to use it elsewhere. The biggest change to consider making is the part where we added the break so the user has to press a key to continue. In Program.cs, you just have to change your SupportMenu() method so it looks like the Listing 5-7.

Listing 5-7. Update to SupportMenu()

```
try {
   result = Convert.ToInt16(cki.KeyChar.ToString());
   if (result == 1) {
      CreateSupportTicket();
   }
   else if (result == 2) {
      SupportTicketLogEntry oSupport = new SupportTicketLogEntry();
      oSupport.UpdateSupportTicket();
   }
   else if (result == 3) {
      SupportTicketLogEntry oSupport = new SupportTicketLogEntry();
      oSupport.ViewSupportTickets();
   }
   else if (result == 9) {
      // We are exiting so nothing to do
      cont = true;
   }
}
catch (System.FormatException) {
   // a key that wasn't a number
}
```

If you run the code and choose Option 3 from the Support menu, you should see results similar to Figure 5-10. Your date and timestamps will obviously be different.

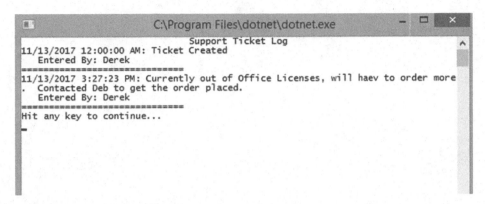

Figure 5-10. *Viewing the support ticket log with the correct date and time*

Summary

This chapter doesn't delve into a lot about database table design, as that would be an entire book to itself. However, I hope that you have a better understanding of what you can do with Entity Framework Core 2.0 when it comes to interacting with your databases and tables. We took a "10,000 foot view" of table and entity design that won't get you any new job or anything, but should at least get you going in the right direction.

We looked at how to create and call stored procedures. Hopefully in a future release, Microsoft will give us more functionality in this department, although if they don't, you at least can handle and work with them. If you are told that you need to call a stored procedure with parameters, you will have something that you can reference to get you started. If you feel you need more practice, go through all of the queries and statements written in this book up to this point and create stored procedures to replace them. That will get you beyond "new guy" status when it comes to working with stored procedures.

We also touched a little bit on SQL Injection and the issues you can run into. If this is something that you need to be concerned with, be sure to do more research on the subject—it could save your job. Remember, data breaches are very expensive. If you can be part of the solution in preventing them, all the better!

Summary

CHAPTER 6

ASP.NET MVC and EF Core 2.0

A good reason to use Entity Framework Core 2.0 is for web development and that is what we are going to look at starting in this chapter. If you have been developing websites or web apps for a while now, you are going to be doing a lot of groaning during this chapter. Since this isn't a book on ASP.NET MVC, we are going to be using the wizards to do a lot of the initial work. However, there is no reason that you can't go back through and recreate the application from scratch for practice, and I highly encourage you to do just that.

We are going to work on a simple MVC application that you can expand on later if you want. We are going to create a web app to keep track of horses, horse shows, and results. If you have no need for this, you can change it to work with just about anything, from soccer games to that newest trading card game.

This isn't a book on creating advanced and truly awesome ASP.NET MVC applications, but you are going to get your feet wet and have a working application by the time you are done. If you want to learn more about it, there are some good books by Apress out there that cover this very topic. However, let's make sure we are all on the same page, as some readers are new to MVC.

MVC stands for Model-View-Controller, which is a design architecture that separates the code into three major areas—the Model, the View, and the Controller. If you are new to programming, this may not mean a lot to you. After the next two chapters, it will make a lot more sense and help you in your future development projects. Up until now we have been talking about entities, since we are dealing with Entity Framework Core 2.0. In MVC, the models are just like the entities we have been working with. Views are used to display information to the user via the user interface. In our new application that we'll be starting shortly, we are going to create a view that displays all the horses we own. It will have some labels and some text boxes, plus a few other controls on the page to display the contents of the database that we get from our model.

© Derek J. Rouleau 2018
D. J. Rouleau, *Beginning Entity Framework Core 2.0*, https://doi.org/10.1007/978-1-4842-3375-7_6

Controllers are the part that took me a bit of time to get my head around, as they handle the user interaction and work with the models, which end up selecting which view is used. The one good thing about MVC applications is they make it easy to set up unit tests to make testing your application much easier. Unit testing is a good thing and something you should do, but people are lazy and sometimes it takes more time to set up the unit test than it does to write the initial code.

Setting Up the Application

We are going to create a new application that we'll be using in this and the following chapter. This time we are going to create an ASP.NET Core web application and call it EquineTracker. Figure 6-1 shows you what it looks like in Visual Studio.

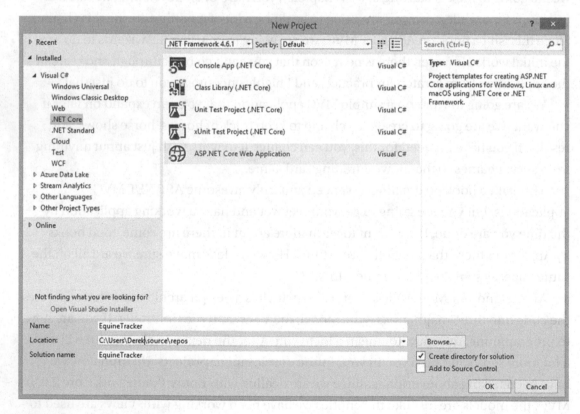

Figure 6-1. Creating a new application

On the next screen, you need to make sure that a couple of things are correct. First make sure that ASP.NET Core 2.0 is selected in the dropdown toward the top. If not, select it. Second, make sure to select Web Application (Model-View-Controller). Lastly, make sure that Authentication is set to No Authentication. Figure 6-2 shows how your selections should look.

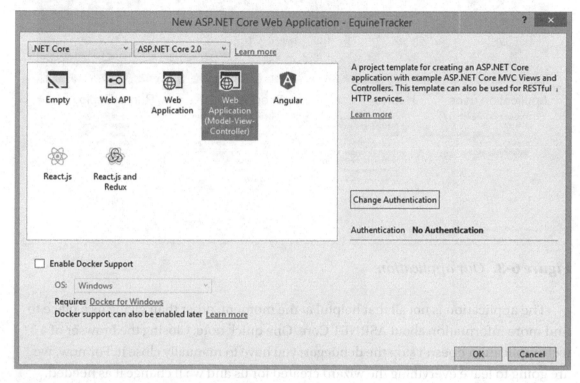

Figure 6-2. *Type of web application*

After you click OK, your application is created and displayed in a window that you can use to learn more about ASP.NET Core. Feel free to click around, as there is helpful information in there. The great part is that we have a working web application that we can run. Press F5 to start the debugger. Depending on how fast your computer is, a web page should appear that looks similar to Figure 6-3.

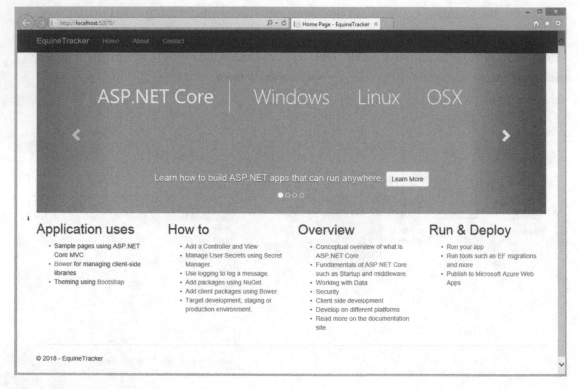

Figure 6-3. *Our application*

The application is not all that helpful at the moment, other than giving us a place to find more information about ASP.NET Core. One quick note: Closing the browser of a web application doesn't stop the debugger; you have to manually close it. For now, we are going to leave everything the wizard created for us and we'll change it as needed.

Now we need to add a couple of NuGet packages to our application just like we did for our console application. Go to the Project menu and select Manage NuGet Packages. This time we'll be adding five packages:

- Microsoft.AspNetCore.Mvc v2.0.0

- Microsoft.AspNetCore.Mvc.Core v2.0.0

- Microsoft.EntityFrameworkCore.SqlServer v2.0.0

- Microsoft.EntityFrameworkCore.Tools v2.0.0

- Microsoft.VisualStudio.Web.CodeGeneration.Design v2.0.0

We have almost everything set up, so we can start making some modifications to our application to make it a bit more useful. A lot of the packages now how a new release (v2.0.1), which should work fine if you choose to use them. If you are using any preview libraries, they will sometimes cause problems with regular libraries and cause errors. If you run into problems, you may need to delete the directory that your NuGet packages are stored in, which is your user directory under .nuget.

Database-First Development

When we created our console application in Chapter 1, we created everything we needed for our database in our code and then we created the database based on our entities. This time, we are going to do the reverse. We are going to connect our application to an existing database. This is called *database-first development*. Appendix A contains the code for creating the database, or you can get it from the website (apress.com).

Once you have created the database, you need to connect to it, which sounds a lot more difficult than it is. The first thing we need to do is open the NuGet Package Manager Console: Tools ➤ NuGet Package Manager ➤ Package Manager Console.

Once you have that open, you need to type the following:

```
Scaffold-DbContext "Server=localhost;Database=BegEFCore; User ID=sa;
Password=*******;" Microsoft.EntityFrameworkCore.SqlServer -OutputDir Models
```

Obviously, your connection string will be different, but the format is Scaffold-DbContext Connection String. Using localhost for the server name will work as long as you are working on the same computer that your database resides. After you press Enter, if you entered everything correctly, you should now have six class files in your Model folder in your application.

Figure 6-4 shows what mine looks like; yours should be similar. We have our DBContext class file, which you should be somewhat familiar with, and then we have the ErrorViewModel.cs file, which we'll talk about later. Then we have four entity classes or, in this case, models. That was less work than when we did it with code, but of course we also don't have quite the level of functionality either. But that's okay, because we can always fix that later.

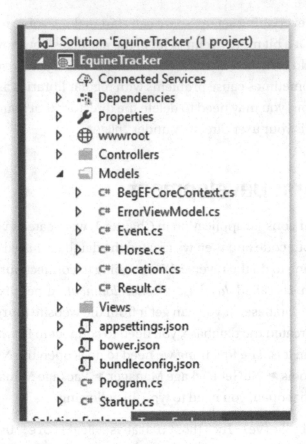

Figure 6-4. Models created by Scaffold-DBContext

The first thing we need to do is fixe a couple of things before we set up our first controller. If you look in BegEFCoreContext.cs, you'll notice that there is a warning in there and that is where we are going to start. The message is somewhat helpful and, if you want, you can follow the link or you can do the following.

What we are going to do is move the code from OnConfiguring and BegEFCoreContext.cs to Startup.cs, although if we were to follow best practices, we would put this into a configuration file. For simplicity's sake, we'll use this method. I do this part a little backwards than some, as I set up Startup.cs and then I remove the code from (in this case) BegEFCoreContext.cs.

Let's do that right now. If it's not already open, open Startup.cs and add the following using statements:

- using EquineTracker.Models;

- using Microsoft.EntityFrameworkCore;

We then need to make the changes to ConfigurationServices() shown in Listing 6-1.

Listing 6-1. Updates to ConfigurationServices()

```
// This method gets called by the runtime. Use this method to add services
to the container.
public void ConfigureServices(IServiceCollection services){
    services.AddMvc();

    var connection = @"Server=localhost;Database=BegEFCore;User
ID=sa;Password=******;";
    services.AddDbContext<BegEFCoreContext>(options =>
options.UseSqlServer(connection));
}
```

Go back to BegEFCoreContext.cs and remove the OnConfiguring() method. We are going to add the constructor in Listing 6-2. You could also comment out the code if you want, but you really should delete it.

Listing 6-2. Adding a Constructor to the DBContext Class

```
public BegEFCoreContext(DbContextOptions<BegEFCoreContext> options) :
base(options) {
}
```

This allows you to use dependency injection. If you are new to ASP.NET Core or MVC, you should become familiar with it, as it's one of the core concepts of ASP.NET Core.

Creating Controllers and Views

We are now ready to create our first controller. We are going to use the wizards to do the work for us since we aren't as concerned with the ASP.NET aspect of the application and it will give us something to look at a lot faster. I find that Visual Studio can sometimes be a bit picky, so the first thing I do is click on the Controllers folder. Right-click on the Controllers folder, choose Add, and then Controller. When the Add Controller window opens, choose MVC Controller with views, using Entity Framework. Figure 6-5 shows you what you should select from the Add Controller window.

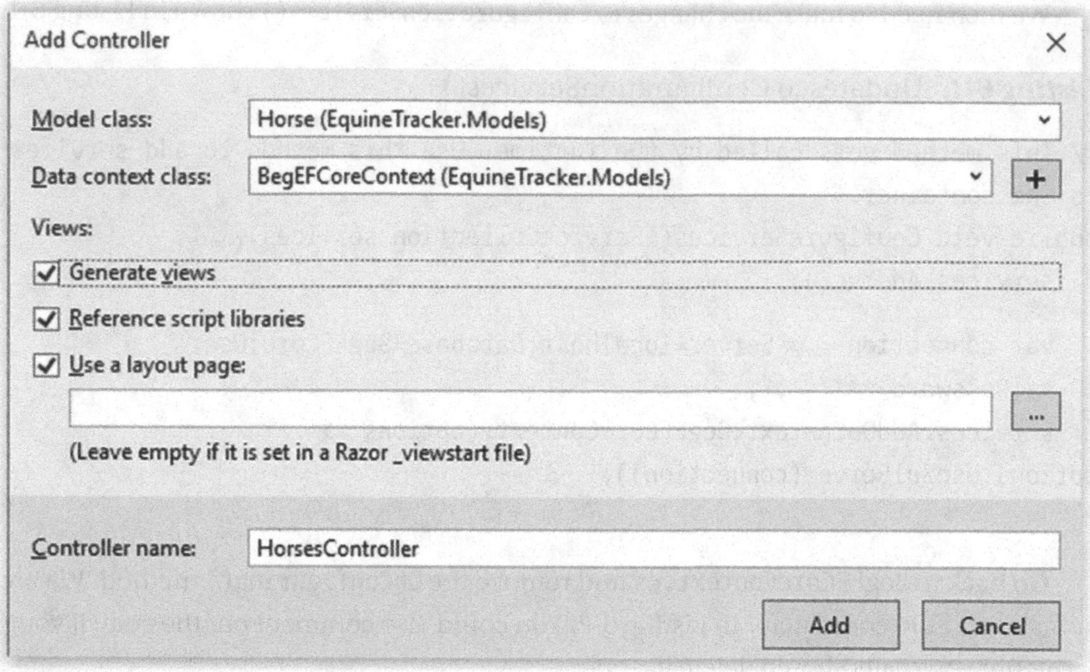

Figure 6-5. *Filling in the Add Controller form*

You can leave the layout page field blank, but make sure that you have all the checkboxes checked. After you click Add, it will create the HorsesController, as well as some View files. Figure 6-6 shows you the files created by Visual Studio.

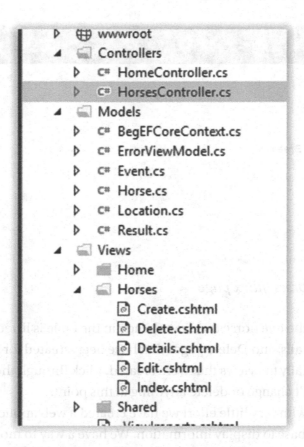

Figure 6-6. *Files created when we create the controller*

Let's take a look at our page first and then we'll take a look at the new files. Since we haven't created any navigation to get to our pages yet we'll have to do some typing to get there but nothing that we can't handle. Press the F5 key to start debugging the project. After your page loads, add /horses to the URL. In my case, it is http:// localhost:60101/horses, although your port number could be different. Once the page loads, you should see results like in Figure 6-7.

Figure 6-7. *The horses Index page*

As you can see, the one horse that was already in the table is listed and it gives us links to the Edit, Details, and Delete pages that have been created for us. Recall that those pages are actually the views that were created. Click through the different pages; just be sure you don't change or delete anything at this point.

As you can see, with very little effort we have created a web application and connected to a database to display information. We have a way to modify, delete, and create new entries in that database. Next we need to create controllers for the other models. Follow the previous directions to create controllers for the Event model.

After it finishes the scaffolding, you may notice that you have a couple of errors that you need to take care of. The first thing you need to do is fix the code that looks like @ => @.Location. We are going to change all of these to x => x.Location. After you make those changes, all of the errors should go away.

Once that is done, create the Location controller and then the Result controller. You shouldn't get any errors or warnings when you create these two controllers. If we had our home page and index working, we could use this web application as is and have it work relatively well. However, that would be a bit boring and as you add more information it would be a bit difficult to navigate the information as well. Some other error handling would need to be added, as there are currently places that will throw errors if you try to do certain actions. After we take care of some basic formatting and some general housekeeping, we'll get to the error handling.

Formatting Output

The first thing we need to do is to make one fix. The height of the horse is 15.10 but it should be 15.1. The good thing is we only need to change it once in order to fix it everywhere. Open the Horse model, Horse.cs, and make changes so it looks like Listing 6-3.

Listing 6-3. Horse.cs

```
using System;
using System.Collections.Generic;
using System.ComponentModel.DataAnnotations;
namespace EquineTracker.Models {
    public partial class Horse {
        public Horse() {
            Result = new HashSet<Result>();
        }

        public int HorseId { get; set; }
        public string Name { get; set; }
        public string Breed { get; set; }
        [DisplayFormat(DataFormatString = "{0:N1}", ApplyFormatInEditMode = true)]
        public decimal? Height { get; set; }
        [DisplayFormat(DataFormatString = "{0:C}")]
        public decimal? Value { get; set; }

        public ICollection<Result> Result { get; set; }
    }
}
```

The changes are in bold. We have added a using statement and the DisplayFormat lines. We need the using statement in order to reference the DisplayFormat attributes. The DisplayFormat attribute displays the height with one decimal place, which is what we want. Then we formatted the value to display as currency. The MVC approach would have up put this at the view level, but since the data should always have just one decimal and it should always be currency, I think it makes more sense to do it at the model level.

One thing to keep in mind when you are doing something like this is the maintainability of the code. A lot of developers will look to the View for this kind of thing. You could always put a note/comment in your view to mention the location of the formatting if you want to make it easier to find it later. To me, it comes down to having to make only one change, which will make my life easier when it comes time to maintaining my applications in the future. The important point to take away from this is you can do any kind of formatting; it doesn't have to be decimals and currency.

Page Navigation

Now that we have taken care of some of the basics, let's take care of some housekeeping to make things a little bit neater before we continue to error handling.

The first thing we'll do is update the navigation so we can get to the right pages. Since we are using a layout, we only need to do our navigation once and the changes will propagated to all of the pages since they all use the same layout. To adjust the Navigation bar, you open _Layout.cshtml. Listing 6-4 shows the portion of _Layout.cshtml that we are going to modify in order to update the navigation.

Listing 6-4. _Layout.cshtml

```
<nav class="navbar navbar-inverse navbar-fixed-top">
   <div class="container">
      <div class="navbar-header">
         <button type="button" class="navbar-toggle" data-toggle="collapse"
         data-target=".navbar-collapse">
            <span class="sr-only">Toggle navigation</span>
            <span class="icon-bar"></span>
            <span class="icon-bar"></span>
            <span class="icon-bar"></span>
            <span class="icon-bar"></span>
            <span class="icon-bar"></span>
            <span class="icon-bar"></span>
            <span class="icon-bar"></span>
         </button>
         <a asp-area="" asp-controller="Home" asp-action="Index"
         class="navbar-brand">EquineTracker</a>
      </div>
```

```
    <div class="navbar-collapse collapse">
        <ul class="nav navbar-nav">
        <li><a asp-area="" asp-controller="Home" asp-
        action="Index">Home</a></li>
        <li><a asp-area="" asp-controller="Horses" asp-
        action="Index">Horses</a></li>
        <li><a asp-area="" asp-controller="Events" asp-
        action="Index">Events</a></li>
        <li><a asp-area="" asp-controller="Results" asp-
        action="Index">Results</a></li>
        <li><a asp-area="" asp-controller="Locations" asp-
        action="Index">Locations</a></li>
        <li><a asp-area="" asp-controller="Home" asp-
        action="About">About</a></li>
        <li><a asp-area="" asp-controller="Home" asp-
        action="Contact">Contact</a></li>
        </ul>
    </div>
    </div>
</nav>
```

The good news is you can copy and paste most of this and then make the changes
you need. In the `<ul class="nav navbar-nav">` section, we are going to add four
`<li>` items. The formatting for these lines is as follows: `<li><a asp-area="" asp-`
`controller="`*Name Of The Controller*`" asp-action="`*View Name*`">`*Text To*
Display`</a></li>`. Because we have decided to show the Index view for each of the
controllers, they all have an `asp-action="Index"` line.

As you can see, we have left the About and Contact items in there so you can get
a better understanding of how they work. As you can see, they both use the Home
controller. When you look in the Home View folder, you'll see that there are three views—
Index, About and Contact. Now when we run our application, the Navigation bar should
be a bit more useful, as seen in Figure 6-8.

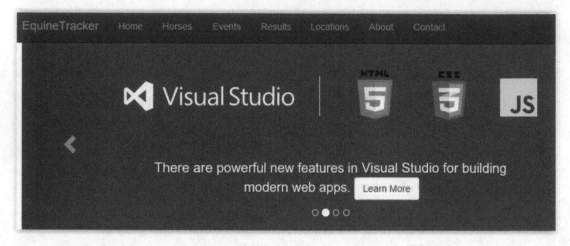

Figure 6-8. *Working navigation*

The Home Page and Adding an Image

Now that the navigation is working, let's clean up the Index page, as I'm pretty sure anyone that is going to want to use this application really doesn't care about all this Visual Studio and ASP.NET Stuff that is currently on it. If you want to take a lot of time to make the page pretty, have at it. We are simply going to put a picture on the page and call it good. Listing 6-5 shows the code for the Home controllers Index page.

Listing 6-5. Index.cshtml in Views ➤ Home

```
@{
    ViewData["Title"] = "Home Page";
}

<div class="body-content">
    <img class="center-block" src="~/images/photo1.jpg" />
</div>
```

In order for this to work, you need a photo. You can download the one from the website where you get the code and examples for this book, or you can use one you have. The key is that you have to put the image in the images folder within the wwwroot folder. Figure 6-9 shows the full path. To easily access it, right-click on the folder and choose Open Folder in File Explorer.

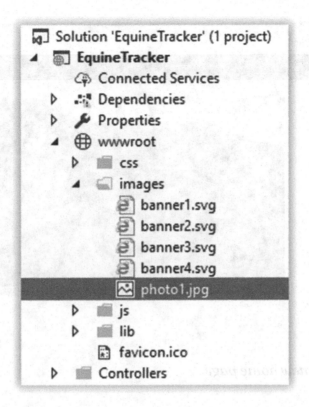

Figure 6-9. *Images folder with the photo in it*

You can run the application again. It looks like something that's related to a horse application, as shown in Figure 6-10.

Figure 6-10.   *Our new home page*

Error Handling

Now that we have our page looking a little bit better, let's take care of a couple of errors. If you have tried to delete the one location that we have created in the database, even though I told you not to, then you have probably already seen the error that we are going to fix. If not, Figure 6-11 shows the error.

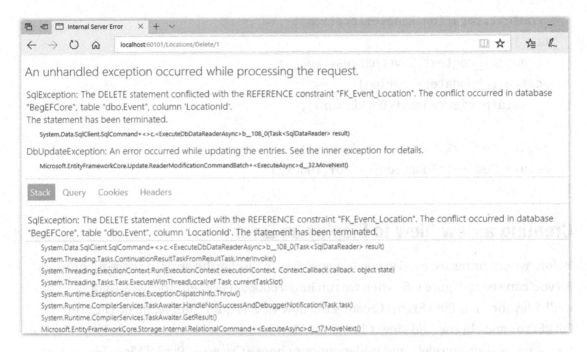

Figure 6-11. *Error when trying to delete a location*

The good news is we have seen this before when we created our console application and tried to delete a record that was referenced by another. The other good news is we really don't have to do a ton here to get some relatively useful functionality out of our application. We are going to add a simple `try catch` block and if that section of code is reached, we are going to display a hardcoded error message to the users explaining that they can't delete the record, as it is being used by one or more events. You could create a dynamic error page, but the experts recommend using a static page, so that is what we are going to do here. Listing 6-6 shows the updated code for handling the error in `LocationsController.cs`.

Listing 6-6. Updated Code to Handle an Error When Deleting a Foreign Key Record

```
// POST: Locations/Delete/5
[HttpPost, ActionName("Delete")]
[ValidateAntiForgeryToken]
public async Task<IActionResult> DeleteConfirmed(int id) {
    var location = await _context.Location.SingleOrDefaultAsync(m =>
    m.LocationId == id);
```

```
    _context.Location.Remove(location);
    try {
        await _context.SaveChangesAsync();
    }catch (DbUpdateException) {
        return View(nameof(DbFkError));
    }
    await _context.SaveChangesAsync();
    return RedirectToAction(nameof(Index));
}
```

Creating a New View to Display an Error

Before we continue, we need to create a new view to display the error message to the users. As you can see in Figure 6-6, when we run into a DbUpdateException we are going to display the view DbFkError. Creating the new view is quite simple. Right-click on DbFkError and choose Add View. Change the View Name to DbFkError, choose Empty for the template (without model), and under options choose Create as Partial View. Figure 6-12 shows what it should look like. Once you are done, click Add to create your new view.

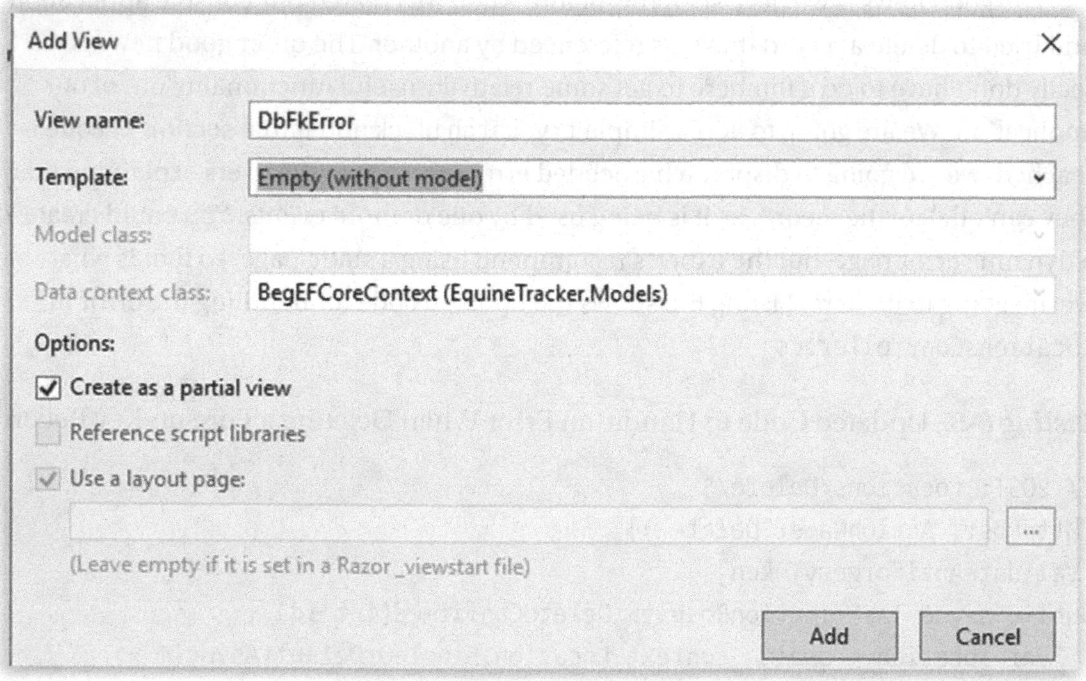

Figure 6-12. *Creating a new view for the error*

Note   Depending on your version of Visual Studio, this may cause an error. If it does, comment out the line `return View(nameof(DbFkError));` and right-click on the Locations folder under Views and add a new View that way. Once you're done, uncomment the line.

Once the view is created, you'll have an empty view that can be modified in any way you see fit. Listing 6-7 shows the contents of `DbFkError.cshtml`.

Listing 6-7. DbFkError.cshtml

```
@{
    ViewData["Title"] = "Error";
}
<h3>Sorry but you are unable to delete the record as it is needed for one
or more events!</h3>
```

If you are still getting an error that `DbFkError` doesn't exist, you need to add one more bit of code to your Locations controller, as shown in Listing 6-7a.

Listing 6-7a. Modifying LocationsController.cs

```
Public LocationsController(BegEFCoreContext context){
    _context = context;
}

Public ViewResult DbFkError(){
    Return View();
}
```

As you can see, you should have a `ViewResult` method for `DbFkError` and if you don't, you won't be able to use it. If the error is gone, fire up the application and try to delete that record again. Figure 6-13 shows you the new result instead of the not-so-nice error message.

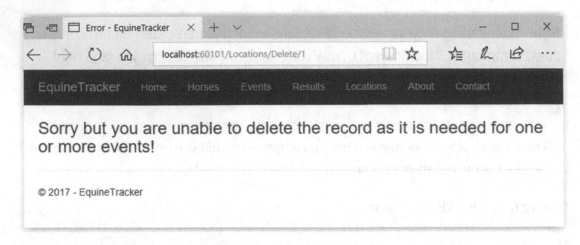

Figure 6-13. *The new error page*

As you can see, this is a better, more helpful message to show the users. We could do a much better job of this than waiting for an error to happen, since we technically don't know what the error is. We simply assumed that the error was caused by trying to delete a record that was associated with another record. In your application, this could be fine and I'll leave that up to you. The next section covers at another way we could handle this problem.

Avoiding Errors

One of the best ways to handle errors is to not hit the error condition in the first place. Obviously, we can't think of every condition that we might hit, but we can try to be as proactive as possible. If you work for a larger company, there is probably a group of people who do this. However, if work for a small company or are working for yourself, you are the group. The downside to doing this yourself is that you are more than likely not going to think of all the problems until you have been doing this a while. But that's okay; that is where general error handling comes in to play, like we just did, although you'd probably want to phrase the wording on your page a bit better.

The first thing we need to do is find out if the location we are trying to delete is needed for any events. The question is, what are we trying to do here? When it comes down to it, we are trying to retrieve a list of events where the location is used, so our code for the retrieval of the list would go into the `EventController.cs` file. Let's open that file and create a new method for retrieving a list of events by `LocationId`.

Listing 6-8 shows the code that we'll be using to retrieve our list. Right now, it's not being returned to a view but that could be changed easily enough.

Listing 6-8. GetEventsByLocation()

```
// "Get" Events by LocationId
public List<Event> GetEventsByLocation(int locationId) {
    List<Event> lEvent = _context.Event.Include(x => x.Location).Where(l =>
    l.LocationId == locationId).ToList();
    return lEvent;
}
```

We don't need to have the include in there but since we might want to display events based on LocationId in the future, why not include it when we first create it? I put "get" in double quotes here, as it's not a true Get statement in the context of ASP.NET. Now we can update the code in LocationsController.cs to capture this condition. Listing 6-9 shows the updated method.

Listing 6-9. Update to Public Async Task<IActionResult> DeleteConfirmed(int id)

```
// POST: Locations/Delete/5
[HttpPost, ActionName("Delete")]
[ValidateAntiForgeryToken]
public async Task<IActionResult> DeleteConfirmed(int id) {
    EventsController ec = new EventsController(_context);
    List<Event> lEvent = ec.GetEventsByLocation(id);
    if(lEvent.Count != 0) {
        return View(nameof(DbFkError));
    }

    var location = await _context.Location.SingleOrDefaultAsync(m =>
    m.LocationId == id);
    _context.Location.Remove(location);
    try {
        await _context.SaveChangesAsync();
    }catch (DbUpdateException) {
        return View(nameof(DbFkError));
    }
    await _context.SaveChangesAsync();
    return RedirectToAction(nameof(Index));
}
```

If you run the application now and try to delete the record, you'll see the same page. However, if you were to put in a breakpoint, you would find that it never tries to delete the record in the first place. This is the method I would use for this situation, as to me it makes more sense compared to letting it try to delete the record and failing. If this was a book on ASP.NET MVC I'd probably get tricky here and display a new page that shows the user the events that the location is currently associated with. This would be good practice for you to do that, and if you don't know how to do it already, it will give you something else you can work on to improve your skills.

Displaying Events by Location

You didn't think we were going to create a way to get a list of events by location and not use it now did you? This process is a bit tricky if you are new to web programming with ASP.NET and/or MVC. The method used here is the one that I know. However, there are other ways to do it and I encourage you to take the time to find them and work them out. The first part of this is going to be the same as before, since the first step is to create our view. So, let's get started. If you don't have EventsController.cs open, open it and add the code shown in Listing 6-10.

Listing 6-10. EventController.cs

```
// GET: Events by LocationID
public ViewResult EventByLocation(int locationId) {
    List<Event> lEvent = GetEventsByLocation(locationId);
    return View(lEvent);
}
```

Nothing too out of the ordinary here. We get our list of events and we pass the list as an argument to our view. Like before, right-click on EventByLocation and choose Add View. This time, we aren't going to create an empty view; we are going to create a "list" so we are going to choose that as the template. Once you have done that, choose Event (EquineTracker.Models) as the Model class. Figure 6-14 shows the wizard window. Once you are done, click Add to create the new view.

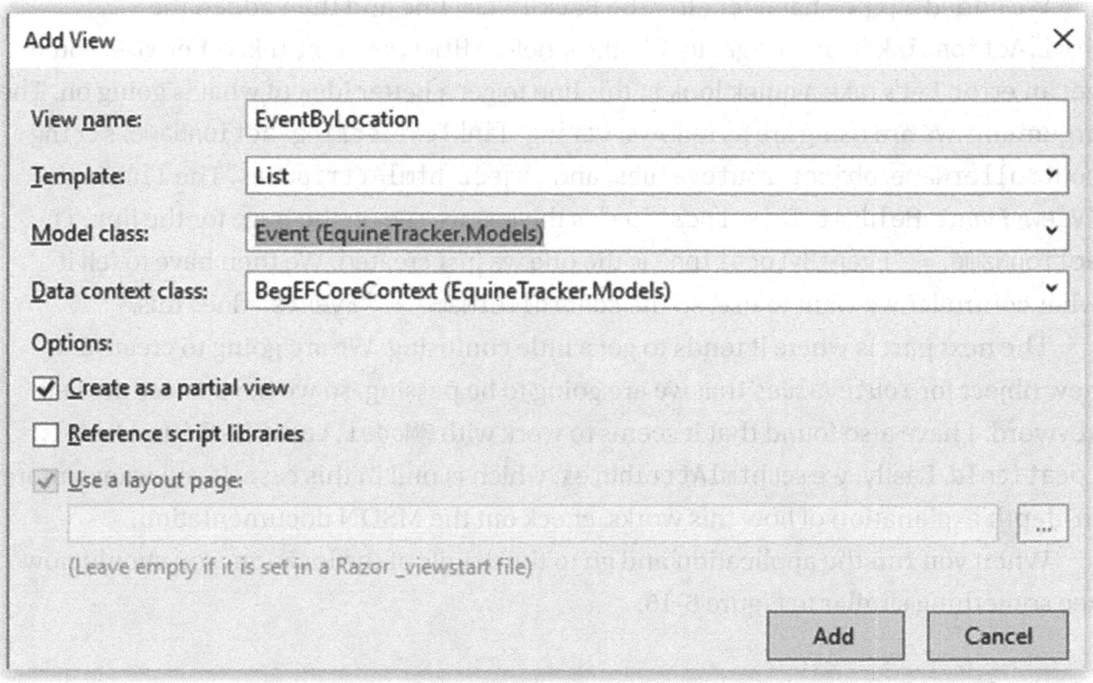

Add View   ✕

View name: EventByLocation

Template: List   ▾

Model class: Event (EquineTracker.Models)   ▾

Data context class: BegEFCoreContext (EquineTracker.Models)   ▾

Options:

☑ Create as a partial view

☐ Reference script libraries

☑ Use a layout page:

[   ] [...]

(Leave empty if it is set in a Razor _viewstart file)

                                              [Add]   [Cancel]

Figure 6-14. *Creating our EventByLocation view*

That was the easy part to figure out if this is new. Now comes the relatively difficult part, or at least it is the first time you do it. For now we'll put the "link" to this in the Details view for the location. Open `Details.cshtml` in the Locations View folder and make the change at the bottom of the page, as shown in Listing 6-11.

Listing 6-11. Changes to Details.cshtml

```
<div>
    <a asp-action="Edit" asp-route-id="@Model.LocationId">Edit</a> |
    <a asp-action="Index">Back to List</a> |
    @Html.ActionLink("View Events Held At This Location", "EventByLocation",
    "Events", new { @LocationId = @Model.LocationId }, null)
</div>
```

We added a pipe character after the Back To List line and then added the `Html.ActionLink`. Don't forget to add the @ before `Html.ActionLink`; otherwise, you'll get an error. Let's take a quick look at this line to get a better idea of what is going on. The arguments we are using are as follows: `string linkText`, `string actionName`, `string controllerName`, `object routeValues`, and `object htmlAttributes`. The `linkText = "View Event Held At This Location"` is the text we see on the page for the link. The `actionName = "EventByLocation"` is the one we just created. We then have to tell it what controller we want to use, so the `controllerName = "Events"` does this.

The next part is where it tends to get a little confusing. We are going to create a new object for `routeValues` that we are going to be passing, so we have to use the new keyword. I have also found that it seems to work with `@Model.LocationId` and `Model.LocationId`. Lastly, we set `htmlAttributes`, which is null in this case. If you want a more in-depth explanation of how this works, check out the MSDN documentation.

When you run the application and go to the details of the location, you should now see something similar to Figure 6-15.

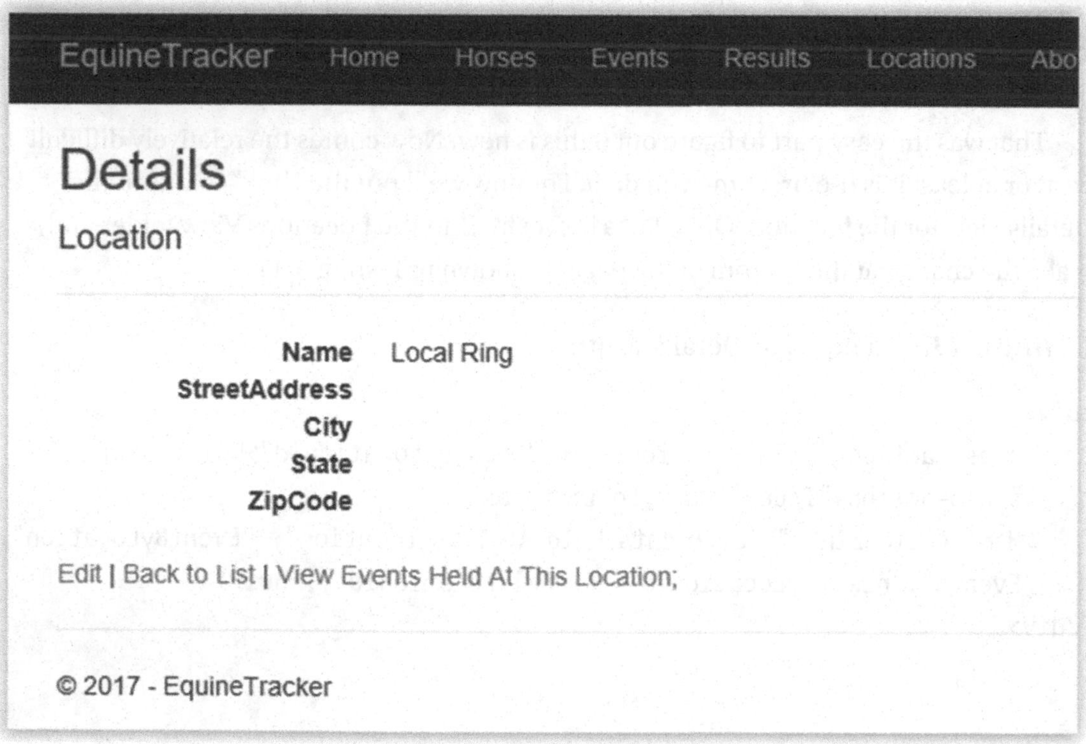

Figure 6-15. *The new Details page for locations*

Figure 6-16 shows you the new page.

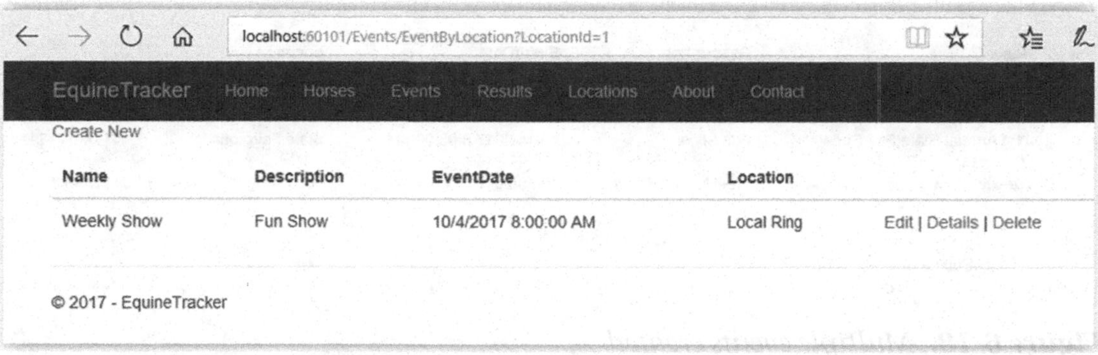

Figure 6-16. *Events by location*

That looks exactly like the Events Index page, since we only have the one show. Now we'll fix that so we can see the difference.

Figure 6-17 shows the locations I added. Feel free to add anything you want here, but add two or three more locations than the initial entry we created.

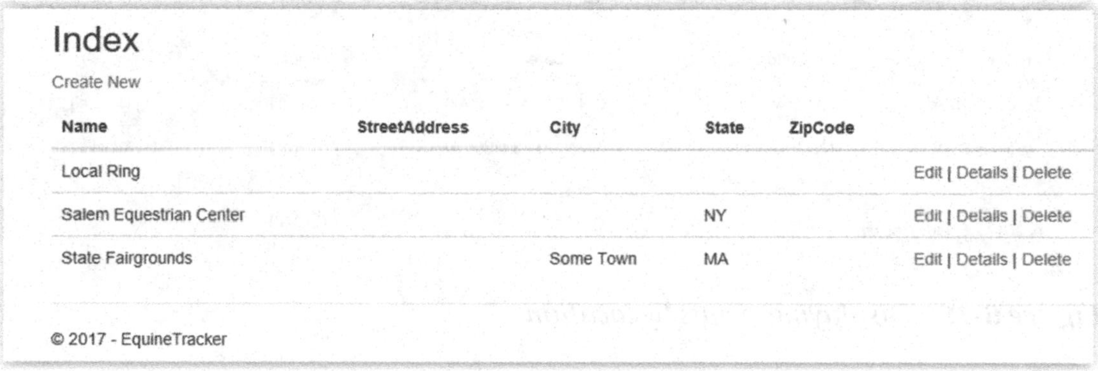

Figure 6-17. *Index of locations*

Now we'll create a couple more events so we can get a better idea of how displaying events by location works, and to prove that it's working. Again, just make sure you create a couple of events in different locations (see Figure 6-18).

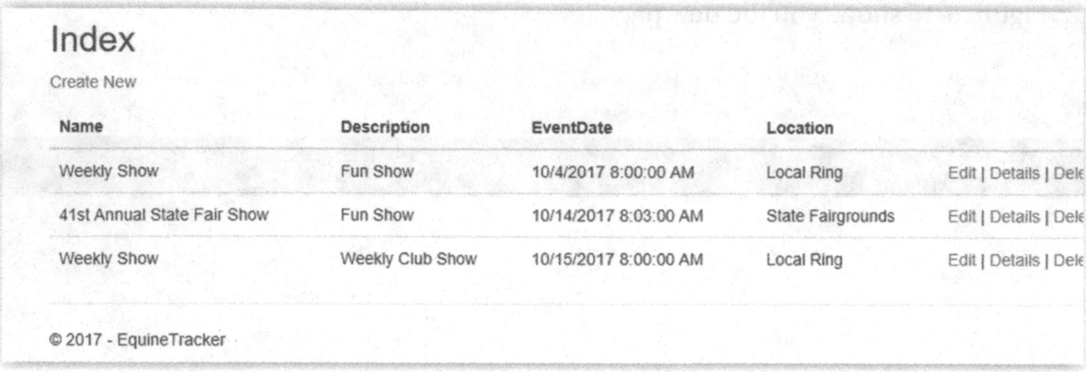

Figure 6-18. *Multiple events created*

Now that we have multiple locations and events, we can verify whether we are seeing the correct data when we try to view the events by location. Figure 6-19 shows that it is working.

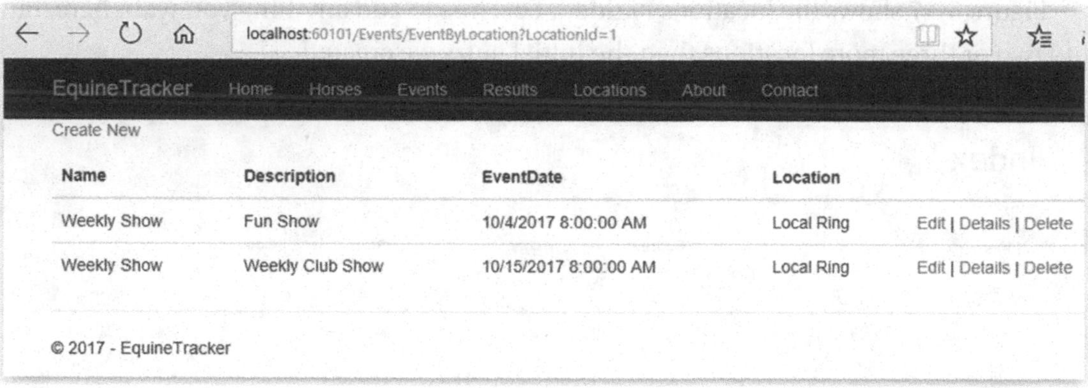

Figure 6-19. *Displaying events by location*

As you can see, it did in fact work, as we are only seeing the two results for that one location. Hopefully, this will give you some ideas as to how you could use this in existing or future projects.

Sorting Results

This section shows you how to display the events in a user-friendly manner. To do this, we'll add a couple more events in random order. For example, create more weekly shows and enter the dates out of order. Figure 6-20 shows the current view with more data entered in random order.

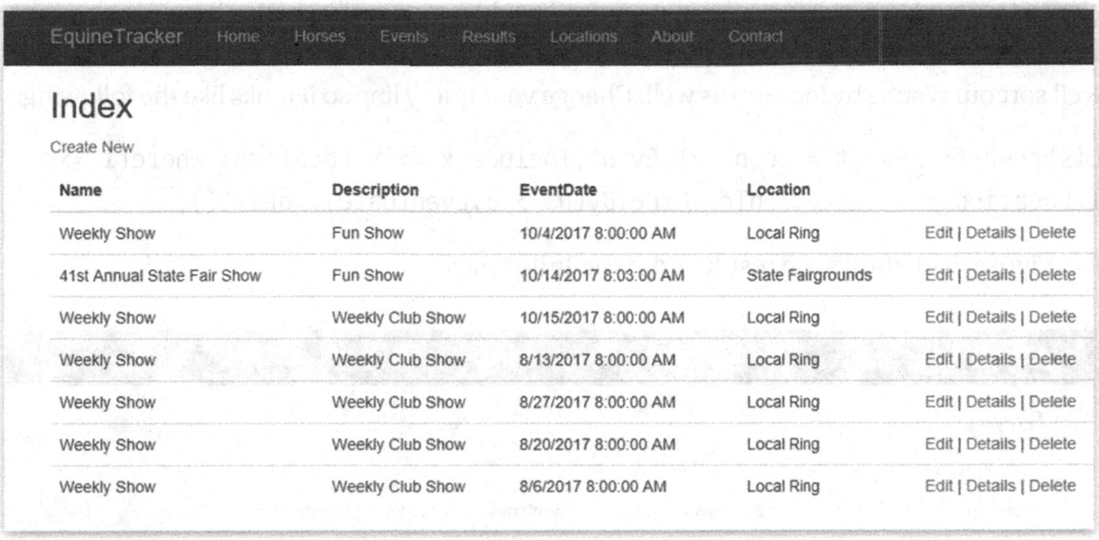

Figure 6-20. *Displaying unsorted results*

As you can see, we entered a couple more results. To determine if there is a show on August 6 is difficult. Imagine if you had 40 or 50 shows listed in some random order by date. We are going to take care of that so it's not a problem. Open EventsController.cs. Without looking at Listing 6-12 first, try to figure how you can achieve the results you want. Remember that you are attempting to sort the results of the Index page for events by the event date.

Listing 6-12. Changes to EventsController.cs.

```
// GET: Events
public async Task<IActionResult> Index() {
    var begEFCoreContext = _context.Event.Include(x => x.Location).OrderBy
    (m => m.EventDate);
    return View(await begEFCoreContext.ToListAsync());
}
```

Were you able to come up with the code shown in Listing 6-12, or something similar? I decided to use .OrderBy to achieve my ordered list. I order by EventDate and I'm done.

Now if I wanted to sort it in descending order, I could just as easily change it to
`.OrderByDescending(m => m.EventDate)`. Since we have done it in the index, we might as
well sort our results by location as well. Change your query line so it looks like the following:

```
List<Event> lEvent = _context.Event.Include(x => x.Location).Where(l =>
l.LocationId == locationId).OrderBy(d => d.EventDate).ToList();
```

Figure 6-21 shows the results from the Index page.

Name	Description	EventDate	Location	
Weekly Show	Weekly Club Show	8/6/2017 8:00:00 AM	Local Ring	Edit | Details | Delete
Weekly Show	Weekly Club Show	8/13/2017 8:00:00 AM	Local Ring	Edit | Details | Delete
Weekly Show	Weekly Club Show	8/20/2017 8:00:00 AM	Local Ring	Edit | Details | Delete
Weekly Show	Weekly Club Show	8/27/2017 8:00:00 AM	Local Ring	Edit | Details | Delete
Weekly Show	Fun Show	10/4/2017 8:00:00 AM	Local Ring	Edit | Details | Delete
41st Annual State Fair Show	Fun Show	10/14/2017 8:03:00 AM	State Fairgrounds	Edit | Details | Delete
Weekly Show	Weekly Club Show	10/15/2017 8:00:00 AM	Local Ring	Edit | Details | Delete

Figure 6-21. *Sorted results*

As you can see, sorting this way makes it easier to find certain shows. The next
chapter covers some more ways of getting the information to the user that may be a little
more useful as this application grows year to year.

ASP.NET MVC Basics

Now that the application has basic functionality and you can fix some of the common
issues, it's time to make the application look a little better. If you look at Figure 6-21, note
that the name of the page is Index. Although that may not bother you, the person using
it might have a different opinion. The good news is it's a simple fix, so let's take care of
it. Since we are talking about Figure 6-21, we'll start with that view. If you don't already
have it open, open `Index.cshtml` from within the Events View folder. Listing 6-13 shows
the code for the first couple of lines that you should see in the file.

Listing 6-13. Index.cshtml (Event)

```
@model IEnumerable<EquineTracker.Models.Event>

@{
    ViewData["Title"] = "Index";
}

<h2>Index</h2>

<p>
    <a asp-action="Create">Create New</a>
</p>
```

We will cover the first line in a moment, but the two lines we are concerned with right now are the ViewData and the <h2>Index</h2> lines. This is where we set the title for the page as well as the label in the browser. If we change Index in both places to Events, the program will make the appropriate changes when we re-launch the browser. Figure 6-22 shows you these changes.

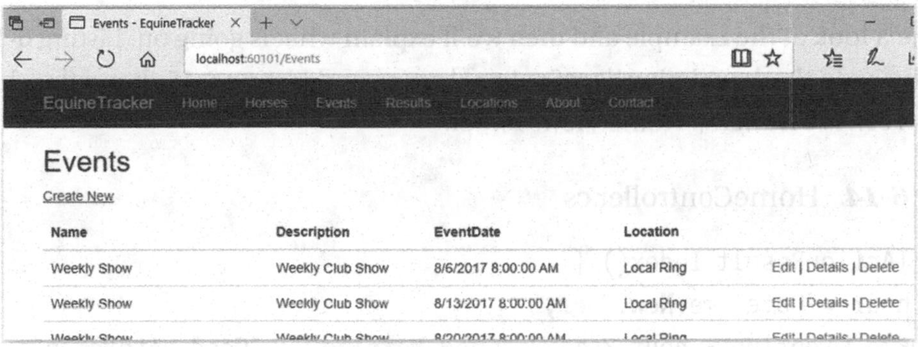

Figure 6-22. *Changes to the Title and Label for the page*

Now you can go to your other views and make similar changes. I will leave it up to you. You don't have to make these changes, but a little practice isn't a bad thing. Don't forget to make the changes to EventByLocation.cshtml as well.

Strongly Typed Views

Look back at Listing 6-13, where the first line is @model IEnumerable<EquineTracker. Models.Event>. This tells us that we have a strongly typed view. What does that mean? We use strongly typed views to render a specific domain type, which in this case is the Events model. Since we want to know about multiple events, we use an IEnumerable. If you look in Details.cshtml in our Events views, you will see that the line is different. It is: @model EquineTracker.Models.Event. That is because we are only working with a single event, so we don't need a list of events. If you look back at Figure 6-14, you will see that we created a strongly typed view when we created EventByLocation.cshtml. We told the wizard that we wanted to use the Event model and that we wanted to use the List template.

Does this mean that you must have all strongly typed views? No, you can create views that aren't strongly typed. Had we not specified a model in Figure 6-14, we would not have had a strongly typed view. So what would something like this look like? The Index page in the Home view is a great example.

Passing Data to a View Using ViewBag

Let's take a look at the example and then we'll explain what is going on. Listing 6-14 shows the code that's updating HomeController.cs and Listing 6-15 shows the changes to Index.cshtml from the Home Views folder.

Listing 6-14. HomeController.cs

```
public IActionResult Index() {
    int hour = DateTime.Now.Hour;
    ViewBag.Greeting = hour < 12 ? "Good Morning" : "Good afternoon";
    return View();
}
```

We added a variable to track the hour of the day and then we created our ViewBag object called Greeting. A ViewBag is a dynamic object that you can assign any value to and pass it along to a view. We are going to add a greeting to the top of the home page and we'll change it based on the time. Listing 6-15 shows how it's used in the view.

Listing 6-15. Index.cshtml

```
@{
    ViewData["Title"] = "Equine Tracker Home Page";
}
<html>
<body>
    <div class="page-header">
        <h3>@ViewBag.Greeting, Welcome To Equine Tracker!</h3>
    </div>
    <div class="body-content">
        <img class="center-block" src="~/images/photo1.jpg" />
    </div>
</body>
</html>
```

As you can see, we added a few lines to our view. If you are new to web programming, this could take a little bit to get used to. We have our ViewBag object right around the middle of our code. What may look strange to Web Form programmers is the comma right after the object. Under the covers, the compiler knows that we want to render the page to read (if it's before noon) "Good Morning, Welcome To Equine Tracker!". If you run the code, you should see a page that looks like Figure 6-23.

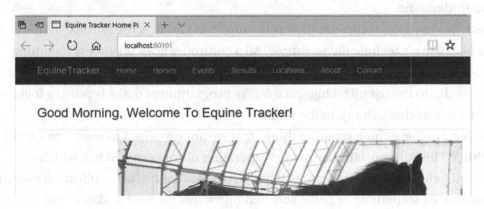

Figure 6-23. *The home page when viewed before noon*

Why Use MVC?

So why take all this time to create models, views, and controllers when you could just get your application up and running in half the time by creating a Smart UI? I'm sure everyone reading this book has created one or more Smart UI applications and perhaps that is all you have ever done. I'm not going to tell you that you should never create a Smart UI application, as I just created a new one the other day. We have a legacy system that can't talk to a new one that we implemented recently so we created an application to be able to modify some data when needed. It's a simple form with a couple of labels, text boxes, and an Enter button. I could have created a couple of class files or I could just put everything in the form code. Since the entire project was under 100 lines I went with everything in the form.

Now if this were an application with several forms and tens of thousands of lines of code, it would obviously make more sense to use something more along the lines of a MVC Pattern application.

We have talked about this briefly before but let's look at it again. What are we talking about when we say model? The model is the data that the user is working with. They can be view models that we use to move data between the views and the controllers. In larger applications, you need to learn more about domain models, which are beyond the scope of this book.

When we talk about views, we are talking about what we are using to render some aspect of the model to the user through a user interface. For example, we created a view to display events only for specific locations. I think the view is probably the easiest of the three to understand.

Lastly we have the controller. This is the one that I think is the hardest to understand, mainly because it's technically so simple. All a controller does is process incoming requests, perform some sort of action on the model if needed, and then decide which view to render to the user. The biggest mistake programmers make is putting logic into the controller, as that belongs in the model.

So we have these three separate things that we are supposed to use to do specific operations. This is important because of separation of concerns (SOC), which we mentioned before, and maintenance. If you have to go back to an application months or years later to fix something or make some changes, this method makes it easier.

If you have a properly set up application and stick to the pattern, it should be easier to fix and maintain down the line. If we do have to make changes, it's more likely that you will only have to make a change in one place.

The other thing that MVC helps you do is unit test. The ASP.NET MVC Framework lends itself well to unit testing and it's something that you really should do.

In the next chapter, we set up a unit test to illustrate the benefits of doing them. Some people complain that setting up these tests takes longer than writing the code. Writing good unit tests does take practice. While it's true that some unit tests I have written took about four times the amount of code than I was actually testing, it still helped me make sure things were working properly, especially compared to testing against a live or semi-live database.

Summary

Although we really didn't do a lot in the way of Entity Framework Code in this chapter, by now you should be comfortable with the everyday aspects of Entity Framework Core. I hope you were able to anticipate the changes we made to our Entity Framework Core code before you read the examples. If not, don't worry. It can take a while to learn something new.

We covered database first development and how to connect to an existing database in an application. You should be able to work with models and controllers as well as modify and create views in an ASP.NET MVC application. You also learned about strongly typed views and how to create and work with them.

You should be able to do some page-to-page navigation and be able to pass data dynamically to a view. The passing of data to views will be very helpful in the future, so if you still aren't sure how to do it, you may want to pick up a book on MVC programming.

The next chapter covers more Entity Framework Core programming as well as ASP.NET MVC programming to make your applications better.

CHAPTER 7

Finishing Our ASP.NET MVC .NET Core 2.0 Project

Now that we have a basic application, let's make it a bit more functional for the end users. Right now we have five controllers; Event, Home, Horse, Location, and Result. We have some data in our tables that we can work with and we have some pages for displaying, editing, creating, and deleting data from our models. This is a good start but we can do better. This chapter focuses on one model at a time and hopefully by the time we get to the last one, you'll be able to do the work without my help. We start with the Location model, as that is where we did a little bit of work in Chapter 6.

Data Validation

A good place to start is by validating the data in our model. After all, if we allow garbage into our database, we'll get garbage out of our database. Let's start by opening Location.cs. Other than the ID field, we have the name, street address, city, state, and zip fields. Of these fields, what makes the most sense to have them as required? I think it would make sense to have the name, address, city, and state be required, so let's make that change first. Listing 7-1 shows the model with the new changes.

Listing 7-1. Location.cs

```
using System;
using System.Collections.Generic;
using System.ComponentModel.DataAnnotations;
```

© Derek J. Rouleau 2018
D. J. Rouleau, *Beginning Entity Framework Core 2.0*, https://doi.org/10.1007/978-1-4842-3375-7_7

```
namespace EquineTracker.Models
{
    public partial class Location
    {
        public Location()
        {
            Event = new HashSet<Event>();
        }

        public int LocationId { get; set; }
        [Required]
        public string Name { get; set; }
        [Required]
        public string StreetAddress { get; set; }
        [Required]
        public string City { get; set; }
        [Required]
        public string State { get; set; }
        public string ZipCode { get; set; }

        public ICollection<Event> Event { get; set; }
    }
}
```

As I hope you remember, we added the using statement so we can use the Required attribute. Then we added the [Required] attribute above the field that we wanted to make required. What happens now if we try to create a new location with the required fields missing? Let's fire up our application and find out. Figure 7-1 shows an example of what you can expect to see.

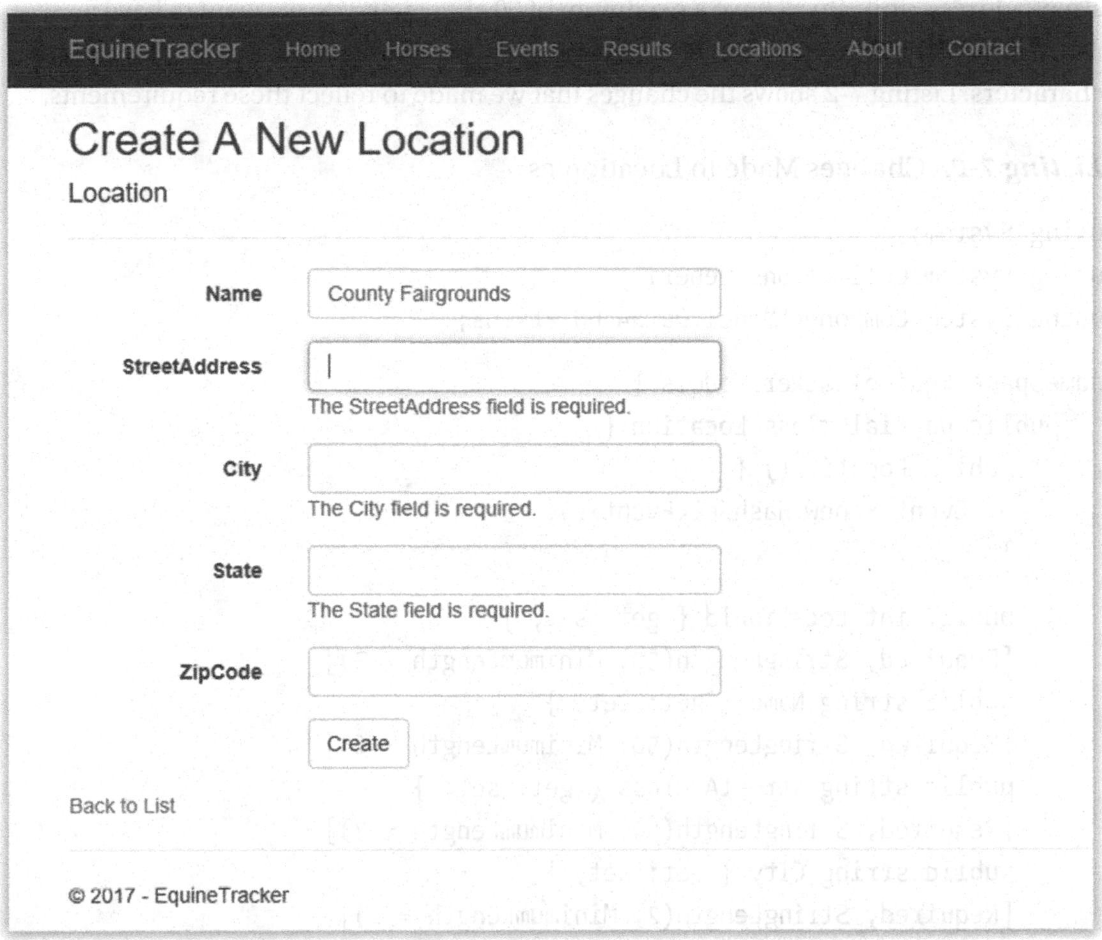

EquineTracker   Home   Horses   Events   Results   Locations   About   Contact

Create A New Location

Location

Name	County Fairgrounds
StreetAddress		
	The StreetAddress field is required.
City	
	The City field is required.
State	
	The State field is required.
ZipCode	

Create

Back to List

© 2017 - EquineTracker

Figure 7-1. *Required fields*

As you can see, with very little effort we are able to have some very basic data validation. It even tells the user what the problem is. Since we let the wizard do a lot of the work for us, there is already some built-in validation functionality. Had we not used the wizard, we would be doing a lot of this work ourselves. If you decide to learn more about ASP.NET MVC, this is something that you will want to look into, as it can help make your web applications look professional.

For now I hope you'll be happy with knowing that this is working because of lines like: `<span asp-validation-for="City" class="text-danger"></span>` within `create.cshtml`. This is a good start, but what if someone tried to enter Conn for Connecticut instead of CT? The good news is that's easy to fix too. Before we do that, lets think of what else we need to do so we can do it all at one time. We know that name,

239

street address, and city all have a maximum of 50 characters; do we want to have a minimum? We also know that ZIP code, even though it's not required, can only hold 10 characters. Listing 7-2 shows the changes that we made to reflect these requirements.

Listing 7-2. Changes Made to Location.cs

```
using System;
using System.Collections.Generic;
using System.ComponentModel.DataAnnotations;

namespace EquineTracker.Models {
    public partial class Location {
        public Location() {
            Event = new HashSet<Event>();
        }

        public int LocationId { get; set; }
        [Required, StringLength(50, MinimumLength = 3)]
        public string Name { get; set; }
        [Required, StringLength(50, MinimumLength = 6)]
        public string StreetAddress { get; set; }
        [Required, StringLength(50, MinimumLength = 3)]
        public string City { get; set; }
        [Required, StringLength(2, MinimumLength = 2)]
        public string State { get; set; }
        [StringLength(10, MinimumLength = 5)]
        public string ZipCode { get; set; }

        public ICollection<Event> Event { get; set; }
    }
}
```

We set some arbitrary values here for minimum lengths, so feel free to adjust them as you see fit. We made the ZIP code field a minimum of five characters and a maximum of 10. We made it 10 characters so the users can add a dash if they want. We also haven't limited them to numbers only, because you may need to accept a foreign address and Canada uses letters in their postal codes.

At this point, we performed basic validation only. You could still enter 15 as a state, for example. Let's take care of that part next.

Using a Regular Expression to Validate a Property

What's nice here is we don't need to add any more using statements and we are going to use a regular expression to accomplish this. This might seem a bit odd for some of you, but once you see it, it should make sense. Once you do it a few times, it will make a lot of sense to you. Listing 7-3 shows the updates we made to Location.cs.

Listing 7-3. Updated Location.cs

```
using System;
using System.Collections.Generic;
using System.ComponentModel.DataAnnotations;

namespace EquineTracker.Models {
  public partial class Location {
    private string _state;

    public Location() {
      Event = new HashSet<Event>();
    }

    public int LocationId { get; set; }
    [Required, StringLength(50, MinimumLength = 3)]
    public string Name { get; set; }
    [Required, StringLength(50, MinimumLength = 6)]
    public string StreetAddress { get; set; }
    [Required, StringLength(50, MinimumLength = 3)]
    public string City { get; set; }
    [RegularExpression("[a-zA-Z][a-zA-Z]", ErrorMessage ="Must Be 2 Alpha
    Characters"),Required]
    public string State {
      get { return _state;}
      set {
        _state = value.ToUpper();
      }
    }
```

```
    [StringLength(10, MinimumLength = 5)]
    public string ZipCode { get; set; }

    public ICollection<Event> Event { get; set; }
  }
}
```

In case you missed it, we added a private string variable called _state. We changed the validation to the State field and removed the min and max length, as we are taking care of that in the regular expression. We left it as a required field. We also gave it a custom error message so it's a bit more user friendly. If we didn't use the custom error message, you would see something like Figure 7-2.

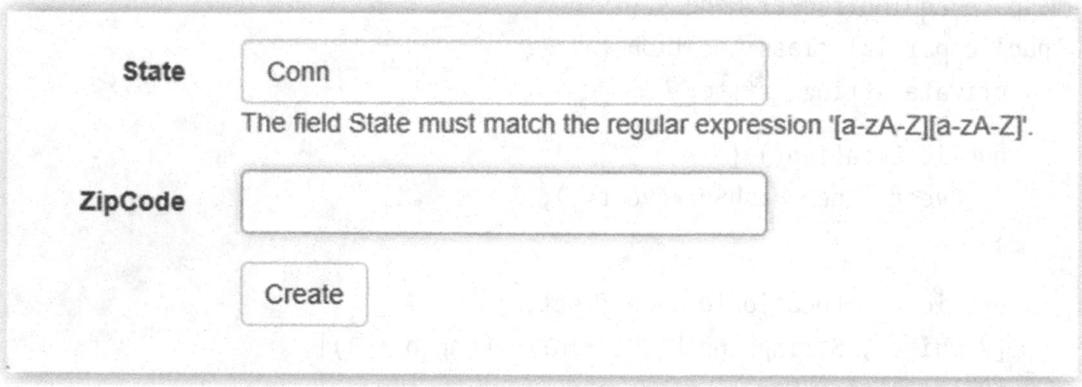

Figure 7-2. *No custom error message*

I'm thinking that most users would be a little confused by that error message, but perhaps it's just me? If we run our application with our custom error message you see a result like in Figure 7-3. The other good thing about our custom error messages is that you can create localized error messages to accommodate people who speak English, French, or Spanish, for example. This is a feature of Data Annotations and not ASP.NET MVC so you can use it in other applications as well. If this is something that you will need, there are some good examples on the web.

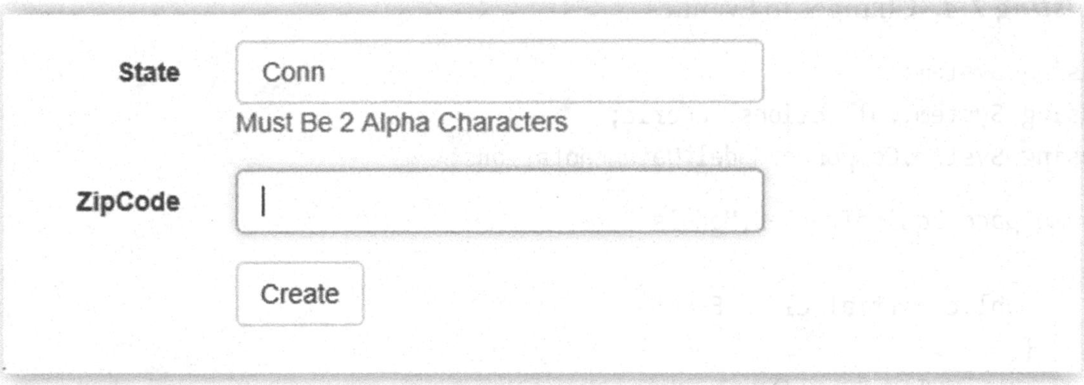

Figure 7-3. *Custom error message*

Your users will appreciate the custom message and you could include an example if you wanted, but try to keep it as compact as possible.

Now that we have this cool new skill, what else could we do? If you were only going to allow U.S. state abbreviations, you could write a regular expression that would accept only the U.S. States. A quick Internet search should give you a couple of examples if you aren't familiar with RegEx. You could write something to validate that the ZIP code, or postal code depending on where you live, is in the correct format. If you want, you could also change the error messages for your other properties. It really comes down to how much custom work you want in your application.

We will leave our Locations.cs file alone for now as I think we performed validation for our model.

Validating the Rest of Our Models

Let's next look at Event.cs and see what we need to do to get some basic validation done. We are concerned with Name, Description, and Event Date. We know Name and Description are both required fields and our table has a max length of 50, so we will make those changes and we also know that our Event Date is nullable (perhaps you know there is an event next year, but not sure the date yet, sounds good right) but we want to be sure it's a DateTime property. Let's make those changes and check out the results. Listing 7-4 shows the changes to Event.cs.

Listing 7-4. Changes to Event.cs

```
using System;
using System.Collections.Generic;
using System.ComponentModel.DataAnnotations;

namespace EquineTracker.Models
{
    public partial class Event
    {
        public Event()
        {
            Result = new HashSet<Result>();
        }

        public int EventId { get; set; }

        [Required, StringLength(50, MinimumLength = 3)]
        public string Name { get; set; }

        public int LocationId { get; set; }

        [Required, StringLength(50, MinimumLength = 3)]
        public string Description { get; set; }

        [DataType(DataType.DateTime)]
        public DateTime? EventDate { get; set; }

        public Location Location { get; set; }
        public ICollection<Result> Result { get; set; }
    }
}
```

There isn't much new here except we now have a property that isn't required. In this case, we are saying that it has to be a data type of DateTime. To test this, we'll start up the application and try to create a new event without entering any data. Figure 7-4 shows how it looks.

Create a New Event

Event

Name	

The Name field is required.

LocationId	Local Ring ⌄

Description	

The Description field is required.

EventDate	mm/dd/yyyy --:-- --

Create

Back to List

Figure 7-4. *Creating a new event and testing our our validation*

We have the two errors we expect and nothing for the Event Date field, as it's not required. Now I hope you can see two small details that we need to fix. Right now the labels are LocationId and EventDate, which isn't correct. We could fix this in different places and sometimes it might make sense to do that, but the good news is for our application we don't need to. However, I'll show you where you could do it in case you ever need to. First, let's fix EventDate so it reads Event Date. We will do this in Event.cs so if you don't have it already open, make sure you open it. We are going to change it so it looks like the following:

```
[Display(Name = "Event Date"), DataType(DataType.DateTime)]
public DateTime? EventDate { get; set; }
```

Display followed by name is a bit misleading but what we are saying is we want to display this as the label text. Here is the best part—any place that there is a label for this property, it will display it as Event Date and not EventDate. Think of all the work you just saved yourself; you have just reduced the chance of missing one of the labels to virtually zero. We are going to do the same thing for LocationId:

```
[Display(Name = "Location")]
public int LocationId { get; set; }
```

Now every place that you saw LocationId you now will see Location (see Figure 7-5). Let's say for the sake of argument that you wanted one of your labels to be different for some reason. How would you do this? Since we have been looking at the create method for our Event model, let's look there. Open Create.cshtml in the Event Views folder. Within that file you will find the following section of code:

```
<div class="form-group">
   <label asp-for="LocationId" class="col-md-2 control-label"></label>
   <div class="col-md-10">
      <select asp-for="LocationId" class ="form-control"
      asp-items="ViewBag.LocationId"></select>
   </div>
</div>
```

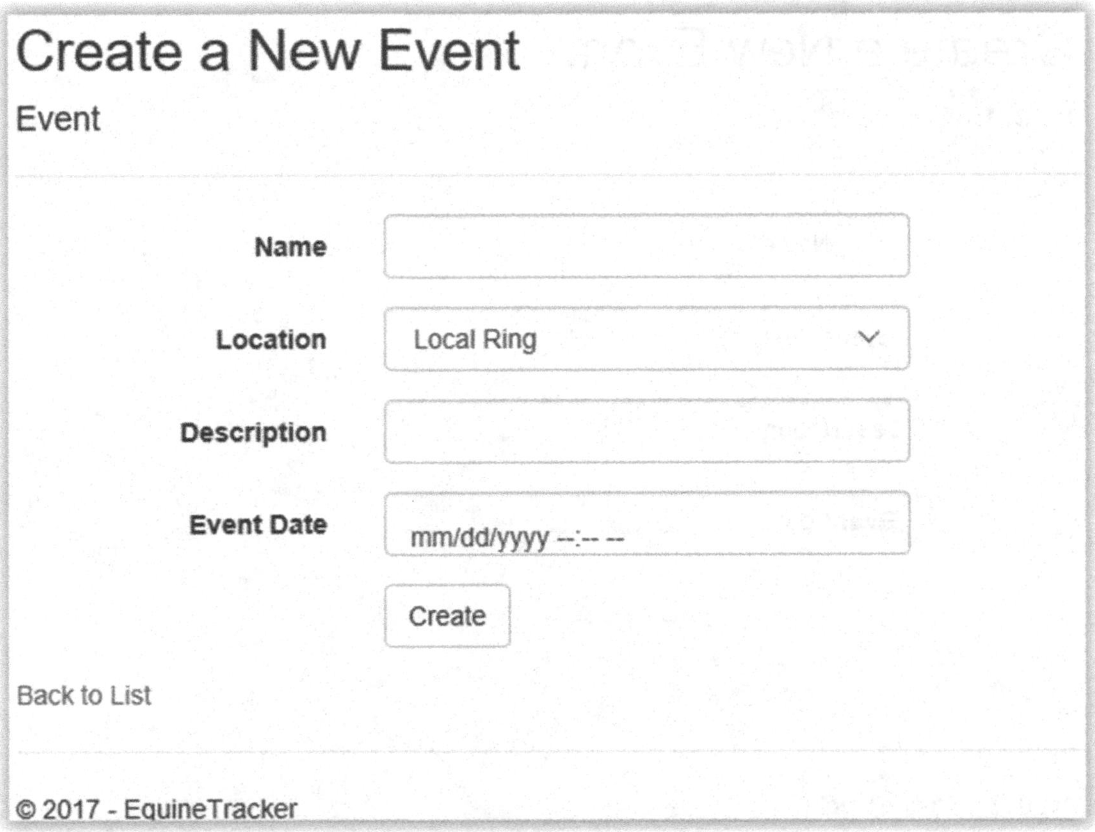

Create a New Event

Event

Name

Location   Local Ring   ∨

Description

Event Date   mm/dd/yyyy --:-- --

                  Create

Back to List

© 2017 - EquineTracker

Figure 7-5. *Our labels updated from the model*

The part that we want is, shockingly enough, the label tag. As you can see, there is nothing between the opening and closing tags, so as a result it uses the name of the property. If you were to change it, even though you already changed the model, it would reflect the change in the view, as that takes precedence. You don't need to do this unless you want it to be some other text, I have changed it so the line now reads:

```
<label asp-for="LocationId" class="col-md-2 control-label">Some Text
</label>
```

You would see that your page now looks like Figure 7-6.

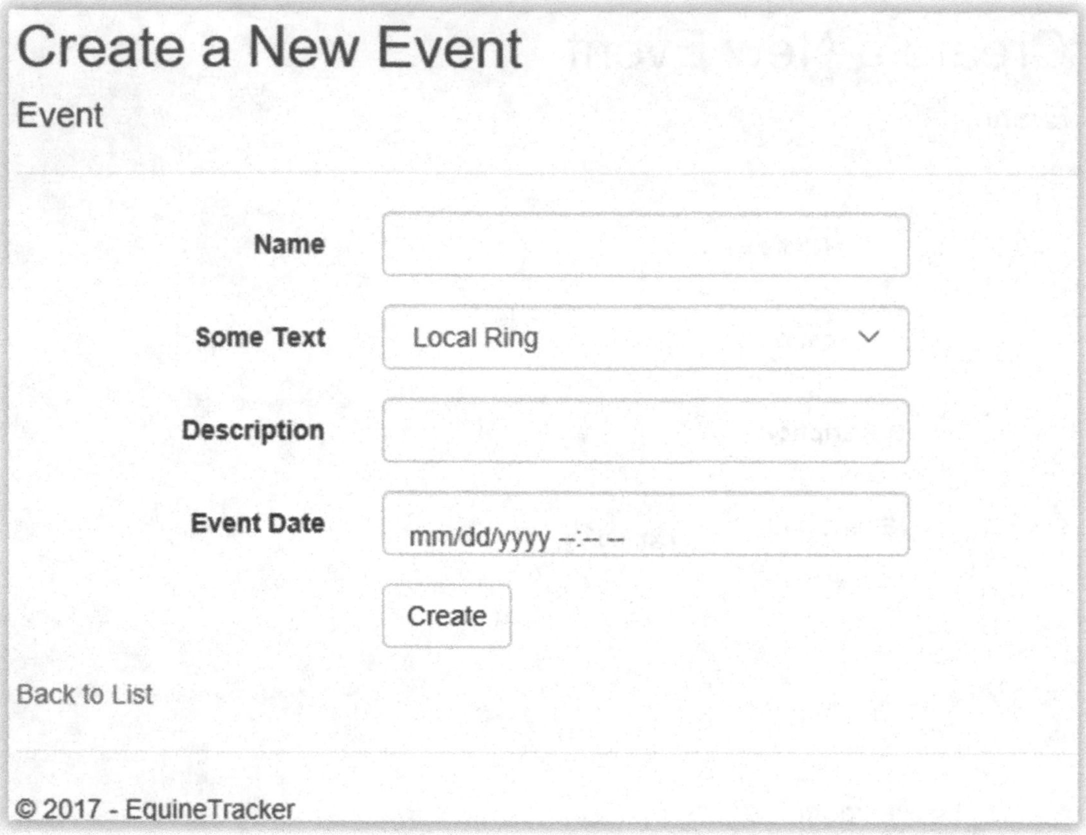

Create a New Event
Event

Name

Some Text   Local Ring   ⌄

Description

Event Date   mm/dd/yyyy --:-- --

Create

Back to List

© 2017 - EquineTracker

Figure 7-6. Changing the label in the view

The method of choice is to set the text in the model and then, if you do need to change it in only one or two locations, make those changes in the appropriate view.

Setting Minimum and Maximum Values for a Property

Let's work on our horse model next, as this is a good place to set a minimum and maximum value for a property. If you don't have it open, open the Horse.cs file. Let's take a look at what we have to work with. If we were to also look at our table we would see that, of the fields we can populate, the only one that is required is the name. The rest can be empty or null, so we will take that into account when we validate our input. Listing 7-5 shows the code that we are going to use. What can you come up with before taking a look at the listing?

Listing 7-5. Horse.cs

```csharp
using System;
using System.Collections.Generic;
using System.ComponentModel.DataAnnotations;

namespace EquineTracker.Models {
    public partial class Horse {
    public Horse() {
        Result = new HashSet<Result>();
    }

    public int HorseId { get; set; }

    [Required]
    public string Name { get; set; }

    public string Breed { get; set; }

    [RegularExpression(@"([1-2]|1[0-9])\.[123]", ErrorMessage = "Enter The
    Height In Hands, for example: 14.0 between 1.0 and 20.3")]
    [DisplayFormat(DataFormatString = "{0:N1}", ApplyFormatInEditMode = true)]
    public decimal? Height { get; set; }

    [Range(0.0, double.MaxValue, ErrorMessage = "Value Must Be Positive"),
    DisplayFormat(DataFormatString = "{0:C}")]
    public decimal? Value { get; set; }

    public ICollection<Result> Result { get; set; }
    }
}
```

How did you do with yours? You may have come up with some things I didn't add to the application and perhaps you missed the height issue. Horses are measured in a unit called *hands*, which is based on 4 inches. So a horse that is 15.2 hands tall is 62" inches tall. That is why we are looking for a number between 1.0 and 20.3. Horses aren't going to be 4 inches tall, but in an effort to not create an overly complicated regular expression, I kept it easy. Feel free to make it equal to or greater than 3.2 hands and less than or equal to 20.3 hands (which are the shortest to tallest recorded horses in the world as of the writing of this book).

We also added a range for the value of the horse of 0.0 to the max value of a double. I'm not going to say that the person using this is going to have a horse worth a few billion dollars, but I wanted to show you that you don't have to use a number and that you can use a constant like `double.MaxValue`. This is something you may find useful in another application. As before, we created some custom error messages. The ones that they would receive otherwise would not be that helpful. If you want to see what I mean, see Figure 7-7, which shows the original error message.

Add A New Horse

Horse

Name	
Breed	
Height	
Value	-2300.00

The field Value must be between 0 and 1.79769313486232E+308.

Create

Figure 7-7. Error not formatted

As with most of the other default error messages, it's not overly helpful to a regular person/end user. We now have two different ways of handling a range of numbers to have a minimum and maximum value—one using a regular expression and the other using the Range attribute.

We saved the easiest one for last and that is `Result.cs` (see Listing 7-6). The three properties that we are concerned about are all required. We aren't going to do any fancy formatting, though you can if you want.

Listing 7-6. Result.cs

```
using System;
using System.Collections.Generic;
using System.ComponentModel.DataAnnotations;

namespace EquineTracker.Models {
    public partial class Result {
        public int ResultId { get; set; }
        public int EventId { get; set; }
        public int HorseId { get; set; }

        [Required]
        public string Class { get; set; }

        [Required]
        public decimal Score { get; set; }

        [Required]
        public string Notes { get; set; }

        public Event Event { get; set; }
        public Horse Horse { get; set; }
    }
}
```

We could probably assume that all scores are going to be positive, but there could be some show some place where the lowest score wins or perhaps the score is seconds from a goal time, so you could have a score of -3.35. You could also set a minimum number of characters for the Class name and the notes if you wanted to.

As you can see, basic validation is pretty easy to incorporate in an ASP.NET MVC Entity Framework Core 2.0 application. In a desktop type application or a more custom ASP.NET MVC application, I would probably put some code in the setter for the properties as well. If you are already familiar with ASP.NET MVC programming, you may already know how to do that. If it's something you want to learn how to do, head out to your local book store or go online and find a good MVC book.

Adding Column Sorting to Results

The sorting of our results is pretty simple, but how do we add the ability to sort our results on our page? We are going to take care of that for our Events page in this section. In the next couple of examples, I'm going to make the changes on one page/view with the thought being that you'll be able to take the example you just did and apply it to the other places within the site. For simplicity, we will sort our events by date and location, and again hopefully with what you are learning here, you can also sort by the other fields if you want to. If it's not already open, open your events controller, which is EventsController.cs. We will add code to our Index method and once we are done with that, we'll make some changes to our view. See Listing 7-7.

Listing 7-7. Updating the Index of EventsController.cs

```
// GET: Events
public async Task<IActionResult> Index(string sortOrder) {
    ViewData["LocationSortParam"] = sortOrder == "loc" ? "loc_desc" : "loc";
    ViewData["DateSortParam"] = string.IsNullOrEmpty(sortOrder) ?
    "date_desc" : "";
    var events = _context.Event.Include(x => x.Location);

    switch (sortOrder) {
      case "loc_desc":
          events = events.OrderByDescending(e => e.Location).Include(x =>
           x.Location);
          break;
      case "loc":
          events = events.OrderBy(e => e.Location).Include(x => x.Location);
          break;
      case "date_desc":
          events = events.OrderByDescending(e => e.EventDate).Include(x =>
          x.Location);
          break;
      default:
          events = events = events.OrderBy(e => e.EventDate).Include(x =>
          x.Location);
          break;
```

252

```
        }
        return View(await events.AsNoTracking().ToListAsync());
}
```

I decided to go with a switch statement because people just don't use them enough. They do a good job of showing you at a quick glance what is going on. This also gives you the ability to have a default value, which again is easy to recognize. First I'll cover the obvious thing, which is the two ViewData elements. Hopefully you have pieced together that these have to do with the view that we'll be working with. These will be used within the view to configure our column headers, which will become hyperlinks. Note that we did add a parameter to our method called sortOrder.

The first thing we are doing is creating an IIncludableQueryable<Event, Location> that we called events. Because we hate ourselves and started with something complex, we have a little extra work to do. For each case statement, we have to add .Include(x => x.Location); otherwise, the compiler will tell us that we are trying to do something we shouldn't. Remove it from one of the lines and you'll see what I mean. If this wasn't a query in which we did a join, you wouldn't need that part. After we get our object, we go through the switch statements and sort our results based on sortOrder. Once we have our results in an ordered list, we pass the list along to the view to be displayed. Before we run our code, however, we need to update our Index view for events. Listing 7-8 shows the table header code for Index.cshtml in our Event Views folder with the changes in bold.

Listing 7-8. Index.cshtml

```
@model IEnumerable<EquineTracker.Models.Event>

@{
    ViewData["Title"] = "Events";
}

<h2>Events</h2>

<p>
    <a asp-action="Create">Create New</a>
</p>
```

```
<table class="table">
  <thead>
    <tr>
      <th>
        @Html.DisplayNameFor(model => model.Name)
      </th>
      <th>
        @Html.DisplayNameFor(model => model.Description)
      </th>
      <th>
        <a asp-action="Index" asp-route-SortOrder=
        "@ViewData["DateSortParam"]"> @Html.DisplayNameFor(model =>
        model.EventDate)</a>
      </th>
      <th>
        <a asp-action="Index" asp-route-SortOrder=
        "@ViewData["LocationSortParam"]"> @Html.DisplayNameFor(model =>
        model.Location)</a>
      </th>
      <th></th>
    </tr>
  </thead>
  <tbody>
    @foreach (var item in Model) {
      <tr>
        <td>
          @Html.DisplayFor(modelItem => item.Name)
        </td>
        <td>
          @Html.DisplayFor(modelItem => item.Description)
        </td>
        <td>
          @Html.DisplayFor(modelItem => item.EventDate)
        </td>
```

```
        <td>
            @Html.DisplayFor(modelItem => item.Location.Name)
        </td>
        <td>
            <a asp-action="Edit" asp-route-id="@item.EventId">Edit</a> |
            <a asp-action="Details" asp-route-id="@item.EventId">
            Details</a> |
            <a asp-action="Delete" asp-route-id="@item.EventId">Delete</a>
        </td>
    </tr>
    }
    </tbody>
</table>
```

As I mentioned, we are using ViewData to set up our hyperlinks. If the user clicks on them, it brings us back to the Index page; now it will be sorted in the order that they selected. Figure 7-8 shows the page when you first enter it and Figure 7-9 shows it sorted by the date field in descending order. I include the address bar in both examples so you can see the difference there as well.

Figure 7-8. *Default view of the Index page*

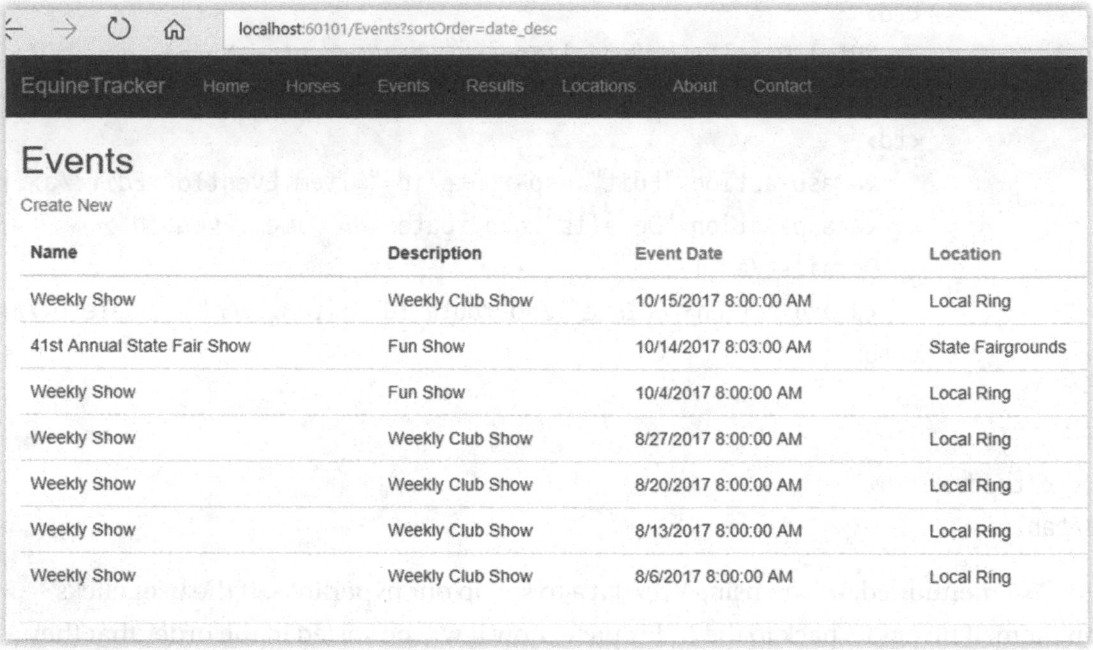

Figure 7-9. *Sorted by descending date*

As you can see, the address changes to `localhost:60101/Events?sortOrder=date_desc`. Now all the shows are sorted by the date in descending order. Don't forget that your port number may be different than mine, so don't try to type in the address.

Adding Search Capabilities

We'll stick with our Events page for the time being so we can keep our code in one place, which should hopefully make your life easier later if you choose to implement this is other locations. Or if you are working on a separate project, you can look in one place to find what you need. Another helpful thing we can offer the users is the ability to search for data. Looking at the Events page, I think the most helpful thing to search for would be the show name. We will be going back to our EventsController.cs file and the Index for this. Listing 7-9 shows the Index method in EventsController.cs with the updates.

Listing 7-9. Index Method in EventsController.cs

```
// GET: Events
public async Task<IActionResult> Index(string sortOrder, string
searchString) {
    ViewData["LocationSortParam"] = sortOrder == "loc" ? "loc_desc" : "loc";
    ViewData["DateSortParam"] = string.IsNullOrEmpty(sortOrder) ?
    "date_desc" : "";
    ViewData["SearchParam"] = searchString;

    var events = _context.Event.Include(x => x.Location);
    // check if searchString is null, if not search the events for the name
    of the event
    if (!string.IsNullOrEmpty(searchString)) {
        events = events.Where(n => n.Name.Contains(searchString)).Include(x =>
        x.Location);
    }
    switch (sortOrder) {
        case "loc_desc":
            events = events.OrderByDescending(e => e.Location).Include(x =>
            x.Location);
            break;
        case "loc":
            events = events.OrderBy(e => e.Location).Include(x => x.Location);
            break;
        case "date_desc":
            events = events.OrderByDescending(e => e.EventDate).Include(x =>
            x.Location);
            break;
        default:
            events = events = events.OrderBy(e -> e.EventDate).Include(x =>
            x.Location);
            break;
    }
    return View(await events.AsNoTracking().ToListAsync());
}
```

The good news is we really didn't have to do a whole lot here in order to add the ability to search. We added another property to our method called searchString. We then added another ViewData property with the same name. Then we needed to make a decision—how are we going to handle our query? Since I don't want to have a super long declaration for my variable, I decided to query the database and then do my SELECT on the results. You could create a variable first and then do your query using that variable, which would look something like this:

```
Microsoft.EntityFrameworkCore.Query.IIncludableQueryable<Event, Location>
events;

if (!string.IsNullOrEmpty(searchString)) {
   events = _context.Event.Where(n => n.Name.Contains(searchString)).
   Include(x => x.Location);
} else {
   events = _context.Event.Include(x => x.Location);
}
```

There are occasions where this would be preferred, and perhaps eventually this application will become large enough to warrant it. This is why I felt it would be good to point it out to you. As I mentioned, if we weren't doing a join on our tables, this would be much shorter. I still prefer the var method for places I know should stay relatively small or if performance isn't much of an issue.

Now we just need to add our search box to our view and we are off to the races. Open Index.cshtml from our Events views and add the code shown in Listing 7-10; the changes are in bold.

Listing 7-10. Changes to Index.cshtml

```
@model IEnumerable<EquineTracker.Models.Event>

@{
   ViewData["Title"] = "Events";
}

<h2>Events</h2>
```

```html
<p>
    <a asp-action="Create">Create New</a>
</p>
<form asp-action="Index" method="get">
    <div>
        <p>
            Search by Event Name: <input type="text" name="searchString"
            value="@ViewData["searchParam"]" />
            <input type="submit" value="Search" class="btn btn-default" />
        </p>
    </div>
</form>
<table class="table">
    <thead>
        <tr>
            <th>
                @Html.DisplayNameFor(model => model.Name)
            </th>
            <th>
                @Html.DisplayNameFor(model => model.Description)
            </th>
            <th>
                <a asp-action="Index" asp-route-SortOrder="@ViewData
                ["DateSortParam"]"> @Html.DisplayNameFor(model => model.
                EventDate)</a>
            </th>
            <th>
                <a asp-action="Index" asp-route-SortOrder="@ViewData
                ["LocationSortParam"]"> @Html.DisplayNameFor(model => model.
                Location)</a>
            </th>
            <th></th>
        </tr>
    </thead>
```

```
    <tbody>
        @foreach (var item in Model) {
            <tr>
                <td>
                    @Html.DisplayFor(modelItem => item.Name)
                </td>
                <td>
                    @Html.DisplayFor(modelItem => item.Description)
                </td>
                <td>
                    @Html.DisplayFor(modelItem => item.EventDate)
                </td>
                <td>
                    @Html.DisplayFor(modelItem => item.Location.Name)
                </td>
                <td>
                    <a asp-action="Edit" asp-route-id="@item.EventId">Edit</a> |
                    <a asp-action="Details" asp-route-id="@item.EventId">
                    Details</a> |
                    <a asp-action="Delete" asp-route-id="@item.EventId">Delete</a>
                </td>
            </tr>
        }
    </tbody>
</table>
```

That's all there is to it. We create a form object in our code because it's good form to do so. I then create a div in case we later want to do some exciting formatting, plus it keeps it grouped together nicely. We then create the text input field, which I named searchString. I normally name them something similar to the variable that will be used with the object. Most importantly, we have our ViewData object, which will be used in the controller just like when we created our hyperlinks. We then have to create a button so the users have something to click on to perform the search. Now let's say we didn't have our handy navigation across the top of the screen and it was a bit harder to get to.

We could also create a hyperlink that would bring us back to the Index page with no search being performed. Like before, you add a tag that would look something like this:

```
<a asp-action="Index">View Complete List</a>
```

Figure 7-10 shows the Events index page when we search for State.

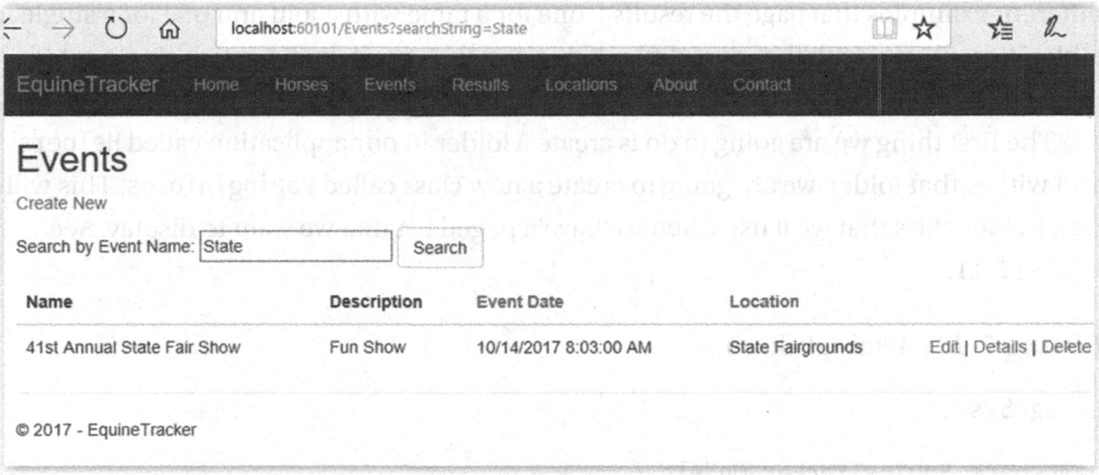

Figure 7-10. *Searching for state in the events*

As you can see, it found the show called 41st Annual State Fair Show. If you were to type state in lowercase, it would still find the fair. If you kept your browser open and searched for week, you would then find that it loads all the shows named Weekly Show.

Something that you may have noticed is that we specified in our form tag that the method is a GET method. By default it would be a POST, which means our parameters would be passed in the HTTP message body and not in the URL as a query string. By using the GET, the parameter is passed in the URL as a query string, which means we could bookmark the page for that particular search. Another reason we did this is that it's considered good practice. Any time the action doesn't result in an update, you should use GET and not POST. If you spend more time working with ASP.NET MVC, you'll come across this. The bookmark will obviously work a lot better when you publish your application rather than run it in debug mode like are doing.

Adding Pagination: Version 1

Back in our console application, we enabled pagination in order to keep our console looking neat and clean. We are going to do the same thing here for the same reasons. The good news is the Entity Framework Core code is pretty much identical; the bad news is this requires some work to get it working on a website. We are going to show two different examples that page the results—one for a table with a join and one for a single table. We will start with the more difficult one and then we'll do the easier, single-table method.

The first thing we are going to do is create a folder in our application called Helpers and within that folder, we are going to create a new class called PagingInfo.cs. This will be a helper class that we'll use when we have a paged list that we want to display. See Listing 7-11.

Listing 7-11. PagingInfo.cs

```
using System;

namespace EquineTracker.Models {
    public class PagingInfo {
        public int TotalObjects { get; set; }
        public int ObjectsPerPage { get; set; }
        public int CurrentPage { get; set; }

        public int TotalPages {
            get {
                return (int)Math.Ceiling((decimal)TotalObjects /
                ObjectsPerPage);
            }
        }

        public bool HasPreviousPage {
            get {
                return (CurrentPage > 1);
            }
        }
```

```
        public bool HasNextPage {
            get { return (CurrentPage < TotalPages); }
        }
    }
}
```

Nothing too complicated here; just a couple of properties that are pretty self-explanatory and a couple of methods to let us know if we have a previous or next page available or how many total pages we are going to have. If you aren't familiar with Math.Ceiling, it's pretty useful as well as a lot of the other Math.Somethings we have access to.

Before you can do the next part, we need to add a new model to our Models folder called EventListViewModel. Right-click on the Models folder and add a new class called EventListViewModel, as shown in Listing 7-12.

Listing 7-12. EventListViewModel

```
using System.Collections.Generic;
using EquineTracker.Helpers;

namespace EquineTracker.Models {
    public class EventListViewModel {
        public IEnumerable<Event> Events { get; set; }
        public PagingInfo PagingInfo { get; set; }
    }
}
```

Next we are going to update our code in EventsController.cs for our Index. I'm going to tell you right now that because of how we handled our events by location, that paging isn't going to work right. Instead, you could add it to the index and check to see if you have a LocationId and if so your query text would be x; otherwise, it would be y. Or you could add the paging logic to EventsByLocation().

With that, let's take a look at the Index method. Before you start, you'll need to add a variable to this class:

```
public int PageSize = 4;
```

As well as another using statement:

```
using EquineTracker.Helpers;
```

This way, if you need to access paging from somewhere else within the class, it will be available. See Listing 7-13.

Listing 7-13. Index() in EventsController.cs

```
// GET: Events
public ViewResult Index(string sortOrder, string searchString, string
currentFilter, int page = 1) {
   ViewData["CurrentSort"] = sortOrder;
   ViewData["LocationSortParam"] = sortOrder == "loc" ? "loc_desc" : "loc";
   ViewData["DateSortParam"] = string.IsNullOrEmpty(sortOrder) ?
   "date_desc" : "";

   if (searchString == null) {
      searchString = currentFilter;
   }
   ViewData["CurrentFilter"] = searchString;

   EventListViewModel model = new EventListViewModel();
   var events = _context.Event.Include(x => x.Location);
   // check if searchString is null, if not search the events for the name
   of the event
   if (!string.IsNullOrEmpty(searchString)) {
      events = events.Where(n => n.Name.Contains(searchString)).Include(x =>
      x.Location);
   }

   switch (sortOrder) {
      case "loc_desc":
         model = new EventListViewModel {
            Events = events.Include(x => x.Location)
            .OrderByDescending(e => e.Location)
             .Skip((page - 1) * PageSize)
             .Take(PageSize)
         };
         break;
```

```
    case "loc":
      model = new EventListViewModel {
        Events = events.Include(x => x.Location)
          .OrderBy(e => e.Location)
          .Skip((page - 1) * PageSize)
          .Take(PageSize),
      };
      break;
    case "date_desc":
      model = new EventListViewModel {
        Events = events.Include(x => x.Location)
          .OrderByDescending(e => e.EventDate)
          .Skip((page - 1) * PageSize)
          .Take(PageSize),
      };
      break;
    default:
      model = new EventListViewModel {
        Events = events.Include(x => x.Location)
          .OrderBy(e => e.EventDate)
          .Skip((page - 1) * PageSize)
          .Take(PageSize),
      };
      break;
  }
  model.PagingInfo = new PagingInfo {
    CurrentPage = page,
    ObjectsPerPage = PageSize,
    TotalObjects = events.ToList().Count()
  };
  return View(model);
}
```

We did quite a few things in this listing. The first thing that you may have missed is that we changed Index to be a ViewResult, which we did so we can return the model that we create to our Index view. We are maintaining our var called events, which we are going to use to query against instead of going back to the database. We are also going to use this in order to calculate our total pages by knowing how many total objects there are in our set.

One of the more annoying things is that you must have .Include(x => x.Location) in all of your queries or you'll get an error. Since we are paging our results, we have to be sure that we use an OrderBy. Otherwise, we could get some pretty whacky results. The .Skip and .Take should look familiar. They are doing the paging from a query standpoint. Once we create our "model" variable, we need to populate the model. PagingInfo property. If we didn't have this, the paging work wouldn't work in our view. You'll see where it's used in our view in just a moment. The last thing we did is change our return to simply be return View(model);.

We now need to update our view. Then we will be ready to run our code and get some paged results for our events. See Listing 7-14.

Listing 7-14. Index.cshtml

```
@*@model IEnumerable<EquineTracker.Models.Event>*@
@model EquineTracker.Models.EventListViewModel
@{
    ViewData["Title"] = "Events";
}

<h2>Events</h2>

<p>
    <a asp-action="Create">Create New</a>
</p>
<form asp-action="Index" method="get">
    <div>
        <p>
            Search by Event Name: <input type="text" name="searchString"
            value="@ViewData["SearchParam"]" />
            <input type="submit" value="Search" class="btn btn-default" />
        </p>
    </div>
</form>
```

```
<table class="table">
    <thead>
        <tr>
            <th>
            Name
            </th>
            <th>
            Description
            /th>
            <th>
                <a asp-action="Index" asp-route-sortOrder="@ViewData
                ["DateSortParam"]" asp-route-currentFilter="@ViewData
                ["CurrentFilter"]"> Event Date</a>
            </th>
            <th>
                <a asp-action="Index" asp-route-sortOrder="@ViewData
                ["LocationSortParam"]" asp-route-currentFilter="@ViewData
                ["CurrentFilter"]"> Location</a>
            </th>
            <th></th>
        </tr>
    </thead>
    <tbody>
    @foreach (var item in Model.Events) {
        <tr>
            <td>
                @Html.DisplayFor(modelItem => item.Name)
            </td>
            <td>
                @Html.DisplayFor(modelItem => item.Description)
            </td>
            <td>
                @Html.DisplayFor(modelItem => item.EventDate)
            </td>
```

```
        <td>
            @Html.DisplayFor(modelItem => item.Location.Name)
        </td>
        <td>
            <a asp-action="Edit" asp-route-id="@item.EventId">Edit</a> |
            <a asp-action="Details" asp-route-id="@item.EventId">Details</a> |
            <a asp-action="Delete" asp-route-id="@item.EventId">Delete</a>
        </td>
    </tr>
  }
  </tbody>
</table>

@{
    var prevPageDisabled = !Model.PagingInfo.HasPreviousPage ? "disabled" : "";
    var nextPageDisabled = !Model.PagingInfo.HasNextPage ? "disabled" : "";
}
<a asp-action="Index" asp-route-sortOrder="@ViewData["CurrentSort"]"
    asp-route-page="@(Model.PagingInfo.CurrentPage - 1)"
    asp-route-currentFilter="@ViewData["CurrentFilter"]" class="btn
    btn-default @prevPageDisabled">Previous</a>
<a asp-action="Index" asp-route-sortOrder="@ViewData["CurrentSort"]"
    asp-route-page="@(Model.PagingInfo.CurrentPage + 1)"
    asp-route-currentFilter="@ViewData["CurrentFilter"]" class="btn
    btn-default @nextPageDisabled">Next</a>
```

As you can see, we made quite a few changes to our page. The most important is right at the top—we commented out the first line and we added a new model declaration: @model EquineTracker.Models.EventListViewModel.

We need to let the view know that we are going to be using our EventListViewModel and not the Event model. This way we can access our PageInfo properties. We could have put this in our original model, but many would say that it's not good form to do so. We statically named our table headers that are not hyperlinks and didn't change anything in the body of the table. We then have our code to check to see if we have a previous or next page and as a result decide if the button with be disabled. If the button needs to be disabled, which means we don't have a previous or next page, I need to set the value to be disabled. We are using the `class` property within the tag to add `disabled` to the class so the button is grayed out and can't be clicked.

It's a little hard to tell in the figures, but the Next button is enabled and the Previous button is disabled in Figure 7-11. Conversely, the Previous button is enabled and the Next button is disabled in Figure 7-12. If you were to search for Weekly and do the same thing, you would find that on page 2, you only have the two results (the two Weekly Show entries).

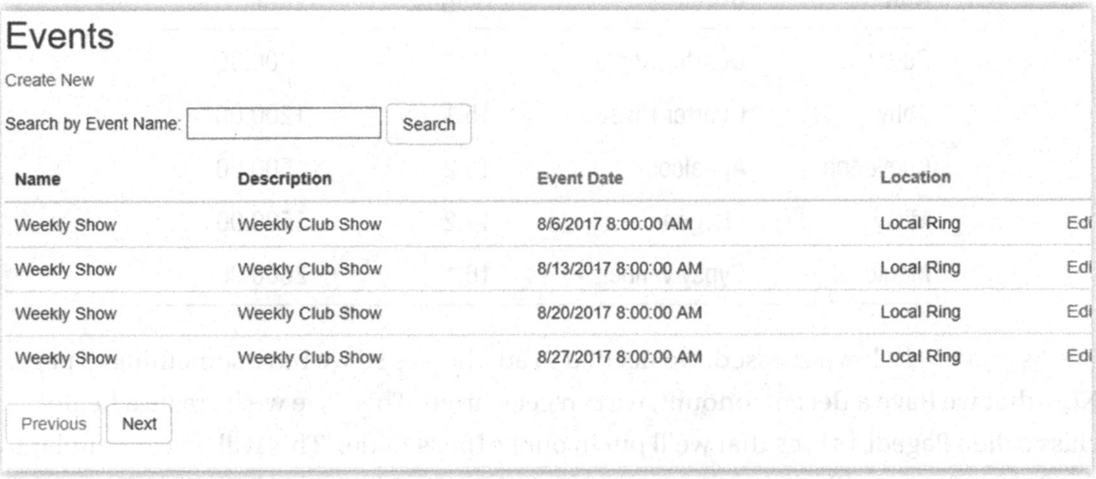

Figure 7-11. *Displaying four records with the Next button enabled*

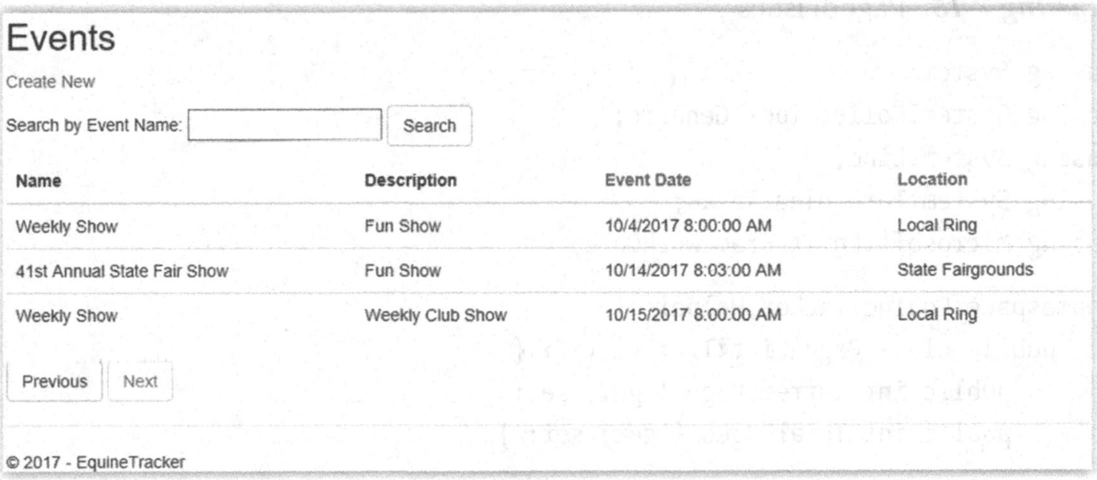

Figure 7-12. *Displaying the remaining three records with the Previous button enabled*

Adding Paging: Version 2

That was the more difficult one, and the main reason it's more difficult is the table join that we are dealing with. Let's try paging results that come from only one table. The first thing we are going to have to do is add some more horses to our table. I'm going to add the following horses to my database:

Name	Breed	Height	Value
Remy	Quarter Horse	15.1	800.00
Abby	Quarter Horse	15.1	1200.00
Cheyenne	Appaloosa	15.2	500.00
Misty	Morgan	14.2	3500.00
Magic	Gypsy Vanner	16.1	2600.00

As you might have guessed, we needed to add horses so we have something to page. Now that we have a decent amount, we can get started. This time we'll create a helper class called `PagedList.cs` that we'll put in our `Helpers` folder. This will be very similar to the `PagingInfo.cs` file that we created before, although it'll work a little bit different as you'll see. See Listing 7-15.

Listing 7-15. PagedList.cs

```
using System;
using System.Collections.Generic;
using System.Linq;
using System.Threading.Tasks;
using Microsoft.EntityFrameworkCore;

namespace EquineTracker.Helpers {
    public class PagedList<T> : List<T> {
        public int CurrentPage { get; set; }
        public int TotalPages { get; set; }
```

```
public PagedList(List<T> items, int count, int currentPage, int
pageSize) {
    CurrentPage = currentPage;
    TotalPages = (int)Math.Ceiling(count / (double)pageSize);

    this.AddRange(items);
}

public bool HasPreviousPage {
    get { return (CurrentPage > 1); }
}

public bool HasNextPage {
    get { return (CurrentPage < TotalPages); }
}

public static async Task<PagedList<T>> CreateAsync(IQueryable<T>
source, int pageIndex, int pageSize) {
    var count = await source.CountAsync();
    var items = await source.Skip((pageIndex - 1) * pageSize).
    Take(pageSize).ToListAsync();
    return new PagedList<T>(items, count, pageIndex, pageSize);
}
}
}
```

Hopefully, you can see what is going on in this class by this point. This time we have two properties one for our current page and one for the total pages in our result set. This time we are passing a List<T> to our class to get our paging instead of doing it in the model like we did in the last example. This is the method I normally use. Once it's working, it does make your life easier. However, I wanted to show you both options so you know what you can do. The other good thing here is we can do it with any List<T> so that is why we called our IQueryable<T> variable source, as it's the source object. I felt that this would help point that out. Feel free to give it a name that means more to you.

Just like before, we need to add this functionality to our Index method. This time we'll be opening HorsesController.cs. Just like before, you'll need to add the following using statement to the controller: using EquineTracker.Helpers;. Once you have done that, we can make the changes shown in Listing 7-16 to Index.

Listing 7-16. HorsesController.cs

```
// GET: Horses
public async Task<IActionResult> Index(int? page) {
    int pageSize = 5;
    var horses = from h in _context.Horse orderby h.HorseId select h;
    return View(await PagedList<Horse>.CreateAsync(horses.AsNoTracking(),
    page ?? 1, pageSize));
    //return View(await _context.Horse.ToListAsync());
}
```

Since we have a lot less going on here, I decided to leave in the old `return` statement but comment it out so you can see the difference. Feel free to delete yours. We create our `IQueryable<Horse>` called `horses` and we pass that with `AsNoTracking()` so the change tracker won't be trying to track any changes to our entity. Not that we are going to be making any changes, but it's always a good idea to do it for read-only type queries like this one, as it reduces the overhead. Lastly, we are checking to see if our nullable `int` page has a value. If not, it passes along a value of 1.

Now we just need to modify our `Index.cshtml` page and we are ready to test. Again make sure you are modifying the `Index.cshtml` file within our Horses Views folder (see Listing 7-17). In order to make my life easier, I usually keep my folders collapsed until I need to use them. I only keep the files open that I'm using since a lot of them tend to have similar names.

Listing 7-17. Index.cshtml in Views ➤ Horses

```
@*@model IEnumerable<EquineTracker.Models.Horse>*@
@model EquineTracker.Helpers.PagedList<EquineTracker.Models.Horse>

@{
    ViewData["Title"] = "Index";
}

<h2>Index</h2>

<p>
    <a asp-action="Create">Create New</a>
</p>
```

```
<table class="table">
    <thead>
        <tr>
            <th>
                Name
            </th>
            <th>
                Breed
            </th>
            <th>
                Height
            </th>
            <th>
                Value
            </th>
            <th></th>
        </tr>
    </thead>
<tbody>
@foreach (var item in Model) {
    <tr>
        <td>
            @Html.DisplayFor(modelItem => item.Name)
        </td>
        <td>
            @Html.DisplayFor(modelItem => item.Breed)
        </td>
        <td>
            @Html.DisplayFor(modelItem => item.Height)
        </td>
        <td>
            @Html.DisplayFor(modelItem => item.Value)
        </td>
```

```
    <td>
        <a asp-action="Edit" asp-route-id="@item.HorseId">Edit</a> |
        <a asp-action="Details" asp-route-id="@item.HorseId">Details</a> |
        <a asp-action="Delete" asp-route-id="@item.HorseId">Delete</a>
    </td>
  </tr>
}
  </tbody>
</table>

@{
  var prevPageDisabled = !Model.HasPreviousPage ? "disabled" : "";
  var nextPageDisabled = !Model.HasNextPage ? "disabled" : "";
}

<a asp-action="Index" asp-route-page="@(Model.CurrentPage - 1)"
  class="btn btn-default @prevPageDisabled">Previous</a>
<a asp-action="Index" asp-route-page="@(Model.CurrentPage + 1)"
  class="btn btn-default @nextPageDisabled">Next</a>
```

The biggest difference with this listing is that we are using PagedList as our model and our buttons require less, as we currently aren't doing any sorting or searching on this page. In the future if you were to add sorting and searching, then you would have to modify it in a similar way as we did in Version 1. We used the same logic for determining if we have a previous or next page and replicated a little bit of code, but I think we'll be able to live through it. See Figure 7-13.

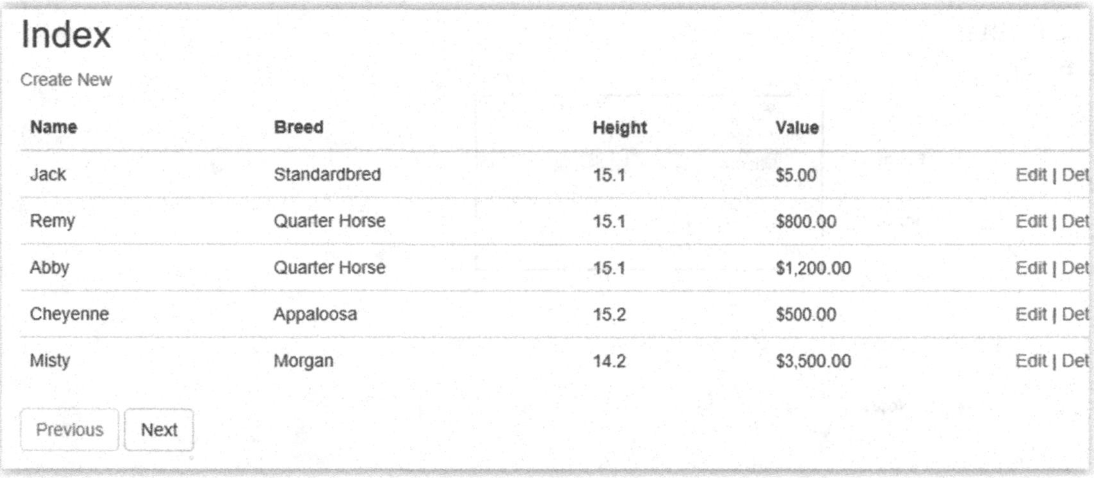

Index

Create New

Name	Breed	Height	Value	
Jack	Standardbred	15.1	$5.00	Edit | Det
Remy	Quarter Horse	15.1	$800.00	Edit | Det
Abby	Quarter Horse	15.1	$1,200.00	Edit | Det
Cheyenne	Appaloosa	15.2	$500.00	Edit | Det
Misty	Morgan	14.2	$3,500.00	Edit | Det

Previous   Next

Figure 7-13. Our paged horses index page

As we would expect, we have five of our six horses listed on the page and the Next button is enabled. If you grew up working on Windows Forms applications, web pages and sites might seem a bit tedious and painful at times. Once you get the hang of it and do it a couple of times, it's really not too bad.

Grouping Results

Right now if we look at our results page, it does just what we asked it to do—it displays all of the results on one page in one giant list. We have only one result in there at the moment, but I think you get what I'm saying. The first thing we are going to do is add a couple more results so that we have some data to work with. This will also act as a way to test the data entry form. Figure 7-14 shows you one issue we currently have with the form.

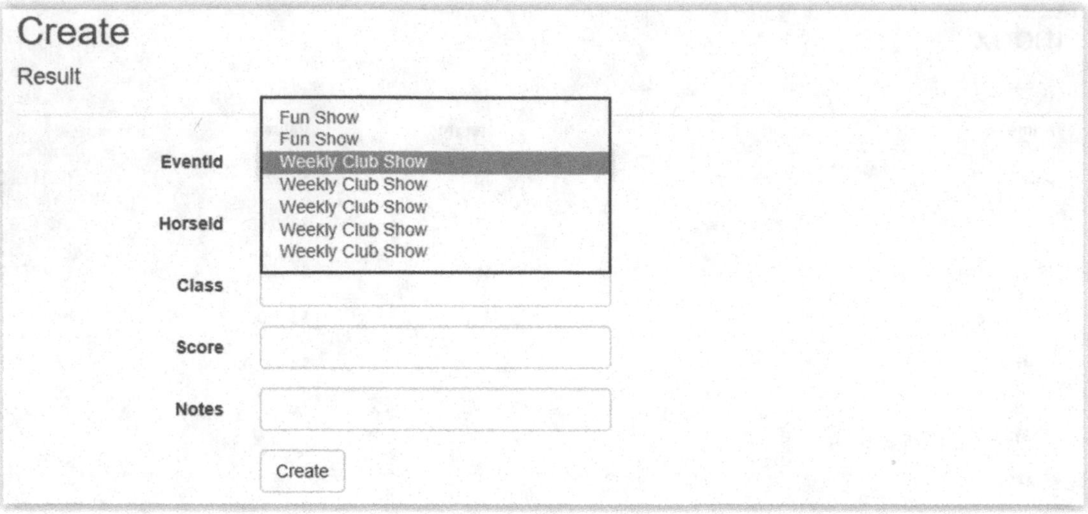

Figure 7-14. *Which show are we picking?*

Think about how we want to handle this problem. Let's say we decide that we are going to put the shows in a dropdown list that the users can pick from. With only seven shows, that's not a big deal. However, what's going to happen in 4 or 5 years when we have 50+ shows? That is going to be quite the list to sift through. What makes the most sense in this case is to create a show result from the show itself. So let's take care of that real quick and then we'll group our results.

To start, we need to open our `Results` controller and change the `Create` method that we are using with our `GET`, as shown in Listing 7-18. We are going to leave the `POST` one alone, as we don't need to make any changes at this point.

Listing 7-18. Modifying Create in the ResultsController.cs File

```
// GET: Results/Create
public IActionResult Create(int EventId) {
    ViewData["EventId"] = new SelectList(_context.Event.Where(e =>
    e.EventId == EventId), "EventId", "Description");
    ViewData["HorseId"] = new SelectList(_context.Horse, "HorseId", "Name");
    return View();
}
```

We added an argument called EventId so we know which event we are looking for. We then modified our ViewData code for EventId in order to select the right one using a where clause. Didn't think we'd be able to do this without adding a little bit of EF Core code, did you? All we are doing with this code is passing a list of one to our view so it can display the proper information as well as maintain the EventId.

We then have to change our Results Create view as a little bit of housekeeping. As you may have noticed when you ran your code, or if you looked at Figure 7-14, it's listed as EventId and our horse is listed as HorseId. This time we'll change the view. Listing 7-19 shows the portion of the view we are concerned with. I removed the rest of the code from the example in an effort to save some space and to make it easier to see the changes.

Listing 7-19. Create.cshtml (Results)

```
@model EquineTracker.Models.Result

@{
    ViewData["Title"] = "Create";
}

<h2>Create</h2>

<form asp-action="Create">
    <div class="form-horizontal">
        <h4>Result</h4>
        <hr />
        <div asp-validation-summary="ModelOnly" class="text-danger"></div>
        <div class="form-group">
            <label asp-for="EventId" class="col-md-2 control-label">Event
            </label>
            <div class="col-md-10">
                <select asp-for="EventId" class ="form-control" asp-items=
                "ViewBag.EventId"></select>
            </div>
        </div>
        <div class="form-group">
            <label asp-for="HorseId" class="col-md-2 control-label">Horse
            </label>
```

```
    <div class="col-md-10">
        <select asp-for="HorseId" class ="form-control" asp-items=
        "ViewBag.HorseId"></select>
    </div>
</div>
<div class="form-group">
    <label asp-for="Class" class="col-md-2 control-label"></label>
    <div class="col-md-10">
        <input asp-for="Class" class="form-control" />
        <span asp-validation-for="Class" class="text-danger"></span>
    </div>
</div>
```

. . .

All we did was add text to the Event and Horse labels. The changes are in bold and the code continues on after this section, but I included it so you could find it easier.. When you run your code, it will now display correctly. We just need a way to call our method and to do that we are going to open Details.cs from our Events view. We are going to do this just like we did in our previous example, although you can add a button if you really want to make it look nice. Listing 7-20 shows the very bottom of the code in Details.cshtml.

Listing 7-20. Details.cshtml in the Events View Folder

```
<div>
    <a asp-action="Edit" asp-route-id="@Model.EventId">Edit</a> |
    <a asp-action="Index">Back to List</a> |
    @Html.ActionLink("Add a Result for this Show", "Create", "Results",
    new { @EventId = @Model.EventId }, null)
</div>
```

Let's do one last thing to help our application work a little bit better. We are going to remove our Create link from the results Index view. We want our users to be able to add results only from the Details view for the event. Remove or comment out (I prefer remove) the following from the view:

```
<p>
    <a asp-action="Create">Create New</a>
</p>
```

Once you do that, you can run the code to be sure it works (see Figure 7-15). This is a great spot for unit testing, but like a lot of people like to say, "everyone has a test environment; it's just some of us are lucky enough to have it separate from production."

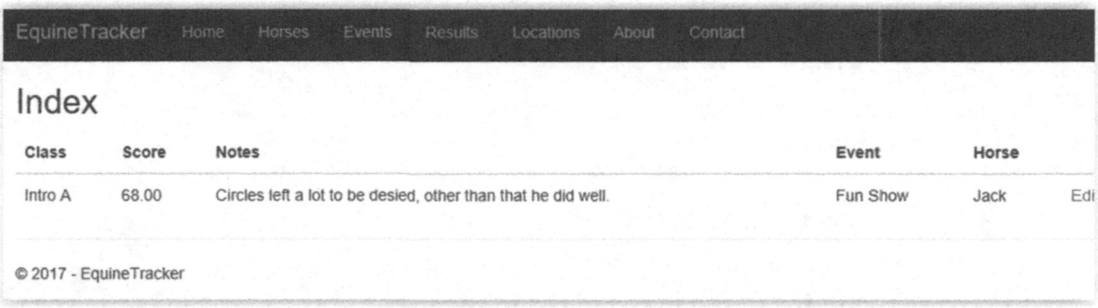

Figure 7-15. *Look mom, no create in our Index view*

The show in Figure 7-16 is the one we are going to add a result to first. When you choose that Hyperlink you should see an empty version of Figure 7-17. Your Event field should read Weekly Show and it should display the first horse in the Horse field. I chose a different horse for this show.

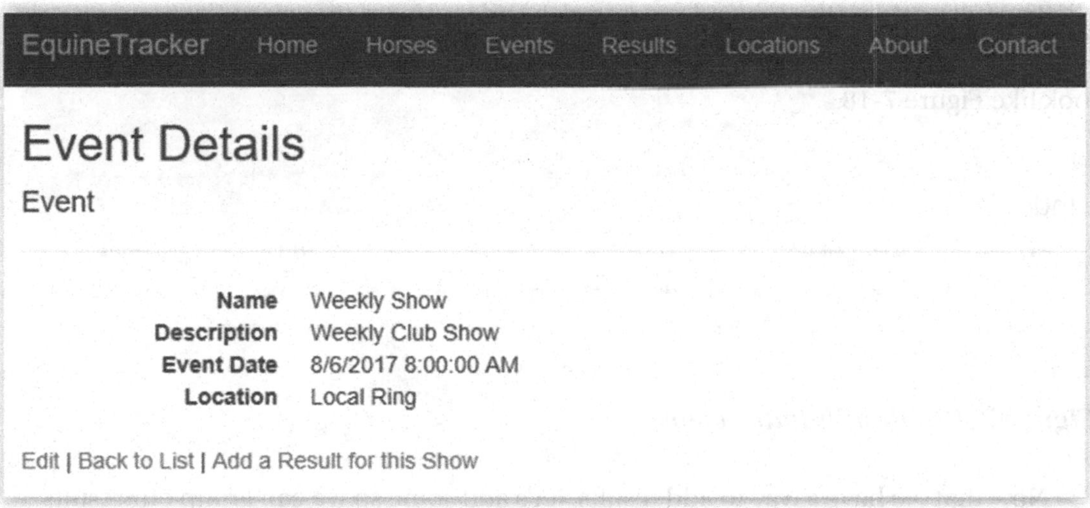

Figure 7-16. *Selecting the 8/6/17 weekly show and viewing the details*

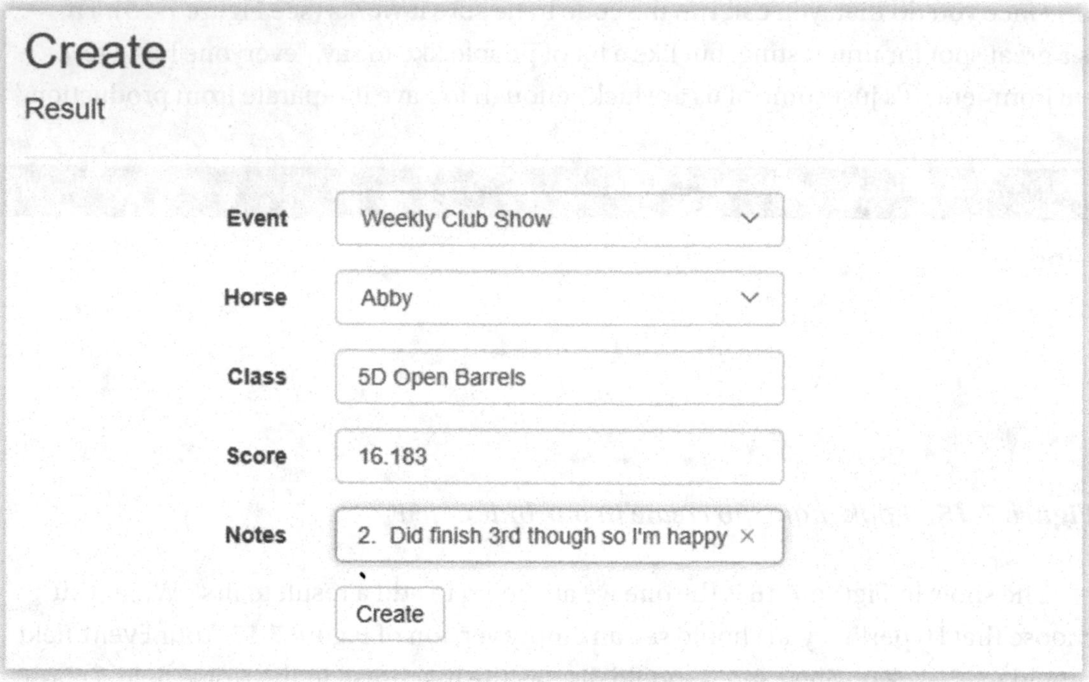

Create

Result

Event	Weekly Club Show ⌄
Horse	Abby ⌄
Class	5D Open Barrels
Score	16.183
Notes	2. Did finish 3rd though so I'm happy ✕

Create

Figure 7-17.   *Adding a result entry*

The full note is: *Way too wide on barrel 2. Did finish 3rd though so I'm happy.*

When we click the Create button, we are brought to the Results Index view. It should look like Figure 7-18.

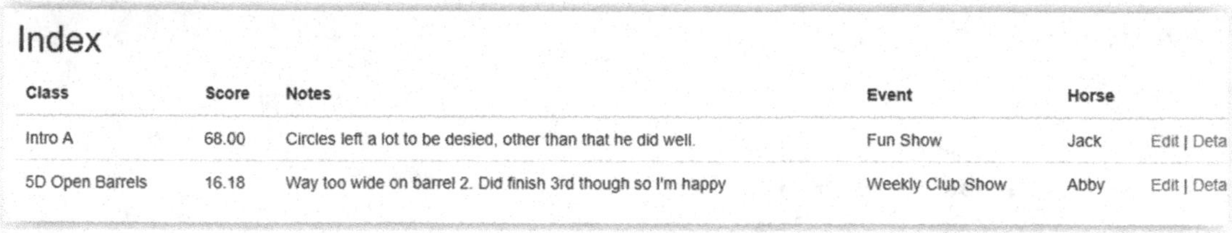

Index

Class	Score	Notes	Event	Horse	
Intro A	68.00	Circles left a lot to be desied, other than that he did well.	Fun Show	Jack	Edit | Deta
5D Open Barrels	16.18	Way too wide on barrel 2. Did finish 3rd though so I'm happy	Weekly Club Show	Abby	Edit | Deta

Figure 7-18.   *Results Index view*

Now that we have a way to add results, let's add some so we can group our results together, which after all is the point of this section.

Event	Horse	Class	Score	Notes
Weekly 8/6/17	Abby	3D Pole Bending	24.21	Slipped on the way back
Weekly 8/20/17	Remy	Training 1	68.34	Spooked at the judge
Weekly 8/20/17	Remy	Training 2	67.62	Car alarm went off at first canter transition
State Fair	Cheyenne	3'3" Low Schooling	0	Didn't touch anything, great round
State Fair	Cheyenne	3'6" High Schooling	4	Came down on 8b

Once we add this information, it will give us some data to work with and show us that it's working. Figure 7-19 shows what the Results Index view will show us before we do any grouping. As you can see, with so few shows, it's not too bad. Imagine how 100+ results and would look. It's true that we could eventually have well over 100 shows listed, but if you were to do two classes per show, that would be 200 results, so I think you can see why we want to group this.

Let's start by creating a class to help. In our `Helpers` folder, we are going to add another class called `ResultGroup.cs`. Listing 7-21 shows the very brief class code.

Listing 7-21. ResultGroup.cs

```
using System;
using EquineTracker.Models;

namespace EquineTracker.Helpers {
    public class ResultGroup {
        public Event _Event { get; set; }
        public int ResultCount { get; set; }
    }
}
```

We have an `Event` property and a `ResultCount` property, which we'll display on our new Index page. The next thing we need to do is make some changes to `ResultsController.cs`. We are going to use our `Index` method to display the individual results for the events and we are going to create a new method to display our grouped list of events for displaying results. This is a bit backwards, but since most of the code was already in place, changing it seemed to be a waste. Listing 7-22 shows the added method and the change to `Index` in our controller.

Listing 7-22. ResultsController.cs

```
// Get: Results grouped together by Event
public ViewResult GroupedResults() {
   var events = _context.Result
     .GroupBy(e => e.EventId)
     .Select(g => new { id = g.Key, count = g.Count() });
   List<ResultGroup> lRg = new List<ResultGroup>();
   foreach(var gRes in events) {
      Event e2 = _context.Event.Where(x => x.EventId == gRes.id).
      FirstOrDefault();
      ResultGroup rg = new ResultGroup() { _Event = e2, ResultCount =
      gRes.count };
      lRg.Add(rg);
   }
   return View(lRg);
}
// GET: Results
public async Task<IActionResult> Index(int EventId) {
   var begEFCoreContext = _context.Result.Include(r => r.Event).Include(r =>
   r.Horse).Where(e=> e.EventId == EventId);
   return View(await begEFCoreContext.ToListAsync());
}
```

If you'll recall, we talked about the joys of grouping before. When we are dealing with MVC, it's just as friendly. The easiest way to accomplish what we need is to create an anonymous type variable and have it hold the EventId and a count of Results for that particular event. We can then use that object to create a List<ResultGroup> variable that we will use to pass to the view. We then loop through our set adding ResultGroup variables to our list that have an event and a count associated with them into our list. Once that is done, we pass our list to our view. For the Index method, we added an argument for the EventId and we changed the query by adding a where clause to look for results that are associated with the specific event.

The next thing we need to do in order to get this to work is create an empty view for GroupedResults, which is our new index page/view. In case you forgot how to do that, right-click on the `return View(lRg);` line (I usually do it on the word view, but so long as it's on the line you'll be okay) and choose Add View. You should then see a window that looks like Figure 7-19.

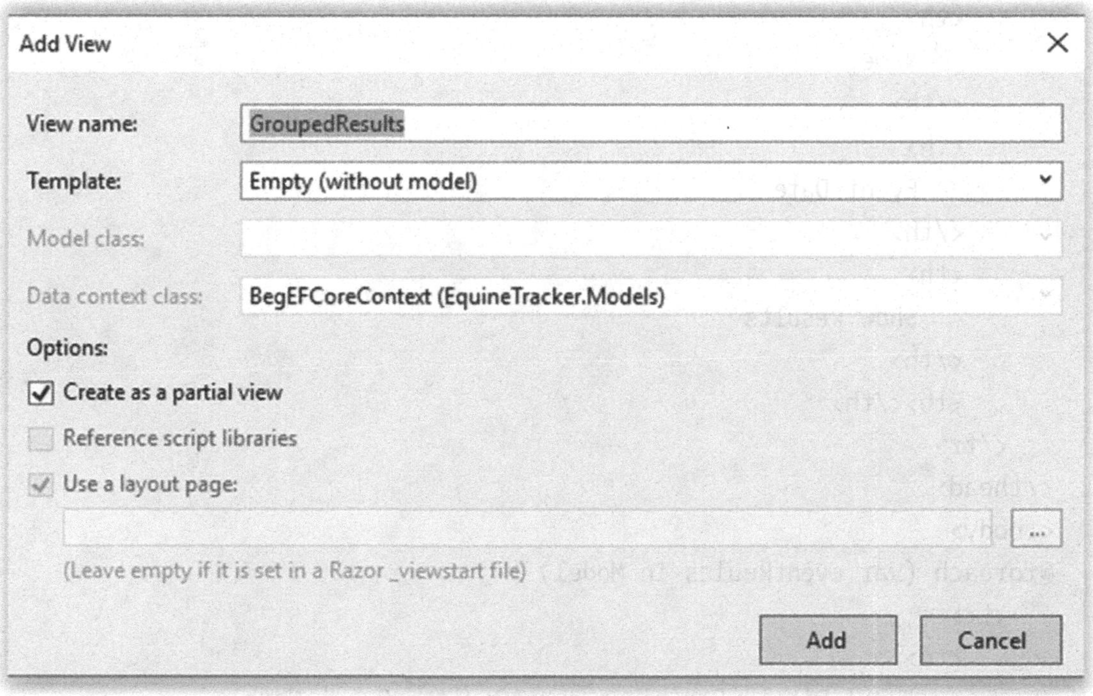

Figure 7-19. *Creating our GroupedResults view*

You can leave the defaults as long as they look like Figure 7-19 and click Add. You will then be presented with an empty view, which we will populate with the code in Listing 7-23.

Listing 7-23. GroupedResults.cshtml

```
@model List<EquineTracker.Helpers.ResultGroup>

@{
    ViewData["Title"] = "Events With Results";
}
```

```
<h2>Event Result Details</h2>
<table class="table">
    <thead>
        <tr>
            <th>
                Name
            </th>
            <th>
                Event Date
            </th>
            <th>
                Show Results
            </th>
            <th></th>
        </tr>
    </thead>
    <tbody>
@foreach (var eventReults in Model) {
        <tr>
            <td>
                @Html.DisplayFor(mi => eventReults._Event.Name)
            </td>
            <td>
                @Html.DisplayFor(mi => eventReults._Event.EventDate)
            </td>
            <td>
                @Html.DisplayFor(mi => eventReults.ResultCount)
            </td>
            <td>
                @Html.ActionLink("View Results", "Index", "Results",
                new { @EventId = eventReults._Event.EventId }, null)
            </td>
        </tr>
    }
    </tbody>
</table>
```

The good news is that there is nothing new that you haven't seen here. The bad news is you have to type it all. The one note is that, as you can see, the model is a List<T>. If you were to just try to pass along just the ResultGroup, it wouldn't work. The other important part is Html.ActionLink, which we use to pass our EventId to the controller so we can display the view and see the results for the event.

Now we just have to make one last change to our program. Can you guess what that is? If you said we need to fix the link to our Results Index page, you would be correct. We need to open _Layout.cshtml, which his found in the View folder, and then in the shared folder. All you have to do is modify:

```
<li><a asp-area="" asp-controller="Results" asp-action="Index">Results
</a></li>
```

To read:

```
<li><a asp-area="" asp-controller="Results" asp-action="GroupedResults">
Results</a></li>
```

That's it. When you click on Results in the menu bar from any of the pages, you'll now see something that looks similar to Figure 7-20.

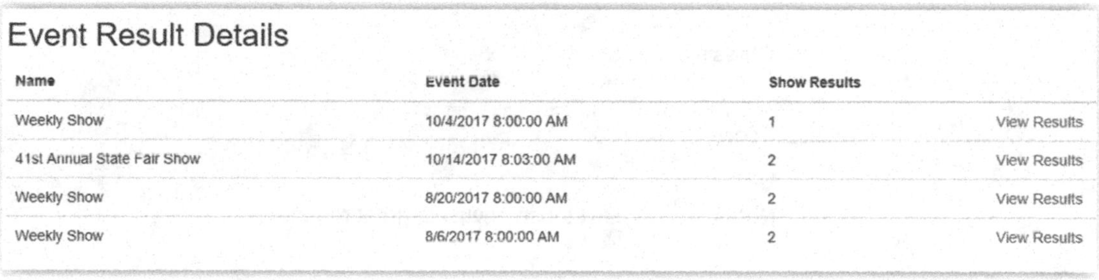

Name	Event Date	Show Results	
Weekly Show	10/4/2017 8:00:00 AM	1	View Results
41st Annual State Fair Show	10/14/2017 8:03:00 AM	2	View Results
Weekly Show	8/20/2017 8:00:00 AM	2	View Results
Weekly Show	8/6/2017 8:00:00 AM	2	View Results

Figure 7-20. Our grouped results

Now if you click on View Results for the 41st Annual State Fair Show, you should see something that looks like Figure 7-21.

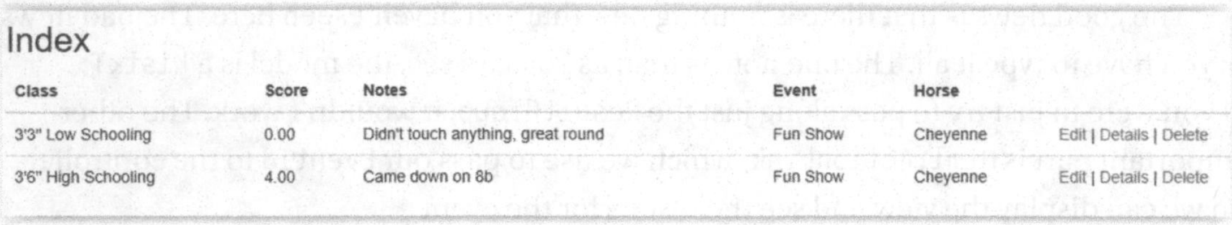

Index

Class	Score	Notes		Event	Horse	
3'3" Low Schooling	0.00	Didn't touch anything, great round		Fun Show	Cheyenne	Edit | Details | Delete
3'6" High Schooling	4.00	Came down on 8b		Fun Show	Cheyenne	Edit | Details | Delete

Figure 7-21. *Results for just one show*

Since we didn't change anything in our view, which we can tell as it still says Index, you'll see that if we click on the Edit hyperlink for 3'3" Low Schooling, it will open the Edit page shown in Figure 7-22.

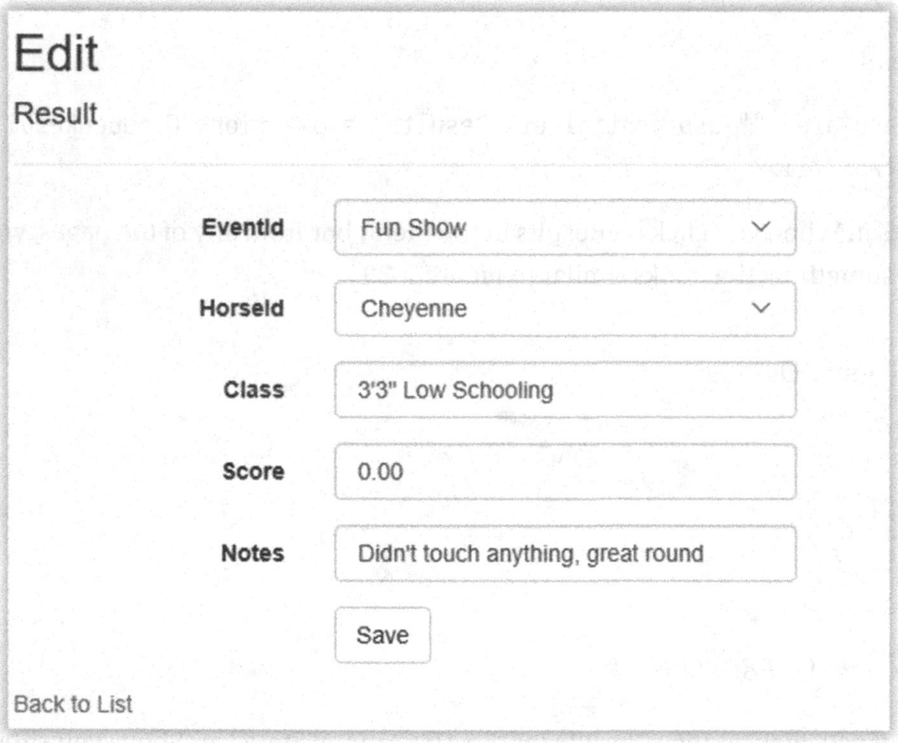

Edit

Result

EventId	Fun Show ⌄
HorseId	Cheyenne ⌄
Class	3'3" Low Schooling
Score	0.00
Notes	Didn't touch anything, great round
	Save

Back to List

Figure 7-22. *Editing the show result*

Now you may notice that we do need to fix one thing. If you were to click on the Back to List hyperlink, you would get a blank page (empty results is more like it). The good thing is you can fix that in a jiffy. Open `Edit.cshtml` from the Results View folder. At the bottom of the page, you should see the following code:

```
<div>
    <a asp-action="Index">Back to List</a>
</div>
```

All you have to do is change it to:

```
<div>
    @Html.ActionLink("Back to List", "Index", "Results", new { @EventId =
    Model.EventId }, null)
</div>
```

Now if you click on Back to List, it will bring you right back where you were. Keep in mind that if you were doing paging, it would require a little bit more effort, but not a ton more. You would just need to keep track of what page you were on.

Summary

We created a very rudimentary website that isn't overly pretty, but has some basic functionality. With a little bit more tweaking, you could use it on a daily basis. If you or someone who lets you spend lots of money of computers and servers (or a monthly cloud hosting bill) isn't into horses, you could easily change it to just about any other sport or hobby and be on your way. We covered basic CRUD (didn't think we could get through the chapter without using that acronym now did you?) operations for our site. You now have a way to validate properties and do some basic error handling when the values aren't correct. You should be able to sort your results, search for values in a table, page your results, and group your results to make it easier to sift through.

Although it's not related to Entity Framework Core 2.0, you should also be able to create classes to help your entities/models and create a custom view to go along with it. By using Entity Framework Core and ASP.NET MVC Core, you should be able to navigate through pages and end up back where you were.

CHAPTER 8

Wrap Up and Where to Go Next

We managed to cover quite a bit of information in the previous chapters, and in very few pages. I hope you found the brief explanations with examples more than sufficient to get you started on your path to working with Entity Framework Core 2.0. We managed to create a database from the code, which I'm sure many of you have never even thought about doing before. When I first learned Entity Framework, the thought of doing a code-first project was daunting, yet that is where we started in Chapter 1. If you can figure out how to do the hard one, then doing the easier one is a snap. When we created our ASP.NET MVC Core Application in Chapter 6, we got our first glimpse of database-first development. As you saw from a getting started perspective, that was a lot easier and required a lot less thought.

Chapters 2 and 3 got you comfortable with LINQ and lambda expressions. If you used just this book to learn those two subjects, you could get by, but you can really do some amazing things if you put in some more time and study the subject. LINQ will make your life a lot easier in many respects once you get the hang of it.

Before you read Chapter 4, you might have wondered what POCOs were. When I started learning Entity Framework and Entity Framework Core, I was a bit disappointed to learn that they are really nothing more than classes. However, you learned a couple of different ways to handle validating your data, which you used again in Chapter 6.

Not Just C# Anymore

One of the features that was added was the ability to not just use C# anymore for your applications. As of now you can only create console applications with Visual Basic and I'm not sure if they are going to extend that out to ASP.NET or not in the future. I'm not much into writing Visual Basic console applications any more, but if you were so

289

© Derek J. Rouleau 2018
D. J. Rouleau, *Beginning Entity Framework Core 2.0*, https://doi.org/10.1007/978-1-4842-3375-7_8

inclined, you would be able to do so now. If you want to write something in Visual Basic, I strongly recommend using Entity Framework 6.x instead of Core. If you know a VB programmer who wants to learn Entity Framework, that will be a much easier path.

To show you what I mean, we'll create a Visual Basic application that connects to the database we created in Chapter 1 in a few short steps.

Step 1. Create a new Visual Basic console application called VBTestApp, as shown in Figure 8-1.

Figure 8-1.   *Creating VBTestApp*

Step 2. Right-click on VBTestApp and choose Add ➤ New Item.

Step 3. From the Wizard, choose Data and then ADO.NET Entity Data Model. Call it MachineModel, as shown in Figure 8-2.

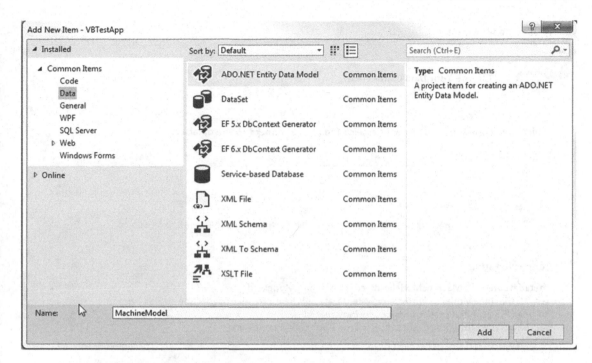

Figure 8-2. *Adding the model*

Step 4. Choose the EF Designer from the database option on the next window. The next thing you will do is choose your data connection. If the one you want isn't in the list, choose New Connection and follow the wizard prompts. Once you find it, click on the Next button. Since I'm not going to use this application, I chose the unsafe option, which is Include the Sensitive Data in the Connection String (see Figure 8-3).

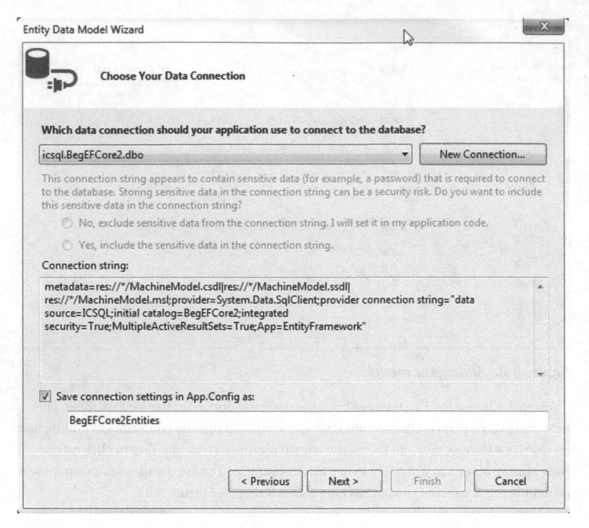

Figure 8-3. *Creating the connection string*

Step 5. Choose Entity Framework 6.x and click Next. In the next window, choose the Tables and Stored Procedures and Functions options. Since we don't have any views, we don't need to check the Views box.

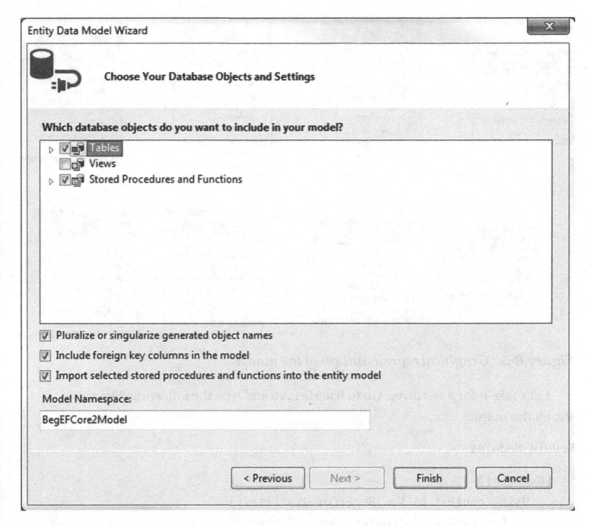

Figure 8-4. Selecting database objects

Step 6. Click on Finish and wait a couple of seconds for everything to be scaffolded. You are done.

It should open up to MachineModel.edmx [Diagram1], which should look similar to Figure 8-5 (although I have moved mine around a little bit to make it easier to follow the links between the tables).

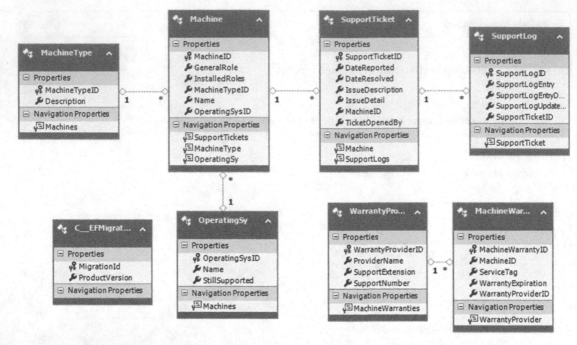

Figure 8-5. *Graphical representation of the model*

Let's take it for a test drive. Go to Module1.vb and type the following. Figure 8-6 shows the output.

```
Module Module1

    Sub Main()
        Using context As New BegEFCore2Entities()
            For Each os In context.OperatingSys
                Console.WriteLine("{0} still supported: {1}", os.Name,
                os.StillSupported)
            Next
        End Using
        Console.WriteLine("Hit any key to continue...")
        Console.ReadKey()
    End Sub

End Module
```

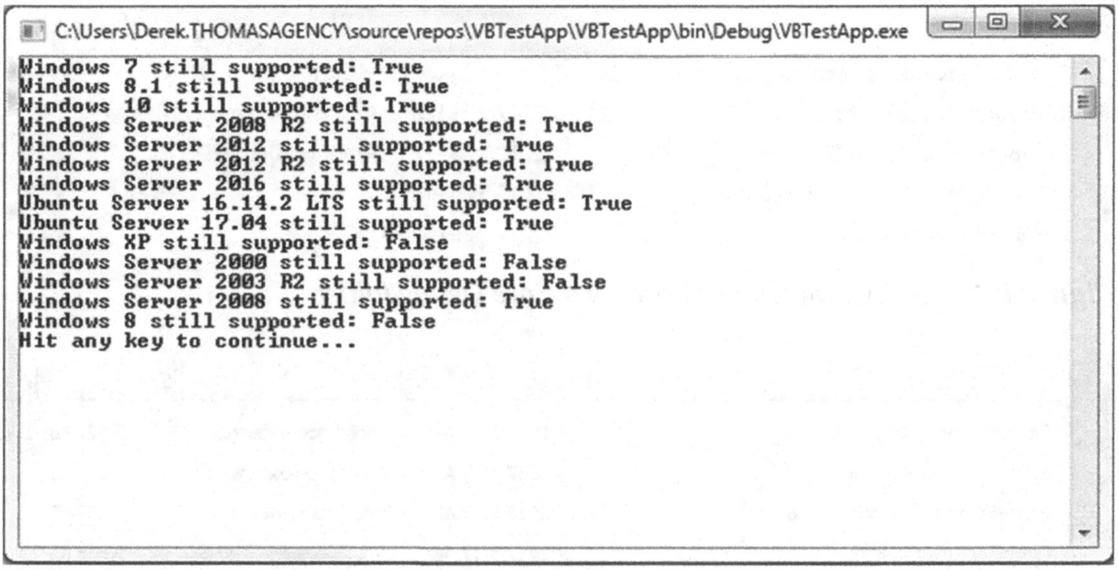

Figure 8-6. *Output from the application*

As you can see, that is a lot easier. Nothing against Visual Basic programmers, but that is a bit easier to work with and probably a better place to start. After all, I think many of us started with Basic or Visual Basic in school and then moved onto some variant of C or Java. You also have a couple more options open to you as well, which will also make things easier. But this is a book on Entity Framework Core, so we'll leave it at that for EF 6.x.

For those who are interested in learning something else, you can also create applications in F#. F# has been supported since .Net Core 1.0, so it's not new. However, they have made some more improvements when it comes to using F#.

Cross Platform

One of the main reasons to use .Net Core and Entity Framework Core is that it is cross platform. You are no longer stuck having to write and use your application on just Windows any more. When you created your Entity Framework Core/.Net Core 2.0 application, you didn't create an EXE file. You created a DLL file. This isn't an apples-to-apples comparison, but Figure 8-7 shows you the Debug folder for our ComputerInventory application and Figure 8-8 shows you the VBTest application we created.

Name	Date modified	Type	Size
ComputerInventory.deps	11/6/2017 1:35 PM	JSON File	38 KB
ComputerInventory.dll	11/13/2017 5:06 PM	Application extens...	107 KB
ComputerInventory.pdb	11/13/2017 5:06 PM	Program Debug D...	27 KB
ComputerInventory.runtimeconfig.dev	11/13/2017 5:06 PM	JSON File	1 KB
ComputerInventory.runtimeconfig	11/13/2017 5:06 PM	JSON File	1 KB

Figure 8-7. *Entity Framework Core/.Net Core Debug folder*

Name ▲	Date modified	Type	Size	
EntityFramework.dll	11/14/2017 8:17 AM	Application extension	5,075 KB	
EntityFramework.SqlServer.dll	11/14/2017 8:17 AM	Application extension	607 KB	
EntityFramework.SqlServer.xml	11/14/2017 8:17 AM	XML Document	152 KB	
EntityFramework.xml	11/14/2017 8:17 AM	XML Document	3,568 KB	
VBTestApp.exe	11/14/2017 8:27 AM	Application	70 KB	
VBTestApp.exe.config	11/14/2017 8:17 AM	XML Configuration File	2 KB	
VBTestApp.pdb	11/14/2017 8:27 AM	Intermediate file	58 KB	
VBTestApp.vshost.exe	11/14/2017 8:29 AM	Application	23 KB	
VBTestApp.vshost.exe.config	11/14/2017 8:17 AM	XML Configuration File	2 KB	
VBTestApp.vshost.exe.manifest	3/18/2013 5:00 PM	MANIFEST File	1 KB	
VBTestApp.xml	11/14/2017 8:27 AM	XML Document	1 KB	

Figure 8-8. *Entity Framework 6.x application*

As you can see, another reason to use EF Core and .Net Core is that you can run your application on Linux and MacOS. There is also a development environment for those operating systems. Microsoft has been doing a lot recently in the open source marketplace, which might come to a shock to some of you. I have read that Red Hat is working on something too, which should hopefully be out soon, so those who are on RHEL (Red Hat Enterprise Linux) or have it in your environment, that is a plus for you. So what's the big deal? We could run C# using mono before. The upside here is it doesn't require any third-party repositories in order to run. I work in a strictly Windows shop and all of my knowledge of Linux could probably fit in a paragraph. But for those of you who use it a lot but also like programming in C#, this could be very helpful.

Unit Testing

It's time for everyone's favorite thing in the whole wide world—unit testing. I bet some of you were hoping I'd forget this part. But it's something that is important and they did a pretty good job of making it easier for us. I'm sure some of you are thinking, "Why do I want to do this? I can just run my code and test it with breakpoints and message boxes or `Console.WriteLines()`." Those methods are okay to an extent, but what happens when you want to start testing your database? Do you want to delete a bunch of records that are either just test data or corrupted data? This is where unit testing helps you, although it's also good for testing general functionality as well. Once you see it in action, I think it will help you understand why.

There is a downside to unit testing and it's the reason people grumble about it. In some cases, it will take you much longer to write the unit test than to write the code you are going to be testing. However, that shouldn't dissuade you from doing it. I'm going to show you the way that I do it, which is only one of many. This was the first way I learned and haven't had the time to learn another method. See how you like it. If you don't, I suggest looking into one of the many other options.

We are going to use the built-in unit testing support that comes with Visual Studio. For more information about the kind of testing capabilities that are available, check out `https://www.visualstudio.com/vs/compare/`. To use it, you need to create a unit testing project, which we are going to add to the ComputerInventory project. To do this, you need to right-click on the project in Solution Explorer and choose Add ➤ New Project. Figure 8-9 shows this process.

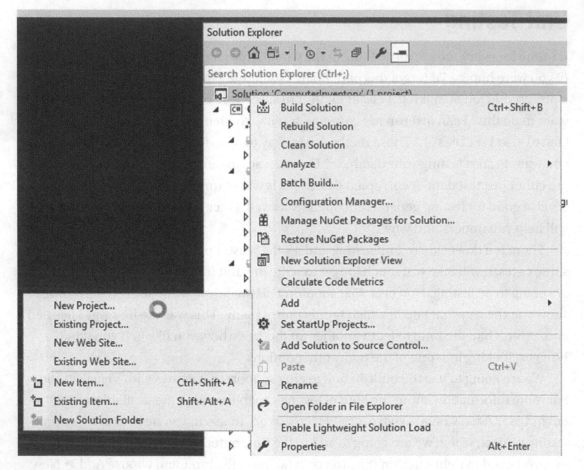

Figure 8-9. *Creating a new project for unit testing*

Once you click on New Project, you should get the Add New Project wizard. From there, choose Visual C# ➤ .NET Core and then choose Unit Test Project (.NET Core). You can use the name UnitTestProject1 for this example. With future projects, you should probably give it a better name (see Figure 8-10).

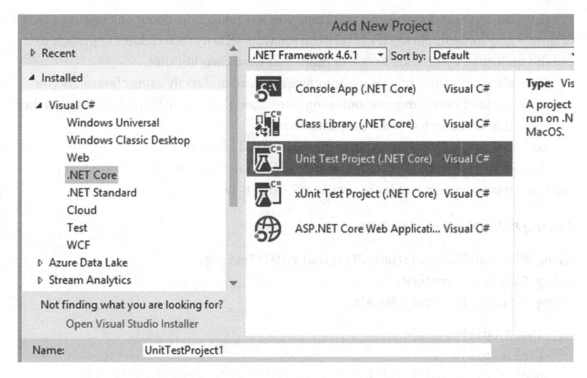

Figure 8-10. Creating the unit test project

We are almost done. Just add a reference to our application so our unit test project can access the classes. Right-click on the UnitTestProject1 project in the Solution Explorer and choose Add ➤ Reference. Then, under Projects ➤ Solution, choose ComputerInventory (see Figure 8-11).

Reference Manager - UnitTestProject1		
▲ Projects		
Solution	Name	Path
	☑ ComputerInventory	C:\Users\Derek.˥
▷ Shared Projects		
▷ Browse		

Figure 8-11. Adding a reference to the original project

One thing I should mention: if you know you are going to be doing unit testing ahead of time—and some might say it's good to do anyway—it is a much cleaner approach to put the majority of your code in one or more .Net Core class libraries.

Note also that a lot of people use interfaces instead of directly using classes. As you know, we created everything without using interfaces. If you were to use interfaces in the future, you would unit test against the interface.

Let's test our BasicValidation method called ValidateYorN();.

If you don't have UnitTest.1.cs open, open it now. Once you have it open, make changes to your project so it looks similar to Listing 8-1.

Listing 8-1. Our First Unit Test

```
using Microsoft.VisualStudio.TestTools.UnitTesting;
using ComputerInventory;
using ComputerInventory.Models;

namespace UnitTestProject1 {
    [TestClass]
    public class UnitTest1 {
        [TestMethod]
        public void Validate_Y_or_N() {
            // Arrange - method is static so no object needed
            //           If you needed an object you would do the following:
            BasicValidation validation = new BasicValidation();

            // Act - Test if ValidateYorN works
            bool bY = BasicValidation.ValidateYorN("Y");
            bool bN = BasicValidation.ValidateYorN("N");
            bool by = BasicValidation.ValidateYorN("y");
            bool bn = BasicValidation.ValidateYorN("n");
            bool bAnyOtherChar = BasicValidation.ValidateYorN("G");
            bool bNumToString = BasicValidation.ValidateYorN(9.ToString());

            // Assert
            Assert.IsTrue(bY, "Validating Y");
            Assert.IsTrue(bN, "Validating N");
            Assert.IsTrue(by, "Validating y");
            Assert.IsTrue(bn, "Validating n");
```

```
            Assert.IsFalse(bAnyOtherChar, "Validating G");
            Assert.IsFalse(bNumToString, "Validating 9");
        }
    }
}
```

As you can see, I added two using statements so we have access to our original project. We haven't used the models yet, but we'll get there, so why not just do it all at once? Each test will start with a [TestMethod] attribute and about 99.9% of the time, they will be voids. I am in the habit of naming my tests the same as the method they are testing, but adding underscores between the logical break. So ValidateYorN becomes Validate_Y_or_N. This is just a personal preference of mine. As you can see, the test is broken into three sections— Arrange, Act, and Assert. In the Arrange section, we are getting everything ready. If we need to create objects, we do so here. We set up variables and values for said variables, basically everything you are going to need to act upon. The Act section is where you do the test; in our case, we passed a string value (one character) to the method and got a value back.

According to the dictionary assert means "to state a fact of belief confidently and forcefully". That is basically what we are doing at this stage—we are saying we expect to get this value. If not, let us know so we can figure out what the heck is going on. There are quite a lot of Assert methods, but the ones I tend to use the most are listed in Table 8-1.

Table 8-1. *Common Assert Methods*

Method	Description
AreEqual<T>(T, T)	Verifies that two specific generic type data are equal by using the equality operator. Fails if they are not equal.
AreEqual<T>(T, T, string)	
AreEqual(String, String, Boolean)	Verifies that two specified strings are equal, ignoring care or not. Fails if they are not equal.
AreSame(T, T)	Verifies that two variables refer to the same object.
AreNotSame(T, T)	Verifies that two variables refer to a different object.
IsTrue(bool)	Verifies that a bool value is true.
IsFalse(bool)	Verifies that a bool value is false.
IsNull(Object)	Verifies that a variable is not assigned an object reference.
IsNotNull(Object)	Verifies that a variable is assigned an object reference.

There are more `Assert` methods than listed here, and there are more choices for each of these. In our code, we have `Assert.IsTrue(bY, "Validating Y");`, which from Table 8-1 is closest to `IsTrue(bool)`, but we have added a string. The string will be displayed in our test output if it fails. I will force one of the tests to fail so you can see it in use. Take some time to read up on MSDN about `Assert` methods, as they will help you greatly during unit testing. Once you do check it out, you'll see why I didn't include the entire list. It's quite long.

Now that you know some basics, let's run the test and see what happens. Before we can do that though, we need to do one more thing. From the menu bar in Visual Studio, choose Test ➤ Windows ➤ Test Explorer. When the Test Explorer opens, you'll see a window similar to the one shown in Figure 8-12. I normally keep mine open at the bottom of the screen.

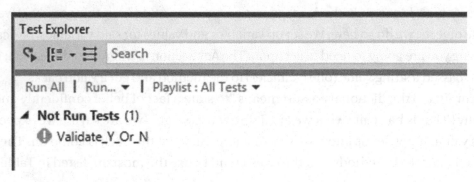

Figure 8-12. *Test Explorer with the test in it*

To run the test, you can click on the Run All or on Run and Run Not Run Tests menu options. See Figure 8-13.

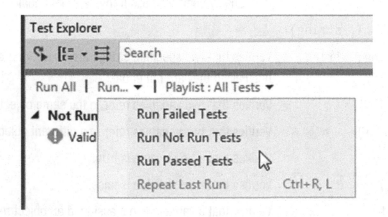

Figure 8-13. *Running the test*

302

It'll take a few seconds to do its thing, as it's got quite a bit to load. Once the test starts, it should be pretty quick. Figure 8-14 shows the test results.

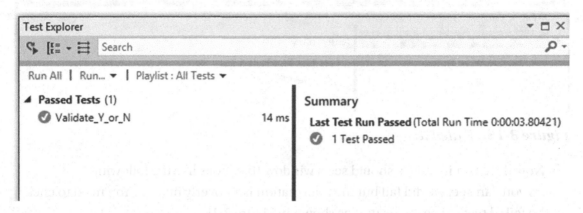

Figure 8-14. *Test results*

As you can see in Figure 8-14, it only lists the test that ran and doesn't list each `Assert` statement. Now let's say that we do our test, but we mess up. Change your code so it looks like Listing 8-2. The text in bold shows what changed. Figure 8-15 shows the failed test.

Listing 8-2. Forcing a Fail

```
// Act - Test if ValidateYorN works
bool bY = BasicValidation.ValidateYorN("Y");
bool bN = BasicValidation.ValidateYorN("N");
bool by = BasicValidation.ValidateYorN("y");
bool bn = BasicValidation.ValidateYorN("n");
bool bAnyOtherChar = BasicValidation.ValidateYorN("G");
bool bNumToString = BasicValidation.ValidateYorN(9.ToString());

// Assert
Assert.IsTrue(bY, "Validating Y");
Assert.IsTrue(bN, "Validating N");
Assert.IsTrue(by, "Validating y");
Assert.IsFalse(bn, message: "Validating n");
Assert.IsFalse(bAnyOtherChar, "Validating G");
Assert.IsFalse(bNumToString, "Validating 9");
```

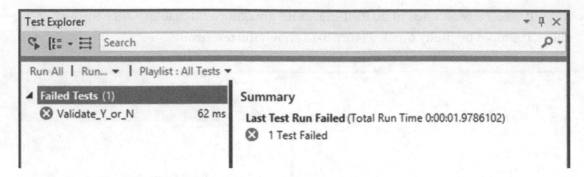

Figure 8-15. *Failed test*

Now if we run it and we should see a window that looks like the following:

As you can see, we did fail but the information isn't overly helpful. You need to click on the failed test to see the results, as shown in Figure 8-16.

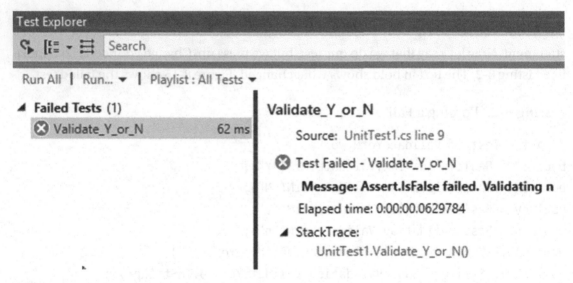

Figure 8-16. *Viewing more detail*

As you can see, Figure 8-16 is a bit more helpful. Not only did we change `Assert.` `IsTrue` to `Assert.IsFalse`, we changed the way we tell the compiler we want a message to be displayed. You can have added the text `message:` in there, which you can use to remind yourself that it's a message and not a value.

Let's try a test against a method in `Program.cs`. Before we can do that, we need to make two changes. First we need to make the class `Program` public and then we need to make the method we are going to test public as well. Listing 8-3 shows the changes we made.

Listing 8-3. Changes to Program.cs for Unit Testing

```
namespace ComputerInventory {
    public class Program {
.
.
.
public static bool CheckForExistingOS(string osName) {
    bool exists = false;
    using (var context = new MachineContext()) {
        var os = context.OperatingSys.Where(o => o.Name == osName);
        if (os.Count() > 0) {
            exists = true;
        }
    }
    return exists;
}
```

Normally, we wouldn't be testing against Program.cs, but in this case, we are going to. That's why we had to make those changes, as there would be a good chance that these would already be public. Now we create a new test. I'm going to include the existing code for this one example, so you can see how your UnitText1.cs file should look. The remaining examples just add to the file. See Listing 8-4.

Listing 8-4. Adding a New Test

```
public class UnitTest1 {
    [TestMethod]
    public void Validate_Y_or_N() {
        // Arrange - method is static so no object needed
        //           If you needed an object you would do the following:
        BasicValidation validation = new BasicValidation();

        // Act - Test if ValidateYorN works
        bool bY = BasicValidation.ValidateYorN("Y");
        bool bN = BasicValidation.ValidateYorN("N");
        bool by = BasicValidation.ValidateYorN("y");
        bool bn = BasicValidation.ValidateYorN("n");
```

```
    bool bAnyOtherChar = BasicValidation.ValidateYorN("G");
    bool bNumToString = BasicValidation.ValidateYorN(9.ToString());

    // Assert
    Assert.IsTrue(bY, "Validating Y");
    Assert.IsTrue(bN, "Validating N");
    Assert.IsTrue(by, "Validating y");
    Assert.IsTrue(bn, message: "Validating n");
    Assert.IsFalse(bAnyOtherChar, "Validating G");
    Assert.IsFalse(bNumToString, "Validating 9");
}

[TestMethod]
public void Check_For_Existing_OS() {
    // Arrange
    string osName = "Windows 7";

    // Act - Test for existing OSName in Database
    bool success = Program.CheckForExistingOS(osName);

    // Assert
    Assert.IsTrue(success);
}
}
```

All you have to do is add your [TestMethod] attribute, followed by the test you want to create and you are good to go. Click on Run All and see what happens (see Figure 8-17).

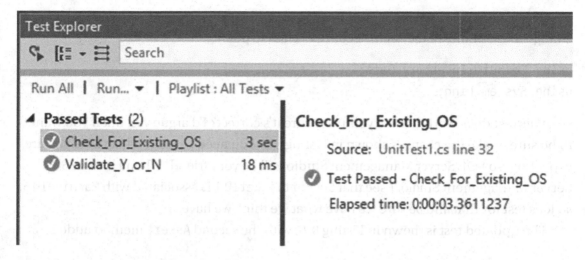

Figure 8-17. *Running two unit tests*

As you can see, we have validated that our database contains an OS named Windows 7. Now let's say we simply wanted to test a query or LINQ query. Well that's pretty simple too. We will do this two different ways. I'll show a simple one first and then one that I normally do. See Listing 8-5.

Listing 8-5. Testing LINQ

```
[TestMethod]
public void Retreive_Support_Ticket_By_ID() {
    // Arrange
    int ticketId = 1;
    SupportTicket sTicket;
    // Act
    using (MachineContext context = new MachineContext()) {
        sTicket = context.SupportTicket.Where(x => x.SupportTicketId ==
        ticketId).FirstOrDefault();
    }

    //Assert
    Assert.AreEqual(1, sTicket.SupportTicketId);
}
```

Before you can run this test, you need to add the following using statements and change the visibility of the MachineContext class to public:

```
using ComputerInventory.Data;
using System.Linq;
```

This test does work, but are you 100% sure it's correct? I'd argue yes, but if you want to be sure, make the changes shown in Listing 8-6. You need to know what value you are expecting, so SQL Server Management Studio will be your friend. When I look in SQL Server Management Studio, I see that SupportTicketID 1 is associated with MachineID 5, so let's test for that and be sure we have what we think we have.

The updated test is shown in Listing 8-6, with the second Assert method added.

Listing 8-6. Updating the Test

```
[TestMethod]
public void Retreive_Support_Ticket_By_ID() {
    // Arrange
    int ticketId = 1;
    SupportTicket sTicket;
    // Act
    using (MachineContext context = new MachineContext()) {
        sTicket = context.SupportTicket.Where(x => x.SupportTicketId ==
        ticketId).FirstOrDefault();
    }

    //Assert
    Assert.AreEqual(1, sTicket.SupportTicketId, message: "TicketId test");
    Assert.AreEqual(5, sTicket.MachineId, message: "MachineId test");
}
```

Running the test should succeed. If not, you either typed something wrong or your entry for SupportTicketId 1 isn't the same as mine, in which case make sure you are testing for the right value. Another thing to keep in mind with testing is that you should be doing it on a test database. So you can add the data you need for testing to be sure you are getting the results you expect. However, if you aren't working against a test database, you need to be careful. But you'll still need to use this approach and look in SSMS to be sure it is correct.

Let's say that we want to test our validation of our support log. We will do this in two steps as well. First, we verify that the "correct" data will validate, then we test for correct errors. See Listing 8-7.

Listing 8-7. Testing the Validation Logic

```
[TestMethod]
public void Validate_Support_Log() {
    // Arrange
    SupportLog supportLog = new SupportLog() {
        SupportLogEntryDate = DateTime.Now,
        SupportLogEntry = "Filler text, just needs to be long enough",
        SupportLogUpdatedBy = "John Smith"
    };
    ModelValidation modelValidation = new ModelValidation();

    // Act
    bool valid = modelValidation.ValidateSupportLog(supportLog, "save");

    // Assert
    Assert.IsTrue(valid);
}
```

You need to add using System; in order to gain access to the datetime data type (but you already knew that, didn't you). We have created a SupportLog object that has valid data in it. The thing with testing is you need to be sure you are testing correctly. Otherwise your test is basically useless and you'll spend a lot of time trying to figure out why something is wrong when it may not be.

Here are two things that you could easily miss when setting up this type of test:

- Creating an invalid datetime by accident (outside of the bounds you are looking for)

- Using update instead of save

If we choose to run the tests, we'll get output that looks like Figure 8-18.

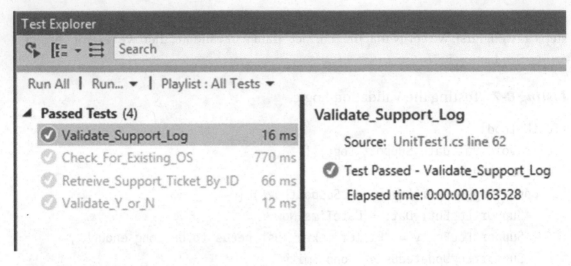

Figure 8-18. *Running just the latest test case*

All of the other tests are grayed out because they didn't run. Now let's test for error conditions. To make this easy, we'll look for all of them in one test. We will modify the last test, as shown in Listing 8-8.

Listing 8-8. Testing for Errors

```
[TestMethod]
public void Validate_Support_Log() {
    // Arrange
    SupportLog supportLog = new SupportLog() {
        SupportLogEntryDate = DateTime.Now,
        SupportLogEntry = "Filler text, just needs to be long enough",
        SupportLogUpdatedBy = "John Smith"
    };
    SupportLog supportLog2 = new SupportLog() {
        SupportLogEntryDate = Convert.ToDateTime("2017-1-1 10:00"),
        SupportLogEntry = "fail",
        SupportLogUpdatedBy = "J"
    };

    ModelValidation modelValidation = new ModelValidation();
```

310

```
// Act
bool valid = modelValidation.ValidateSupportLog(supportLog, "save");
bool invalid = modelValidation.ValidateSupportLog(supportLog2, "save");

// Assert
Assert.IsTrue(valid);
Assert.IsFalse(invalid);
Assert.AreEqual("Date is not valid", modelValidation.errorList[0].Error.
ToString());
Assert.AreEqual("Enter at least 10 characters.", modelValidation.
errorList[1].Error.ToString());
Assert.AreEqual("Enter at least 2 characters", modelValidation.
errorList[2].Error.ToString());
}
```

The trick to getting this one to test correctly is making sure we are testing in the right order. Since we are forcing all of our values to fail, we just test right down the line, starting at position 0 going up through position 2, also known as the third value.

Note   This used to be more confusing for people who went between Visual Basic and just about any other language, as it used to be one-based and not zero-based. If you did a lot of programming in VB and in something else, you probably messed that up more than a few times.

Another feature you can use is mock and mock repositories. Mock is a little confusing at first, yet it works well with interfaces. I strongly suggest that if you do want to do a lot more unit testing, you look into Mock—and using interfaces probably isn't a bad idea either. We didn't use either in this book in the interest of focusing more on interacting with the database through Entity Framework Core 2.0.

There are things to be careful about while unit testing. As you can see, we didn't insert anything, delete anything, or update anything in the database. If you wanted to test that kind of functionality, you would need to, excuse the term, mock up an object to be able to insert, update, or delete against. As you saw with the last example, you can test against your models/entities, so you should be able to do most of your testing that way. At some point, you'll have to work with a database. The goal is to do that as little as possible.

I'm not going to get into unit testing an ASP .NET Core MVC application, as there are many good sources out there that cover the subject and it's pretty involved. The good thing is you can unit test your views, which is quite helpful.

More on LINQ

Throughout the book, we have used LINQ and we have covered quite a bit. Table 8-2 is a list of the methods that I used most when I started using LINQ. I wrote them on a piece of paper that I kept on the wall next to my desk so I could remember them. Once I had used them enough, I noticed I was using that sheet less and less.

Table 8-2. *Common LINQ Extension Methods*

Extension Method	Description	Deferred
All	Returns true if all the elements in a collection match a specified condition.	No
Any	Returns true if a least one element in a collection matches a specified condition.	No
Contains	Returns true if a data source contains a specified value or item.	No
Count	Returns the number of items in a data source.	No
First	Returns the first item from a data source.	No
FirstOrDefault	Returns the first item from a data source or if there are no items, you get the default value.	No
Last	Returns the last item from a data source.	No
LastOrDefault	Returns the last item from a data source or if there are no items you get the default value	No
Max	Returns the largest value specified by a lambda expression.	No
Min	Returns the smallest value specified by a lambda expression.	No
OrderBy	Sorts the source data in ascending order (smallest to largest) based on a lambda expression.	Yes
OrderByDescending	Sorts the source data in descending order (largest to smallest) based on a lambda expression.	Yes

(continued)

Table 8-2. (*continued*)

Extension Method	Description	Deferred
Reverse	Reverses the order of the items from the data source.	Yes
Select	Produces a result set from a query. If you return anything other than a copy of the source element, it's called a projection.	Yes
Single	Returns the first match from a data source. If there are more than one, it will throw an error.	No
SingleOrDefault	Returns the first match from a data source or the default value. If there are more than one, it will throw an error.	No
Skip	Skips over a specified number of elements.	No
Sum	Totals the values that are selected by the predicate.	No
Take	Selects a specified number of elements from the start of a data source.	Yes
ToArray	Converts the data source to an array.	No
ToList	Converts the data source to a list.	No
Where	Filters items from the data source, removing those that don't match the predicate.	Yes

One important point that we need to cover with LINQ is that some of the methods that we use have something called *deferred execution*. The best example of this is when you have a query that iterates though a list. The query code isn't actually run until you start to iterate through the list. Even though you may have created the query and got past that section of code, the query variable only holds the commands and not the results. Let's take a look at an example; it'll start to make more sense once you see it.

We have used most of these at some point in this book, so you should have a pretty good understanding of how most of them work. However, let's take a look at an example of a deferred LINQ query to give you a better idea of what's going on.

Let's say we have a product table and we want to get the sum of the table and list the items in it. We might have something that looks like the following pseudocode:

```
Product Table
Name = "Widget1", Price 200M
Name = "Widget2", Price 300M
```

```
Name = "Widget3", Price 400M
var result = context.Products.OrderByDescending(e => e.Price)
    .Select(x => new {
        x.Name,
        x.Price
    };
var sumResult = products.Sum(e => e.Price);
Console.WriteLine(sumResult);
foreach (var p in result){
    Console.WriteLine($"{p.Name} {p.Price}");
}
```

We would expect to see something along the lines of this:

```
900
Widget1 200
Widget2 300
Widget3 400
```

This seems reasonable. However, let's say that just as you hit the line in which you are writing the result, the finance department updates Widget3 to 500. Your results will then be:

```
900
Widget1 200
Widget2 300
Widget3 500
```

This is because of the deferred execution of the query. The good and the bad part of this is that the query is executed from scratch every time the results are enumerated.

One downside to using Entity Framework Core 2.0 is that it currently doesn't provide LINQ to XML capability. You could still read through an XML document using the string properties of the columns, but none of the other LINQ functionality is available. Hopefully, we'll see that in an update or a later version.

SQL Server Profiler

Depending on the version of SQL Server you are using, you may be able to use the SQL Server Profiler (not available in SQL Server Express). One of the things you can do with the SQL Server Profiler is see how your LINQ queries are being executed in SQL.

Think back to when we were listing the information about machines to the user. We created the following query:

```
var mach = (from mac in context.Machine
    join mw in context.MachineWarranty on mac.MachineId equals mw.MachineId
    where mac.MachineId == machineId
    select new {
        mac.Name, MacType = mac.MachineType.Description, osName =
        mac.OperatingSys.Name, mac.OperatingSys.StillSupported,
        mw.WarrantyProvider, mw.WarrantyExpiration, mac.MachineType.
        Description }).FirstOrDefault();
```

If you were to look in SQL Server Profiler (see Figure 8-19), you would see that code converted into the following SQL code:

```
exec sp_executesql N'SELECT TOP(1)
    mw.WarrantyProvider].[WarrantyProviderID],
    [mw.WarrantyProvider].[ProviderName],
    [mw.WarrantyProvider].[SupportExtension],
    [mw.WarrantyProvider].[SupportNumber], [mac].[Name] AS [Name0],
    [mac.MachineType].[Description] AS [MacType],
    [mac.OperatingSys].[Name] AS [osName],
    [mac.OperatingSys].[StillSupported], [mw].[WarrantyExpiration]
FROM [Machine] AS [mac]
INNER JOIN [OperatingSys] AS [mac.OperatingSys] ON [mac].[OperatingSysID] =
[mac.OperatingSys].[OperatingSysID]
INNER JOIN [MachineType] AS [mac.MachineType] ON [mac].[MachineTypeID] =
[mac.MachineType].[MachineTypeID]
INNER JOIN [MachineWarranty] AS [mw] ON [mac].[MachineID] = [mw].
[MachineID]
```

```
INNER JOIN [WarrantyProvider] AS [mw.WarrantyProvider] ON [mw].
[WarrantyProviderID] = [mw.WarrantyProvider].[WarrantyProviderID]
WHERE [mac].[MachineID] = @__machineId_0',N'@__machineId_0 int',
@__machineId_0=5
```

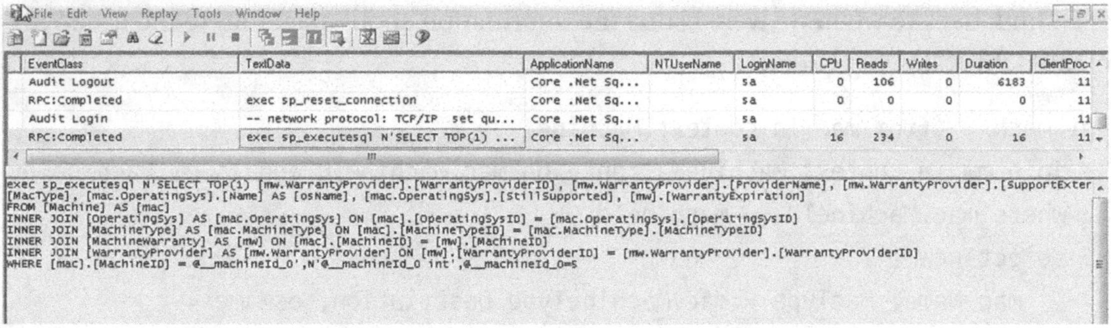

Figure 8-19. *SQL Server Profiler*

It's hard to see in Figure 8-19, but you can get quite a lot of information out of the profiler. If you are looking to tune your queries, this is the place to go. You can see how things are working and the effect that making a change to your query has on the execution of that query. If you are having problems with your database, look to the Profiler to figure it out. If you haven't used it before, the Microsoft website is a great place to get information about how to use it and what you can do with it.

Change Tracking

One of the things that we haven't covered directly yet is change tracking in Entity Framework Core. Any query that we run by default that returns an entity type is tracked. So what does that mean? As you have seen in many instances, we have called some form of DBContext.SaveChanges(). The reason that does anything is because of change tracking. Any time we modify the entity that we are working with, those changes will be pushed back to the database when we call .SaveChanges(). Why would we want to change that since it seems to be pretty helpful?

If your goal is to retrieve a large amount of data that you are going to present to the user in the form of a report, then you would probably be doing a read-only type query since you aren't going to be writing anything back to the database.

In this case, why would you want to waste the overhead and setup time for the system to get change tracking going if you aren't going to use it? Throughout the code in this book, we have used anonymous types instead of strongly typed objects because they are generally easier and require less typing. Just because we are using an anonymous type and not an entity object doesn't mean that change tracking isn't still on. Some people think that by using the anonymous types, they don't have to worry about it, but think of all the times we used one and then called .SaveChanges().

So if you don't want to use change tracking, how do you turn it off? I'm glad you asked. Let's take a look at some code we already created, shown in Listing 8-9.

Listing 8-9. Change Tracking Enabled

```
static void DisplayMachineNameAndIdOnly() {
    using (var context = new MachineContext()) {
        var machines = (from m in context.Machine
            where m.MachineTypeId == 1
            select new { m.MachineId, m.Name });

        foreach (var m in machines) {
            Console.WriteLine($"{m.MachineId} {m.Name}");
        }
    }
}
```

This is a great example of a query where we aren't doing anything with the results other than displaying them to the user. In ASP .NET MVC, this is quite common. We have two choices that we can use to turn off change tracking. For this example, we'll turn it off at the context-instance level, as shown in Listing 8-10.

Listing 8-10. Turning Off Change Tracking at the Context Instance Level

```
static void DisplayMachineNameAndIdOnly() {
    using (var context = new MachineContext()) {
        context.ChangeTracker.QueryTrackingBehavior = QueryTrackingBehavior.
        NoTracking;
        var machines = (from m in context.Machine
            where m.MachineTypeId == 1
            select new { m.MachineId, m.Name });
```

```
      foreach (var m in machines) {
        Console.WriteLine($"{m.MachineId} {m.Name}");
      }
   }
}
```

That's all there is to it. Now if we had multiple queries that we were running, none of them would have change tracking enabled. That is pretty helpful, but what if you want to turn off tracking only for a specific query. This could be because you need to retrieve two sets of data—one that you want to make changes to and one you don't. To do this, we'll take a look at the UpdateMachineDetails() method, , shown in Listing 8-11. Note that I removed part of the method, as there were quite a few Console.WriteLines in there.

Listing 8-11. UpdateMachineDetails().

```
static void UpdateMachineDetails() {
  Console.Clear();
  List<Machine> lMachine = GetListOfMachines();
  WriteHeader("Update Machine Details");

  string machineId = DisplayAllMachines("Enter the MachineId followed by
  the Enter Key for more information.");
  if (machineId.Length > 0) {
    int mId = Convert.ToInt32(machineId);
    Machine mach;
    MachineWarranty mWar;
    using (MachineContext context = new MachineContext()) {
      mach = context.Machine
        .Include(o => o.OperatingSys)
        .Include(t => t.MachineType)
        .Where(x => x.MachineId == mId).FirstOrDefault();

      mWar = context.MachineWarranty
        .Include(p => p.WarrantyProvider)
        .Where(x => x.MachineId == mach.MachineId).FirstOrDefault();
    }
```

```
    ...
    UpdateMachine(mach.MachineId);
  }
  Console.ReadKey();
}
```

In this example we update it outside of the context, but we can use our imaginations here and pretend that we are doing it within. In this example, we only need to be able to update mach. mWar is only used to display some information to the users, which we have cut out in the interest of saving space. Listing 8-12 shows the update, which turns off tracking for one query.

Listing 8-12. Turning Off Change Tracking for One Query

```
static void UpdateMachineDetails() {
  Console.Clear();
  List<Machine> lMachine = GetListOfMachines();
  WriteHeader("Update Machine Details");

  string machineId = DisplayAllMachines("Enter the MachineId followed by
  the Enter Key for more information.");
  if (machineId.Length > 0) {
    int mId = Convert.ToInt32(machineId);
    Machine mach;
    MachineWarranty mWar;
    using (MachineContext context = new MachineContext()) {
      mach = context.Machine
        .Include(o => o.OperatingSys)
        .Include(t => t.MachineType)
        .Where(x => x.MachineId == mId).FirstOrDefault();

      mWar = context.MachineWarranty
        .Include(p => p.WarrantyProvider)
        .Where(x => x.MachineId == mach.MachineId).AsNoTracking().
        FirstOrDefault();
    }
```

```
    ...

    UpdateMachine(mach.MachineId);
  }
  Console.ReadKey();
}
```

We didn't make any changes to mach, but we did add .AsNoTracking() to mWar. This is all we have to do. As you start to work with bigger and bigger datasets and tables, it will become important that you consistently use one of the two methods mentioned to turn off change tracking. What does a query look like that doesn't have change tracking enabled by default? That would be an anonymous type that returns values from an entity but not an instance of an entity. The good news is that we have already done this, although it's not the simplest of examples. You have been working with Entity Framework Core 2.0 and LINQ long enough that this should be simple for an old pro like you. See Listing 8-13.

Listing 8-13. No Change Tracking by Default

```
static void GroupMachinesByOS() {
    using (var context = new MachineContext()) {
        var mli = (from m in context.Machine
            join o in context.OperatingSys on m.OperatingSysId
            equals o.OperatingSysId
            group new { m, o } by m.OperatingSysId into grouped
            select new { grouped.Key, count = grouped.Select(x => x.m.Operating
            SysId).Count(), Name = grouped.Select(ma => ma.o.Name) });

        foreach (var m in mli) {
            Console.WriteLine($"OS ID: {m.Key} Machine Count W/OS: {m.count}
            OS Name: {m.Name.ElementAt(0)}");
        }
    }
}
```

Even though we are using multiple entities, we aren't using actual instances of those entities in our query results. A simple example of what it looks like to have a query with a SELECT statement is shown in Listing 8-14.

Listing 8-14. Select That Has Change Tracking Enabled

```
using (var context = new SomeContext()){
   var prod = context.Products
      .Select(p =>
      new {
         Product = p,
         Items = p.Items.Count()
   });
}
```

As you can see in this pseudocode, we are working with instances of entities from the table. I don't normally use `.Select` for queries unless I have to, so that is why we don't have an example from earlier in the book.

Summary

I hope that you have enjoyed this new way of learning about a new programming method. I hope that got enough out of it to get you started and have a good foundation with Entity Framework Core 2.0 and with using LINQ. When you head off to hone your skills and you come across topics about DBContext, models, and creating interfaces for your entities, you'll have a basic understanding and not get caught up in the lingo.

I can't even begin to tell you how many times I had to read the chapter on pointers when I was first learning C++ because there was just so much there but not a lot of examples. Or when I was first learning how to use something that called for delegates. For some reason, that took a bit of time to click, which again was the result of way too much talk and not a lot of examples.

Some people say the best way to learn is by doing, so getting some examples of what something is, working on them for a while, and then learning the background (the how and why) is a bit easier. I've probably forgotten more about Visual Basic in the last couple of years than most of the new Visual Basic programmers out there know. However, if I took a week or so to refresh my memory, I'd probably be able to pick most of it right back up. The hope is that you can read past the parts you already know to learn the things that you need to in order to expand your knowledge of Entity Framework Core 2.0 and, as a result, your knowledge of LINQ.

Thank you for taking the time to read through this book. I hope you found it to be interesting and I hope it's helpful to your future programming endeavors.

APPENDIX A

Database Script for Chapter 6

This appendix lists the script for creating the database in Chapter 6. Keep in mind that you may need to change the location of the mdf and ldf files.

```
/*      ==Scripting Parameters==

    Source Server Version : SQL Server 2014 (12.0.2269)
    Source Database Engine Edition : Microsoft SQL Server Express Edition
    Source Database Engine Type : Standalone SQL Server

    Target Server Version : SQL Server 2017
    Target Database Engine Edition : Microsoft SQL Server Standard Edition
    Target Database Engine Type : Standalone SQL Server
*/
USE [master]
GO
/****** Object:  Database [BegEFCore]    Script Date: 1/8/2018 4:22:30 AM
******/
CREATE DATABASE [BegEFCore]
 CONTAINMENT = NONE
 ON  PRIMARY
( NAME = N'BegEFCore', FILENAME = N'C:\Program Files\Microsoft SQL
Server\MSSQL12.MSSQLSERVER\MSSQL\DATA\BegEFCore.mdf' , SIZE = 3072KB ,
MAXSIZE = UNLIMITED, FILEGROWTH = 1024KB )
 LOG ON
```

© Derek J. Rouleau 2018
D. J. Rouleau, *Beginning Entity Framework Core 2.0*, https://doi.org/10.1007/978-1-4842-3375-7_9

```
( NAME = N'BegEFCore_log', FILENAME = N'C:\Program Files\Microsoft SQL
Server\MSSQL12.MSSQLSERVER\MSSQL\DATA\BegEFCore_log.ldf' , SIZE = 1024KB ,
MAXSIZE = 2048GB , FILEGROWTH = 10%)
GO
ALTER DATABASE [BegEFCore] SET COMPATIBILITY_LEVEL = 120
GO
IF (1 = FULLTEXTSERVICEPROPERTY('IsFullTextInstalled'))
begin
EXEC [BegEFCore].[dbo].[sp_fulltext_database] @action = 'enable'
end
GO
ALTER DATABASE [BegEFCore] SET ANSI_NULL_DEFAULT OFF
GO
ALTER DATABASE [BegEFCore] SET ANSI_NULLS OFF
GO
ALTER DATABASE [BegEFCore] SET ANSI_PADDING OFF
GO
ALTER DATABASE [BegEFCore] SET ANSI_WARNINGS OFF
GO
ALTER DATABASE [BegEFCore] SET ARITHABORT OFF
GO
ALTER DATABASE [BegEFCore] SET AUTO_CLOSE OFF
GO
ALTER DATABASE [BegEFCore] SET AUTO_SHRINK OFF
GO
ALTER DATABASE [BegEFCore] SET AUTO_UPDATE_STATISTICS ON
GO
ALTER DATABASE [BegEFCore] SET CURSOR_CLOSE_ON_COMMIT OFF
GO
ALTER DATABASE [BegEFCore] SET CURSOR_DEFAULT  GLOBAL
GO
ALTER DATABASE [BegEFCore] SET CONCAT_NULL_YIELDS_NULL OFF
GO
```

```
ALTER DATABASE [BegEFCore] SET NUMERIC_ROUNDABORT OFF
GO
ALTER DATABASE [BegEFCore] SET QUOTED_IDENTIFIER OFF
GO
ALTER DATABASE [BegEFCore] SET RECURSIVE_TRIGGERS OFF
GO
ALTER DATABASE [BegEFCore] SET  DISABLE_BROKER
GO
ALTER DATABASE [BegEFCore] SET AUTO_UPDATE_STATISTICS_ASYNC OFF
GO
ALTER DATABASE [BegEFCore] SET DATE_CORRELATION_OPTIMIZATION OFF
GO
ALTER DATABASE [BegEFCore] SET TRUSTWORTHY OFF
GO
ALTER DATABASE [BegEFCore] SET ALLOW_SNAPSHOT_ISOLATION OFF
GO
ALTER DATABASE [BegEFCore] SET PARAMETERIZATION SIMPLE
GO
ALTER DATABASE [BegEFCore] SET READ_COMMITTED_SNAPSHOT OFF
GO
ALTER DATABASE [BegEFCore] SET HONOR_BROKER_PRIORITY OFF
GO
ALTER DATABASE [BegEFCore] SET RECOVERY SIMPLE
GO
ALTER DATABASE [BegEFCore] SET  MULTI_USER
GO
ALTER DATABASE [BegEFCore] SET PAGE_VERIFY CHECKSUM
GO
ALTER DATABASE [BegEFCore] SET DB_CHAINING OFF
GO
ALTER DATABASE [BegEFCore] SET FILESTREAM( NON_TRANSACTED_ACCESS = OFF )
GO
ALTER DATABASE [BegEFCore] SET TARGET_RECOVERY_TIME = 0 SECONDS
GO
```

```
ALTER DATABASE [BegEFCore] SET DELAYED_DURABILITY = DISABLED
GO
USE [BegEFCore]
GO
/****** Object:  Table [dbo].[Event]    Script Date: 1/8/2018 4:22:30 AM ******/
SET ANSI_NULLS ON
GO
SET QUOTED_IDENTIFIER ON
GO
CREATE TABLE [dbo].[Event](
        [EventId] [int] IDENTITY(1,1) NOT NULL,
        [Name] [nvarchar](50) NOT NULL,
        [LocationId] [int] NOT NULL,
        [Description] [nvarchar](50) NOT NULL,
        [EventDate] [datetime] NULL,
 CONSTRAINT [PK_Event] PRIMARY KEY CLUSTERED
(
        [EventId] ASC
)WITH (PAD_INDEX = OFF, STATISTICS_NORECOMPUTE = OFF, IGNORE_DUP_KEY = OFF,
ALLOW_ROW_LOCKS = ON, ALLOW_PAGE_LOCKS = ON) ON [PRIMARY]
) ON [PRIMARY]
GO
/****** Object:  Table [dbo].[Horse]    Script Date: 1/8/2018 4:22:30 AM ******/
SET ANSI_NULLS ON
GO
SET QUOTED_IDENTIFIER ON
GO
CREATE TABLE [dbo].[Horse](
        [HorseId] [int] IDENTITY(1,1) NOT NULL,
        [Name] [nvarchar](50) NOT NULL,
        [Breed] [nvarchar](50) NULL,
        [Height] [decimal](3, 1) NULL,
        [Value] [decimal](18, 0) NULL,
```

```
   CONSTRAINT [PK_Horse] PRIMARY KEY CLUSTERED
(
        [HorseId] ASC
)WITH (PAD_INDEX = OFF, STATISTICS_NORECOMPUTE = OFF, IGNORE_DUP_KEY = OFF,
ALLOW_ROW_LOCKS = ON, ALLOW_PAGE_LOCKS = ON) ON [PRIMARY]
) ON [PRIMARY]
GO
/****** Object:  Table [dbo].[Location]  Script Date: 1/8/2018 4:22:30 AM ******/
SET ANSI_NULLS ON
GO
SET QUOTED_IDENTIFIER ON
GO
CREATE TABLE [dbo].[Location](
        [LocationId] [int] IDENTITY(1,1) NOT NULL,
        [Name] [nvarchar](50) NOT NULL,
        [StreetAddress] [nvarchar](50) NULL,
        [City] [nvarchar](50) NULL,
        [State] [varchar](2) NULL,
        [ZipCode] [varchar](10) NULL,
 CONSTRAINT [PK_Location] PRIMARY KEY CLUSTERED
(
        [LocationId] ASC
)WITH (PAD_INDEX = OFF, STATISTICS_NORECOMPUTE = OFF, IGNORE_DUP_KEY = OFF,
ALLOW_ROW_LOCKS = ON, ALLOW_PAGE_LOCKS = ON) ON [PRIMARY]
) ON [PRIMARY]
GO
/****** Object:  Table [dbo].[Result]   Script Date: 1/8/2018 4:22:30 AM ******/
SET ANSI_NULLS ON
GO
SET QUOTED_IDENTTFIER ON
GO
```

```
CREATE TABLE [dbo].[Result](
        [ResultId] [int] IDENTITY(1,1) NOT NULL,
        [EventId] [int] NOT NULL,
        [HorseId] [int] NOT NULL,
        [Class] [nvarchar](50) NOT NULL,
        [Score] [decimal](18, 4) NOT NULL,
        [Notes] [nvarchar](max) NULL,
 CONSTRAINT [PK_Result] PRIMARY KEY CLUSTERED
(
        [ResultId] ASC
)WITH (PAD_INDEX = OFF, STATISTICS_NORECOMPUTE = OFF, IGNORE_DUP_KEY = OFF,
ALLOW_ROW_LOCKS = ON, ALLOW_PAGE_LOCKS = ON) ON [PRIMARY]
) ON [PRIMARY] TEXTIMAGE_ON [PRIMARY]
GO
SET IDENTITY_INSERT [dbo].[Event] ON

INSERT [dbo].[Event] ([EventId], [Name], [LocationId], [Description],
[EventDate]) VALUES (1, N'Weekly Show', 1, N'Fun Show', CAST(N'2017-10-
04T08:00:00.000' AS DateTime))
SET IDENTITY_INSERT [dbo].[Event] OFF
SET IDENTITY_INSERT [dbo].[Horse] ON

INSERT [dbo].[Horse] ([HorseId], [Name], [Breed], [Height], [Value]) VALUES
(1, N'Jack', N'Standardbred', CAST(15.1 AS Decimal(3, 1)), CAST(5 AS
Decimal(18, 0)))
SET IDENTITY_INSERT [dbo].[Horse] OFF
SET IDENTITY_INSERT [dbo].[Location] ON

INSERT [dbo].[Location] ([LocationId], [Name], [StreetAddress], [City],
[State], [ZipCode]) VALUES (1, N'Local Ring', NULL, NULL, NULL, NULL)
SET IDENTITY_INSERT [dbo].[Location] OFF
SET IDENTITY_INSERT [dbo].[Result] ON
```

```
INSERT [dbo].[Result] ([ResultId], [EventId], [HorseId], [Class], [Score],
[Notes]) VALUES (1, 1, 1, N'Intro A', CAST(68.0000 AS Decimal(18, 4)),
N'Circles left a lot to be desied, other than that he did well.')
SET IDENTITY_INSERT [dbo].[Result] OFF
ALTER TABLE [dbo].[Event]  WITH CHECK ADD  CONSTRAINT [FK_Event_Location]
FOREIGN KEY([LocationId])
REFERENCES [dbo].[Location] ([LocationId])
GO
ALTER TABLE [dbo].[Event] CHECK CONSTRAINT [FK_Event_Location]
GO
ALTER TABLE [dbo].[Result]  WITH CHECK ADD  CONSTRAINT [FK_Result_Event]
FOREIGN KEY([EventId])
REFERENCES [dbo].[Event] ([EventId])
GO
ALTER TABLE [dbo].[Result] CHECK CONSTRAINT [FK_Result_Event]
GO
ALTER TABLE [dbo].[Result]  WITH CHECK ADD  CONSTRAINT [FK_Result_Horse]
FOREIGN KEY([HorseId])
REFERENCES [dbo].[Horse] ([HorseId])
GO
ALTER TABLE [dbo].[Result] CHECK CONSTRAINT [FK_Result_Horse]
GO
USE [master]
GO
ALTER DATABASE [BegEFCore] SET  READ_WRITE
GO
```

Database Diagrams

Figures A-1 and A-2 show the database diagrams of the BegEFCore and BegEFCore2 tables, respectively.

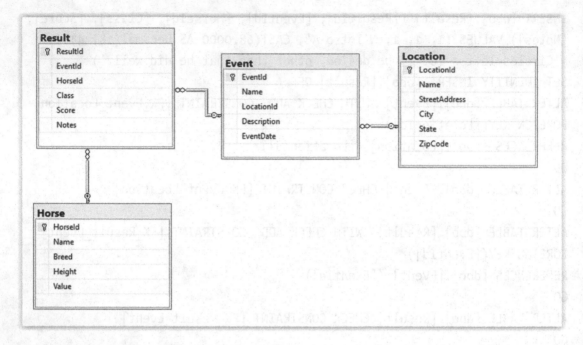

Figure A-1. *Diagram of BegEFCore tables*

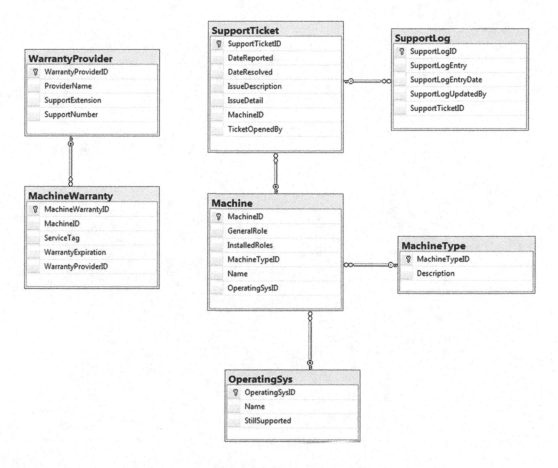

Figure A-2. *Diagram of BegEFCore2 tables*

Index

© Derek J. Rouleau 2018
D. J. Rouleau, *Beginning Entity Framework Core 2.0*, https://doi.org/10.1007/978-1-4842-3375-7

P, Q

R

S

Get the eBook for only $5!

Why limit yourself?

With most of our titles available in both PDF and ePUB format, you can access your content wherever and however you wish—on your PC, phone, tablet, or reader.

Since you've purchased this print book, we are happy to offer you the eBook for just $5.

To learn more, go to http://www.apress.com/companion or contact support@apress.com.

Apress®

Printed in the United States
by Bookmasters

Printed in the United States
By Bookmasters